The Fathers of American Presidents

The Fathers of American Presidents

From Augustine Washington to William Blythe and Roger Clinton

by Jeff C. Young

McFarland & Company, Inc., Publishers
Jefferson, North Carolina, and London

The present work is a reprint of the library bound edition of The Fathers of American Presidents: From Augustine Washington to William Blythe and Roger Clinton, *first published in 1997.*

*For my parents,
Marvin Clair Young and
Charlotte Lou Hanna*

LIBRARY OF CONGRESS CATALOGUING-IN-PUBLICATION DATA

Young, Jeff C., 1948–
    The fathers of American presidents : from Augustine Washington to William Blythe and Roger Clinton / by Jeff C. Young.
      p.   cm.
    Includes index.

    ISBN 0-7864-1699-8 (softcover : 50# alkaline paper)

    1. Presidents — United States — Fathers — Biography. I. Title.
E176.25.Y68   2003
973'.099 — dc20   96-20497

British Library cataloguing data are available

©1997 Jeff C. Young. All rights reserved

No part of this book may be reproduced or transmitted in any form or by any means, electronic or mechanical, including photocopying or recording, or by any information storage and retrieval system, without permission in writing from the publisher.

Manufactured in the United States of America

*McFarland & Company, Inc., Publishers
  Box 611, Jefferson, North Carolina 28640
    www.mcfarlandpub.com*

Table of Contents

Acknowledgments	ix
Preface	1

Augustine Washington • *George Washington*	3
John Adams Sr. • *John Adams*	7
Peter Jefferson • *Thomas Jefferson*	11
James Madison Sr. • *James Madison*	16
Spence Monroe • *James Monroe*	22
John Adams • *John Quincy Adams*	25
Andrew Jackson Sr. • *Andrew Jackson*	33
Abraham Van Buren • *Martin Van Buren*	36
Benjamin Harrison V • *William Henry Harrison*	40
John Tyler Sr. • *John Tyler*	45
Samuel Polk • *James K. Polk*	50
Richard Taylor • *Zachary Taylor*	54
Nathaniel Fillmore • *Millard Fillmore*	58
Benjamin Pierce • *Franklin Pierce*	63
James Buchanan Sr. • *James Buchanan*	68
Thomas Lincoln • *Abraham Lincoln*	73
Jacob Johnson • *Andrew Johnson*	79
Jesse Root Grant • *Ulysses Simpson Grant*	82
Rutherford Hayes Jr. • *Rutherford B. Hayes*	89
Abram Garfield • *James A. Garfield*	94
William Arthur • *Chester A. Arthur*	97
Richard Falley Cleveland • *Grover Cleveland*	102
John Scott Harrison • *Benjamin Harrison*	107
William McKinley Sr. • *William McKinley*	114
Theodore Roosevelt Sr. • *Theodore Roosevelt*	118

Alphonso Taft • *William Howard Taft*	127
Joseph Ruggles Wilson • *Woodrow Wilson*	134
George Tyron Harding II • *Warren G. Harding*	142
John Calvin Coolidge • *Calvin Coolidge*	149
Jesse Clark Hoover • *Herbert Hoover*	155
James Roosevelt • *Franklin D. Roosevelt*	160
John Anderson Truman • *Harry S Truman*	167
David Jacob Eisenhower • *Dwight D. Eisenhower*	173
Joseph P. Kennedy Sr. • *John F. Kennedy*	180
Sam Ealy Johnson Jr. • *Lyndon B. Johnson*	190
Francis Anthony Nixon • *Richard M. Nixon*	197
Leslie Lynch King Sr. • *Gerald R. Ford Jr.*	205
Gerald R. Ford Sr. • *Gerald R. Ford Jr.*	208
James Earl Carter Sr. • *Jimmy Carter*	212
John Edward Reagan • *Ronald Reagan*	218
Prescott Sheldon Bush • *George Bush*	223
William Jefferson Blythe III • *Bill Clinton*	230
Roger Clinton • *Bill Clinton*	235
Index	239

Acknowledgments

Thanks to the interest and encouragement of my friends and family and the aid and assistance of writers, historians, librarians, archivists, journalists, and authors, I have been able to complete this book.

First of all, I wish to thank Ralph W. Stark, Al P. Nelson, and Steve Blackwell. Long before I even dreamed of being an author, they encouraged me to learn the craft of writing. I also wish to thank my former Ball State history professor, Dr. Dwight W. Hoover. Words of encouragement from such an eminent scholar went a long way in motivating me to finish this book.

Three books I repeatedly referred to were invaluable in my writing and research: Joseph Nathan Kane's *Facts About the Presidents,* Doris Faber's *The Mothers of American Presidents,* and William DeGregorio's *The Complete Book of U.S. Presidents.* The Orange County (Florida) Public Library has been of great help in expeditiously filling my interlibrary loan requests and quickly answering my reference questions.

Others who have been very helpful in answering queries and providing articles, obituaries, photos, and other vital information include: Scott M. Brown of the Belle Grove Plantation in Middletown, Virginia; Janet B. Schwarz of the Virginia Historical Society in Richmond, Virginia; Jeff K. Walters of the James K. Polk Association in Columbia, Tennessee; Mary F. Bell of the Buffalo and Erie County Historical Society in Buffalo, New York; Elizabeth Hamlin-Morin of the New Hampshire Historical Society in Concord, New Hampshire; Ron D. Bryant of the Kentucky Historical Society in Frankfort, Kentucky; Carolyn Texley of the Lincoln Museum in Fort Wayne, Indiana; Kim Cumber of the North Carolina State Archives in Raleigh, North Carolina; Wayne Onkst of the Kenton County Public Library in Covington, Kentucky; the Rutherford B. Hayes Presidential Center in Fremont, Ohio; Sharon Farrell of the Grover Cleveland Birthplace in Caldwell, New Jersey; Linda Bailey of the Cincinnati Historical Society in Cincinnati, Ohio; W. J. Weber of the William McKinley Museum in Canton, Ohio; Wallace Dailey of the Houghton Library at Harvard University; Janet Campbell of the Woodrow Wilson Birthplace and Museum in Staunton, Virginia; William W. Jenney of the President Calvin Coolidge Birthplace in Plymouth, Vermont; Meg Page of the Vermont Department of Libraries in Montpelier, Vermont; Dwight W. Miller and Cindy Worrell of the Herbert Hoover Library in West Branch, Iowa; the Franklin D.

Roosevelt Library in Hyde Park, New York; the Prints and Photographs Division of the Library of Congress in Washington, D.C.; the Harry S. Truman Library in Independence, Missouri; the Dwight D. Eisenhower Library in Abilene, Kansas; the John F. Kennedy Library in Boston, Massachusetts; E. Phillip Scott of the Lyndon B. Johnson Library in Austin, Texas; Susan Naulty of the Richard Nixon Library and Birthplace in Yorba Linda, California; Janet Peters of the Tucson Public Library in Tucson, Arizona; Jacquelyn Cenacveira of the Los Angeles Times Library; Richard L. Holzhausen and Nancy Mirshah of the Gerald R. Ford Library in Ann Arbor, Michigan; David J. Stanhope of the Jimmy Carter Library in Atlanta, Georgia; Mrs. Alton Bryce of the Lake Blackshear Regional Library in Americus, Georgia; the Ronald Reagan Library in Simi Valley, California; Steve Rice of the Connecticut Historical Society in Hartford, Connecticut; Wendy Coleson of the *Sikeston (Missouri) Standard-Democrat;* the Reference Department of the Garland County Arkansas Public Library.

Special thanks to Bill Penmann of Sarasota, Florida, and to my Hoosier friends, Rick Jones, Angie Jones, and Chris Otterman, for providing me with a quiet, comfortable place to work on this book during the summer of 1994.

I am indebted to each and every one of you.

Preface

The best quote that I ever read on the subject of fathers and sons came from author-playwright Margaret Turnbull. She wrote: "No man is responsible for his father. That is entirely his mother's affair."

The Fathers of American Presidents examines and reviews the lives of the 43 men who were fathers of a United States president. Using presidential biographies, correspondence, journals, speeches, autobiographies, and obituaries of their fathers, I have tried to determine how each father may have shaped and influenced his famous son's life and what kind of a father-son relationship they had. The book is not a psychohistory. I think that history is too complex to say that a president made a certain decision or acted in a particular way because of his father's influence.

Fathers has its origins in an article I researched, but never wrote. Several years ago, I began researching an article on George Washington's father, Augustine. I kept my notes and after reading Doris Faber's fine work, *The Mothers of American Presidents,* and finding in *Books in Print* no book on presidential fathers, I decided that the fathers deserved a book of their own. I also decided that I wanted to be the person to write it.

For about two years, I frequented public and academic libraries and contacted presidential libraries, historical societies, archivists, librarians, journalists and other sources of information. After hundreds of hours of reading, writing, phone calls, research, writing, editing and rewriting, a magazine-article-turned-book-idea was completed.

I hope that the reader will enjoy reading this book as much as I enjoyed researching and writing it.

Jeff C. Young
Winter Haven, Florida
November 1995

Augustine Washington (1694–1743)

Farmer, planter, sheriff, justice of the peace, businessman, and father of President George Washington

Augustine Washington fathered the man known and revered as the "father of his country," but he did little parenting after George Washington was born. A perusal of Washington biographies indicates that Augustine spent little time with his one day famous son and paid scant attention to him.

The tale of George chopping down Augustine's cherry tree is of dubious veracity. Even if it did happen, Augustine was most likely too preoccupied with his farms, his slaves, his iron business, and his other children to notice that a tree was missing.

George Washington's feelings for his father remain a mystery over two-and-a-half centuries after Augustine's death. According to Bernhard Knollenberg's book, *George Washington: The Virginia Period, 1732–1775*, George Washington mentioned his father in only three of his twenty-thousand surviving letters, memos, and diary entries. In a letter written in 1784, George described himself as "early deprived of a father." On another occasion, George recollected that Augustine "died when I was only ten years old" (actually he was eleven). In a statement of lineage written in 1792 George recorded Augustine's birth and death dates, parents, wives, and children, but nothing else about his father.

Some historians and Washington scholars believe that Augustine had little effect or influence on George's life. In *The Invention of George Washington*, Paul K. Longmore suggests that George Washington's drive for public fame was a result of Augustine dying when George was so young.

The first Washingtons to emigrate to America were a pair of brothers, John and Lawrence. John was the grandfather of Augustine. The Washington brothers came to America from the north of England around 1657. They settled at Bridge's Creek on the Potomac River in the Virginia county of Westmoreland. John served the Virginia colony as a soldier and legislator. He held the rank of colonel while commanding Virginia forces in the Indian War of 1675, and he later represented Westmoreland County in the Virginia House of Burgesses.

Captain Lawrence Washington was the eldest son of Colonel John and the father of Augustine. According to *Burke's Presidential Families of the United States of America,* Captain Lawrence was also a legislator. He likewise served in the House of Burgesses and on the Governor's Council. At one time, he also served as the acting governor of Virginia.

Captain Lawrence married Mildred Warner in 1689. They had three children, Lawrence, Mildred, and Augustine. Captain Lawrence died in 1697 when Augustine was three. The widow, Mildred, married George Gale in 1700, and the Washington children moved to England with their mother and stepfather. Augustine attended the Appleby School in England until he was nine.

Mildred had come into considerable property when Colonel Lawrence died. Before marrying George Gale she had received the legal authorization to turn that property over to Gale. Mildred was pregnant when she moved to England. She died either shortly after giving birth to her last child or during childbirth. Augustine thus became an orphan at the tender age of six.

All that is known of Augustine between the ages of nine and twenty-one is that he returned to Virginia and lived with his cousin, John Washington of Chotank, and that cousin John was embroiled in protracted litigation in an attempt to seize control of Mildred's estate from George Gale.

On April 20, 1715, Augustine married Jane Butler, a teenaged daughter of a well-to-do planter. Four of the ten children that Augustine would sire were by his first wife. Three boys and one girl were born to Augustine and Jane between the years of 1716 and 1722.

While biographers of Washington do not provide a physical description of Jane Butler Washington, they describe Augustine in some detail. According to Douglas Southall Freeman's *George Washington,* George remembered Augustine as "tall, fair of complexion, well proportioned and fond of children." In *The Mother of Washington,* Nancy Byrd Turner recounts that one of Augustine's grandsons heard an unnamed acquaintance of his grandfather describe him as "six feet in height . . . of noble and manly proportions, with the most extraordinary muscular power. Over at Principio Iron Works, where he acted as agent, he used to lift up and place in a wagon a mass of iron that two ordinary men could hardly have raised from the ground." Augustine's second wife, Mary Ball Washington, remembered him as "a noble-looking man of distinguished bearing, tall and athletic, with florid complexion, brown hair and gray eyes." John Thomas Flexner's biography, *George Washington: The Forge of Experience, 1732–1775,* describes Augustine as "a blonde giant, fabulously strong but miraculously gentle." Flexner also fleshes out Augustine's personality, characterizing him as "a nervous businessman, much concerned with land speculation, prone to lawsuits; given increasingly, the larger the reward offered, to hesitation and procrastination." W. E. Woodward, in his book, *George Washington: The Image and the Man,* calls Augustine "a bustling person, without imagination or intellectual urge."

The composite image of Augustine Washington that emerges from all these sources is that of a tall, muscular, virile, strong but gentle man, fond of children, but irresolute and litigious in his business affairs.

During his marriage to Jane Butler, Augustine became more prosperous and more prominent in the government and politics of the Virginia colony. He served as a justice of the peace, church warden, and sheriff. For the latter position, he received a stipend of 1,080 pounds of tobacco a year.

The discovery of iron ore on his property thrust Augustine into the iron manufacturing and exporting business. In the summer of 1729 he left Jane and his three children to travel to England for a face-to-face meeting with his business partners. When Augustine returned home on May 26, 1730, he was informed that Jane had died on November 24, 1729.

Augustine's second wife was Mary Ball. According to an entry in the Washington family Bible, they were wed on March 6, 1731. She was then in her early twenties and Augustine in his late thirties. There are two different stories about their first meeting.

The first version is a romantic tale of a chance encounter when Augustine was in England on a business trip. According to that story, Mary was sitting in her stepbrother's house sewing. When she looked out the window, she saw a handsome equestrian struggling to control his skittish mount. Augustine was thrown from his horse and carried into the nearby house. A tireless and compassionate Mary Ball nursed him back to health. Augustine and Mary discovered that they were both visitors from Virginia. The couple took that startling coincidence as an omen that they were destined to spend the rest of their lives together. The less romantic, but more probable, account is that they met at the Virginia home of George Eskridge, a friend of the Ball family.

By June of 1731 Mary Ball Washington knew that she was pregnant and that the child would arrive by midwinter. On February 22, 1732, at 10 o'clock in the morning a large healthy boy whom they named George was born. George was the first of six children (four boys and two girls) born from the union of Augustine and Mary.

For the first three years of George's life, Augustine and his family lived at the family estate on Popes Creek, Virginia. In 1735 the Washingtons moved to a 2,500-acre tract of land Augustine had purchased from his sister Mildred. The new Washington home was known as Little Hunting Creek Farm. It would later become known as Mount Vernon.

In 1738 Augustine uprooted his family once again so he could be closer to his ironworks. He purchased the 260-acre Ferry Farm, which was located across from Fredericksburg, Virginia, on the Rappahannock River. Augustine would spend the rest of his life there.

On an April day in 1743, Augustine was caught in a heavy rainstorm while riding over his plantation. He caught a cold and then died on April 12, 1743, after a brief illness. Gout of the stomach is generally believed to have been the cause of death. Throughout his life, Augustine had displayed a pronounced fondness for rich food and fine wine.

When Augustine became ill, George was visiting some cousins in the Chotank district of the Potomac. He was summoned home, and he arrived in time to see his father one last time. It is not known if Augustine was still conscious when George arrived.

Legend has it that as Augustine lay dying, he thanked God that he had never struck a man in anger. Augustine reputedly said, "For if I had, I am sure that from my remarkable muscular powers I should have killed my antagonist and then his blood would have lain heavily on my soul. As it is, I die in peace with all men."

Bibliography

Bellamy, Francis Rufus. *The Private Life of George Washington*. New York: Crowell, 1951.
Cunliffe, Marcus. *George Washington: Man and Monument*. Boston: Little, Brown, 1958.
Donavan, Frank. *The George Washington Papers*. New York: Dodd, Mead, 1964.
Faber, Doris. *The Mothers of American Presidents*. New York: New American Library, 1968.
Ferling, John E. *The First of Men*. Knoxville, Tn.: University of Tennessee Press, 1968.
Flexner, James T. *George Washington: The Forge of Experience, 1732–1775*. Boston: Little, Brown, 1965.
Freeman, Douglas Southall. *George Washington: A Biography*. Vol. 1, *Young Washington*. New York: Scribner's, 1948.
Irving, Washington. *Life of George Washington*. New York: Putnam, 1862.
Knollenberg, Bernhard. *George Washington: The Virginia Period, 1732–1775*. Durham, N.C.: Duke University Press, 1964.
Longmore, Paul K. *The Invention of George Washington*. Berkeley, Ca.: University of California Press, 1988.
Montgomery-Massingbred, Hugh, editor. *Burke's Presidential Families of the United States of America*. London: Burke's Peerage, 1975.
Turner, Nancy Byrd. *The Mother of Washington*. New York: Dodd, Mead, 1930.
Woodward. W. E. *George Washington: The Image and the Man*. New York: Fawcett, 1956.

John Adams Sr. (1691–1761)

Farmer, leather crafter, public official, and father of President John Adams

In his *Autobiography*, John Adams delineated the near boundless admiration he felt for his father, Deacon John Adams. John Adams wrote, "He was the honestest Man I ever knew. In wisdom, piety, benevolence and charity. In proportion to his Education and Sphere of Life, I have never seen his Superior."

Deacon John was the great-grandson of Henry Adams, a Puritan who had emigrated to America with his wife and nine children in 1636. The Adamses came from the small town of Barton St. David in Somerset County, England. Upon arriving in America, Henry began working as a tenant farmer. After two years of tenant farming, Henry was able to purchase a forty-acre farm in Braintree, Massachusetts. Succeeding generations of Adamses lived in Braintree and added additional acreage and a brewery to Henry's forty acres. Deacon John was one of eight children born to Joseph Adams and Hannah Bass.

The father of America's second president was born on February 8, 1691, presumably at the family farm in Braintree. Little has been written or recorded about Deacon John's early life. In *John Adams and the American Revolution*, Catherine Drinker Bowen records that Deacon John left school when he was twelve. In an eighteenth-century farm village such as Braintree it was common for children to leave school before their teens. Boys were expected to help out on the farm once they were sufficiently healthy and robust to perform the manual labor. Deacon John Adams was no exception.

Biographers of President Adams also provide few details about Deacon John's life prior to his marriage, mentioning only that he joined the local militia when he was fifteen. Adams biographers also record that Deacon John got the title of deacon by serving in that office at the Congregational Church. In addition, Deacon John is described as a farmer and leather crafter (shoes, harnesses, and other salable goods). Deacon John also served his church and community as a tithingman, tax collector, and selectman (city councilman). According to John Ferling's *John Adams:*

A Life, John Adams recalled that no public business was transacted in Braintree without Deacon John's consent.

On October 31, 1734, Deacon John Adams married Susanna Boylston. She was twenty-five and Deacon John was forty-three. Adams biographers do not record how and when they met but only that the Boylstons were a prominent and prosperous family and that Deacon John's marriage improved his financial and social status. As Peter Shaw put it in his book, *The Character of John Adams*, "he [Deacon John] set a precedent for later Adamses of social advance through marriage instead of business."

Exactly one day before their first wedding anniversary, Deacon John and Susanna became parents. Assisted by a midwife, Susanna gave birth to John Adams at the family farmhouse in Braintree on October 30, 1735. Deacon John and Susanna had two more children, Peter Boylston in 1738 and Elihu, born in 1741. Even before John was born, his parents had agreed that their firstborn son would get a college education. Deacon John taught John to read when his son was a preschooler. John Adams's formal education began when he was about six. John first attended a boys' and girls' academy that held classes in the teacher's house. A short time later, his parents transferred him to the academically more demanding Latin School in Braintree.

Forcing all that schoolwork and studying on a stubborn, strong-willed boy like John Adams eventually led to a father-son conflict. The result is related in an anecdote that appears in several biographies of President Adams. When John was around ten, Deacon John was discouraged and dismayed by his son's lackadaisical performance in school. Deacon John asked the boy what he would do if he did not go to college.

"Be a farmer," John quickly replied.

"A farmer!" exclaimed Deacon John. "I'll show you what it is to be a farmer."

Early the next morning, Deacon John took John with him to a marsh to gather thatch. They worked from sunup to sundown in knee-deep mud and under a blazing sun, cutting, bundling, and tying large bundles of thatching. Deacon John worked relentlessly and John gamely struggled to match his father's pace. After dinner that evening, Deacon John confidently asked his weary son how he liked farming now.

"I like it very well, sir," John obstinately replied.

As fathers usually do, Deacon John had the last word.

"Aye, but I don't like it so well," Deacon John said. "So you shall go to school." That was a commandment Deacon John frequently repeated.

Along with his emphasis and insistence upon a good education for John, Deacon John raised his children in a strictly religious environment. Deacon John led his family in daily prayers. In the Adams home, the Sabbath began at noon on Saturday. Attendance at Sunday services (both morning and afternoon) was mandatory. Sermons lasted from two to four hours. Hour-long prayers were not uncommon, and the congregation prayed standing up, as kneeling for prayer was considered popery.

It was not until he was fourteen that John Adams began to take his studies seriously. He wrote in his *Autobiography* that he told his father: "Sir, I don't like my schoolmaster. He is so negligent and cross that I can never learn anything under him. If you will be so good as to persuade Mr. Marsh to take me, I will apply myself to my studies as closely as my nature will admit, and go to College as soon as I can be prepared."

The next day, Deacon John told John that he had persuaded Mr. Marsh to take him as a student. John Adams studied under Marsh for a year before entering Harvard College in 1751. He graduated from Harvard four years later, thus becoming the first American president to earn a college degree.

Both Deacon John and Susanna impressed upon John the Puritan virtue of chastity. John later recalled that his parents "held every species of Libertinage in . . . Contempt and horror." When John was around twelve, Deacon John gave John a sex education lecture. The Deacon quoted scripture: "Cursed be the fornicator, an abomination to the Lord." Deacon John also reminded John that John's grandfather had seen a man hung for his sexual indiscretions. Even if the sinner escaped punishment on earth, he would surely burn in hell after facing his judgment day. As proof, Deacon John quoted chapter and verse. However, Deacon John was not a complete prude. According to Shaw, the deacon was known to tell off-color stories, but it is unlikely that he ever told one to John. It is believed that John Adams remained celibate until marriage.

The family conflicts of Deacon John were not exclusively with John. According to *John Adams: A Life*, John's parents "bickered to an unusual degree." John noticed that his mother usually had her way. He wrote that she "frets, squibs, scolds, rages, raves," until she has her way.

Probably the last conflict John Adams had with his father was after he graduated from Harvard. Deacon John had made sacrifices to send his son to college. He had sent John to Harvard with the expectation that John would enter the ministry. Once again, what Deacon John wanted and what John wanted were two different things. John wanted to be a lawyer.

John graduated from Harvard in 1755, but he waited until sometime in 1756 to tell his father about his career plans. According to Bowen, the news was received calmly by both his parents: "Mr. Adams showed neither shock nor disappointment." There is some evidence that John had known all along that Deacon John would acquiesce to his forsaking the ministry for a career in law. In his *Diary*, John wrote, "Although my Father's general Expectation was that I should be a Divine, I knew him to be a Man of so thoughtful and considerate turn of mind, to be possessed of so much candor and moderation, that it would not be difficult to remove any objections he might make to my pursuit of Physick or Law or any other reasonable course."

In May of 1761 Braintree was plagued by an influenza epidemic. According to Page Smith's book, *John Adams*, "the epidemic that hit Braintree put half the town to bed." Deacon John Adams was one of the epidemic's seventeen recorded victims. He died on May 25, 1761, at the age of seventy.

Susanna and Deacon John's three sons were all at the Deacon's bedside when he died. Ferling writes, "For a time thereafter, John was despondent and introverted." Smith also notes the father's influence on his famous son: "The father's influence on the son was strong and enduring. The boy loved him and admired him and sought, in all things, to imitate him." As Shaw describes Deacon John's influence on John, "Adams owed his father a debt for having launched him out of the Braintree orbit without preventing him from choosing his own way."

Attorney John Adams was the executor of Deacon John's estate, which was inventoried at 1,330 pounds, 9 shillings, and 8 pennies. John's inheritance was a small house a few yards away from the Deacon's farmhouse and thirty acres.

Because he was now a man of property, John Adams was entitled to participate in Braintree's town meetings. Thus, the Deacon's legacy enabled John to embark upon a career in politics.

During his term as vice president, John Adams recalled his father with admiration: "My father was an honest man, a lover of his Country and an independent spirit and the example of that father inspired me with the greatest pride of my life."

Bibliography

Bowen, Catherine Drinker. *John Adams and the American Revolution*. Boston: Little, Brown. 1950.
Ferling, John. *John Adams: A Life*. Knoxville, Tn.: University of Tennessee Press, 1992.
Gilbert, Chinard. *Honest John Adams*. Boston: Little, Brown. 1933.
Hess, Stephen. *American Political Dynasties: From Adams to Kennedy*. Garden City, N.Y.: Doubleday, 1966.
Peabody, James Bishop, editor. *John Adams: A Biography in His Own Words*. New York: Newsweek, 1976.
Shaw, Peter. *The Character of John Adams*. Chapel Hill, N.C.: University of North Carolina Press, 1976.
Shepherd, Jack. *The Adams Chronicles, 1750–1900*. Boston: Little, Brown. 1975.
Smith, Page. *John Adams*. New York: Doubleday, 1962.
Stefoff, Rebecca. *John Adams: Second President of the United States*. Ada, Okla.: Garrett Educational Corporation, 1988.

Peter Jefferson
(1708–1757)

Farmer, surveyor, soldier, public official, magistrate, legislator, and father of President Thomas Jefferson

Although he was a prolific writer, Thomas Jefferson had little to say about his father, Peter. In his *Autobiography,* the man often considered as the most learned and scholarly of all American presidents wrote about his father's lack of education and thirst for knowledge: "My father's education had been quite neglected; but being of a strong mind, sound judgement, and eager after information, he read much and improved himself." Jefferson concluded his memories of his father by giving Peter credit for sending him to school: "He placed me at the English School at five years of age; and at the Latin at nine, where I continued until his death."

The father of America's third president was born in Virginia on February 29, 1708. Peter was the fourth child of six (three boys and three girls) born to Thomas Jefferson II and Mary Field Jefferson. Thomas Jefferson II was a prominent, well-to-do landowner and public official who served as a militia captain, justice of the peace, and county sheriff.

Mary died when Peter was eight. Thomas II died in 1731. Upon the death of his father, Peter inherited his father's lands, a chest of clothes, six silver spoons, weapons, furniture, livestock, and "two Negroes, Farding and Pompey." Peter took his inheritance and settled on some undeveloped land in the area of Fine Creek, Virginia. For the next ten years, Peter cleared the land, built a house, and supported himself as a farmer and surveyor. During that decade Peter also achieved some prominence in the colonial government. At various times he served as a justice of the peace, sheriff of Goochland County, and as county surveyor.

Either while working as a surveyor or while serving as a justice of the peace, Peter Jefferson met and befriended William Randolph of Tuckahoe. The Randolphs were among the most politically and socially prominent families in the Virginia colony. Through this friendship Peter became acquainted with William's cousin, Jane. It is not known how and when they first met, nor how long Peter courted

Jane. What is known is that they were married in October of 1739 when Peter was thirty-two and Jane was nineteen.

Over a span of eighteen years the Jeffersons had ten children (six girls and four boys), but only eight of them survived infancy. Thomas, their third child and first son, was born at Shadwell, the family estate, on April 13, 1743.

Sometime in 1745 William Randolph suddenly died at his Tuckahoe home. Under the provisions of his will, William had entrusted the care of his two children and the management of his estate to his "dear and loving friend," Peter Jefferson. Peter left his home and lands in the care of an overseer and moved his family to the Tuckahoe plantation.

Acceding to the wishes of William's will was a completely unselfish act on Peter's part. When William Randolph died, Peter had four children of his own and a growing estate to administer. Peter received no financial compensation for being the executor of William's estate. According to Willard Sterne Randall's biography, *Thomas Jefferson: A Life*, the only compensation Peter received was food, lodging, and schooling for his children. Nevertheless, Peter served as the caretaker of the estate and guardian of the Randolph children for about six or seven years, and according to Dumas Malone's book, *Jefferson the Virginian*, Peter "was unquestionably a more prosperous man after this period than he had been before."

Although he had a long record of service as a public and elected official, Peter Jefferson became best known for his work as a surveyor and map maker. When Thomas was three, Peter worked with a forty-man surveying crew mapping an area of Virginia that became known as the Fairfax Line. The survey took seven weeks, and Peter crossed mountains "prodigiously full of fallen timber and ivey," precipices where horses lost their footing, and swamps of laurel that a less determined man would have found impenetrable. During the expedition, some of the crew's horses died and several of the crew members were stricken with fevers and dysentery. But according to Malone, the only sign of weakness Peter showed was once being "much indisposed." For his seven weeks of hard labor, Peter reportedly was paid twenty pounds.

In 1749 Peter Jefferson and Joshua Fry, who had been Peter's partner in the Fairfax Line survey, were commissioned to continue the dividing line between Virginia and North Carolina, which had first been established by William Byrd in 1728. They crossed rivers, streams, and mountain ranges to extend the line an additional ninety miles to the east. In 1751 Jefferson and Fry completed their survey and drew a map of "the most inhabited part of Virginia containing the whole province of Maryland with parts of Pennsylvania, New Jersey and North Carolina." In his book, *Thomas Jefferson: A Biography*, Nathan Schachner describes their map as still "the fundamental map of Virginia and its environs, and [it] remained for many years the sole geographical arbiter for the territory it presumed to cover."

Peter and Joshua were handsomely rewarded for their landmark surveying and cartography. Peter was paid 300 pounds plus expenses for his surveying, and he earned an additional 150 pounds for drawing the map. After Peter returned home, young Thomas Jefferson spent hours listening to his father's tales of the adventures, hardships, and dangers he had encountered and endured during the survey. Stories of defending himself against wild beasts, of sleeping in trees, and of having to eat raw meat to survive were passed on from father to son. Young Thomas was duly impressed by his father's courage, daring, and fortitude.

Peter also passed on to Thomas his love of nature and the outdoors. Peter taught Thomas about the flora and fauna around them as well as how to swim, fish, ride a horse, and stalk game. Peter's education of Thomas was intellectual as well as physical. As Jefferson biographer Willard Sterne Randall put it, Peter "taught his son his own exquisite penmanship, his veneration for books, his love of mathematics." Peter read the works of Addison, Swift, Pope, and Shakespeare. According to Jefferson family legend, Thomas read all of his father's books by the age of five, including the Bible and Rapin's *History of England*. In short, Peter expected Thomas to exercise both mind and body and not neglect one to the detriment of the other. Peter would remind Thomas that "It is the strong in body who are both the strong and free in mind." Peter also emphasized self-reliance. One of his favorite sayings was "Never ask another to do for you what you can do for yourself."

Like his fellow presidential father, Augustine Washington, Peter Jefferson was reputed to be a man of prodigious physical strength. That is illustrated by two anecdotes appearing in several biographies of President Jefferson. The first anecdote tells of three slaves tugging on a rope in a futile effort to pull down a dilapidated shed. When Peter saw this, he took the rope from them and proceeded to single-handedly demolish the structure. The second anecdote claims that Peter Jefferson could simultaneously "head up" (raise from their sides to an upright position) two hogsheads of tobacco weighing nearly 1,000 pounds each.

Although there is no surviving portrait or likeness of Peter Jefferson, evidence suggests that there was a physical resemblance between Thomas and Peter. Henry Randall's 1865 biography, *The Life of Thomas Jefferson*, states, "There was some physical resemblance between them. According to tradition, the calm, thoughtful, firm eye of the son, and the outlines of his face, were those of his father; his physical strength, too, was beyond that of ordinary men; but his slim form and delicate fibres were those of his mother's family." Other Jefferson biographers describe both Peter and Thomas as "tall and sinewy."

Randall also provides some insights into Peter Jefferson's personality: "His judgement was swift and solid. His neighbors sought his advice; his friends soon learned to esteem it unerring. His mind once made up, no danger could turn him aside...." Randall also characterizes Peter as "a tender husband, a devoted father."

Peter Jefferson unexpectedly died at his home on August 17, 1757. He was forty-nine years old. The cause of death is not known. Jefferson biographers mention that Peter's neighbor, an unlicensed physician named Dr. Thomas Walker, frequently treated Peter during the summer of 1757.

Peter's will made generous provisions for his widow and eight children. His wife got lifetime use of the house, the plantation, and a significant portion of the crops, livestock, and slaves. Each child inherited a servant, and the daughters were bequeathed a stipend of 200 pounds to be paid within a year of their marriage or their twenty-first birthday. The most important material goods Peter left to Thomas were a forty-volume library, his bookcase, and his writing desk. Most importantly, Peter's dying wish was for Thomas to continue his classical education.

Natalie S. Bober describes Thomas Jefferson as "overwhelmed by a sense of sadness and loss," and according to Willard Sterne Randall, Thomas "missed his father terribly, and he transferred his grief into blaming his mother."

There is no extant correspondence between Peter and Thomas. In a letter to his grandson, Thomas Jefferson Randolph, Thomas Jefferson alluded to his father's death: "When I recollect that at fourteen years of age the whole care and direction of myself was thrown on myself entirely, without a relative or friend qualified to advise or guide me, and recollect the various sorts of bad company with which I associated from time to time, I am astonished that I did not turn off with some of them and become as worthless to society as they were."

Exactly how profound and pervasive was the influence of Peter on Thomas? As previously mentioned, Thomas Jefferson's *Autobiography* offers scant insight. Perhaps that is because Thomas Jefferson was seventy-seven years old when he wrote it. Peter died when Thomas was fourteen, and more than six decades of fatherlessness greatly obscured Thomas's memories of Peter.

According to Malone, Thomas "may have imbibed democratic attitudes from his father, for the Colonel had associated with crude men on the frontier." Merrill D. Peterson's *Thomas Jefferson and the New Nation* provides the most detailed analysis of how and why Peter influenced Thomas's life: "He owed his father a great deal, not in companionship, for they were frequently apart, perhaps not even in affection, but in the tone and direction given to his life. Habits of industry, system and responsibility are acquired early, and in Jefferson's case they were learned first from his father."

Bibliography

Bober, Natalie S. *Thomas Jefferson: Man on a Mountain.* New York: Atheneum, 1988.
Brodie, Fawn M. *Thomas Jefferson: An Intimate History.* New York: Bantam, 1974.
Cunningham, Noble E., Jr. *In Pursuit of Reason: The Life of Thomas Jefferson.* Baton Rouge, La.: Louisiana State University Press, 1987.
Fleming, Thomas. *The Man from Monticello: An Intimate Life of Thomas Jefferson.* New York: Morrow, 1969.
Koch, Adrienne and William Peden, editors. *The Life and Selected Writings of Thomas Jefferson.* New York: Modern Library, 1972.
Lisitzky, Gene. *Thomas Jefferson.* New York: Viking Press, 1933.
Malone, Dumas. *Jefferson the Virginian.* Boston: Little, Brown, 1948.

Peterson, Merrill D. *Thomas Jefferson and the New Nation*. New York: Oxford University Press, 1970.
Randall, Henry S. *The Life of Thomas Jefferson*. Philadelphia: Lippincott, 1865.
Randall, Willard Sterne. *Thomas Jefferson: A Life*. New York: Macrae, 1993.
Schachner, Nathan. *Thomas Jefferson: A Biography*. New York: Yoseloff, 1951.

James Madison Sr. (1723–1801)

Farmer, justice of the peace, vestryman, sheriff, soldier, public official, and father of President James Madison

The letters James Madison wrote to his father, James Sr., indicate the immense respect America's fourth president had for his father. James invariably began his letters with the salutation "Honored Sir" and closed with "Your dutiful son."

The first ancestor of James Sr. to emigrate to America was a ship's carpenter named John Maddison. John had left England in the early 1650s. Upon arriving in America, John acquired the rights to six hundred acres of land in what is now Gloucester County, Virginia. John worked hard, prospered, and used the capital he earned to acquire more land. When he died in the 1680s, his estate had expanded to 1,900 acres. John II dropped a "d" from the surname and worked as a tobacco planter, sheriff, and magistrate in colonial Virginia. One of his three sons, Ambrose, was the father of James Sr. and the grandfather of President James Madison. In 1721 Ambrose married Francis Taylor. Francis was the sister of Zachary Taylor, whose namesake grandson would serve as twelfth president of the United States. Thus President James Madison and President Zachary Taylor were second cousins.

When James Madison Sr. was born on March 27, 1723, Ambrose received a dowry of 2,240 acres in Orange County, Virginia. Ambrose expanded upon that tract by claiming and acquiring an additional 5,333 acres. By 1729 he had some land cleared and had a house built for his growing family. Ambrose Madison died in 1732 when James Sr. was nine. Ambrose was survived by a widow, three children, and twenty-nine slaves. His will decreed that Francis would manage the estate until James Sr. turned eighteen.

With the death of Ambrose, the carefree childhood of James Madison Sr. abruptly ended. James Sr. became second in command in the operation and maintenance of the family plantation. Among other chores, he helped to plant, cultivate, cure, and ship the tobacco crop. Virginia Moore succinctly sums up James Sr.'s early years in her book, *The Madisons: A Biography*: "He was a man before he was a boy."

James Sr. first met his future bride when he was delivering some tobacco to a warehouse. Nelly Conway was the daughter of Francis Conway, the prosperous merchant and planter who owned the warehouse. Exactly where and when James Sr. and Nelly met is not known. It is known that they were wed on September 15, 1749, when she was eighteen and James Sr. was twenty-six.

Their first child, James, was born at midnight on March 16, 1751, in the home of his maternal grandparents in Port Conway, Virginia. James Sr. and Nelly eventually had twelve children, and seven of them lived to maturity.

James spent his childhood at Montpelier, the family plantation. His chief companions and playmates were the children of his father's slaves. The childhood friendships he formed later caused him to become an outspoken foe of slavery. James's lifelong interest in politics, law, and public service was nurtured by his father's involvement in the colonial government. James Sr. served the Virginia colony as both a magistrate and as an officer of the law. While serving as a vestryman of the Anglican church, James Sr. collected taxes and doled out alms to the poor. He was also responsible for arresting drunkards, profaners, and any scofflaws found horseback riding on the Sabbath. James came to see his father as a conservative enforcer of the mores and laws of the colony.

James Sr. was a reluctant magistrate. For three years, he refused to accept an appointment as justice of the peace, citing the demands of overseeing a plantation, building a mansion, and tending to the needs of an ever-growing family. When he finally accepted the office, James Sr. became justice of the king's peace and presiding magistrate of Orange County. Acceptance of the office also made James Sr. commander of the king's militia in Orange County. James Madison Sr. thus became the most politically powerful and influential citizen of Orange County. In effect, he was responsible for the county government and was answerable only to the colonial governor.

While immersing himself in the life of the colonial gentleman/planter/politician, James Sr. made sure that his son would receive the best possible education. When James was eleven, James Sr. enrolled him in a private school run by a scholarly Scottish schoolmaster named Donald Robertson. James studied the classical curriculum of the time. He studied Latin, Greek, world history, geography, geometry, and algebra. He read Virgil, Ovid, Cervantes, and Montesquieu. James would later say of Robertson: "All I have been in life, I owe largely to that man."

Besides providing James with a quality education, James Sr. raised James and his other children in a religious household. James Sr. led his family in daily prayers and Bible readings. Every Sunday when there were services, James Sr. would hitch up the carriage and the Madisons would travel four miles to attend services at the Brick Church.

James unhappily left Robertson's tutelage in 1761. James Sr. withdrew him from school because the rector of the Brick Church, the Reverend Thomas Martin, had established residence at Montpelier and became a live-in tutor for the Madison children. Martin is credited with convincing James to forsake William and Mary College and to attend Princeton instead.

While James was getting an education, James Sr. was becoming more alienated

James Madison Sr. Courtesy of Belle Grove, Inc.

and estranged from England. According to Moore, after the news of the Boston Tea Party reached Montpelier in December of 1773, Justice of the King's Peace James Madison Sr. had to decide whether to uphold the King's law or "on the ground of a higher law — to oppose it." James Sr. conferred with James before making a decision.

By December of 1774 it was apparent that James Sr. had decided to follow what he perceived as a higher law. He organized the Orange County committee on public safety with his son James as his principal aide. The committee raised and organized troops and stockpiled firearms and ammunition in anticipation of an impending war with England. Following the battles of Lexington and Concord, the committee officially voiced its support of the revolutionaries. A May 9, 1775, letter to Patrick Henry written by James Sr. and signed by the committee's eleven members stated, "The blow struck in the Massachusetts government is a hostile attack on this and every other colony, and is a sufficient warrant to use violence and reprisal in all cases in which it may be expedient for our security and welfare."

Both James Sr. and James Madison were ardent supporters of the revolutionary cause. Both Madisons held the rank of colonel in the militia, but health problems ostensibly prevented either of them from engaging in combat. James Sr. was in his early fifties when the fighting started. James's delicate health limited his participation to drilling, recruiting, and target practice.

By 1778, James Sr. was feeling too old and weary to continue serving as the county lieutenant of Orange County. At the time, James was serving as a member of Virginia's Council of State. When he heard of his father's possible resignation, he wrote James Sr. and appealed to his father's sense of patriotism: "Although I well know how inconvenient and disagreeable it is to you to continue to act as the lieutenant of the county, I cannot help informing you that a resignation at this juncture is here to have a very unfriendly aspect on the execution of the draft, and consequently, to betray at least a want of patriotism and perserverance." The letter had the desired effect, and James Sr. continued to serve as the county lieutenant.

Because of his father's financial support, James Madison was able to pursue a career in politics and public service. According to Irving Brant's biography, *The Fourth President: A Life of James Madison*, James did not receive any salary during his first three years as a member of the Continental Congress: "In his first year, Virginia sent him 39,000 pounds in paper currency for expenses. Its case value was 547.16.3 pounds, a bit over half of his living costs. Small remittances from his father kept him going for the next two years."

Madison biographers agree that James Sr. had a profound and pervasive influence on the life and character of America's fourth president. As Ralph Ketcham puts it in *James Madison: A Biography*, "The father had made an immense contribution to the moral and practical education of his son, and deserves therefore an important share of the credit for the sensible, humane qualities of the son's statesmanship." According to Moore, James Sr.'s reserved manner was something he passed on to his eldest son: "The 'old Colonel' and the 'young Colonel' did not share that slightly long upper lip for nothing. The father's reticence had been fostered by heavy early farm responsibilities, and later by his position as magistrate and county lieutenant; the son's by an example of a father he greatly esteemed and by his own experience in office holding."

There may have been some conflict between the father and son over the issue of slavery. James Madison abhorred slavery, but both he and James Sr. apparently regarded the peculiar institution as a necessary evil in the management of the family plantation. James Sr. was known for his humane treatment of his slaves and for regarding them as human beings rather than chattel. James Sr. made sure that his slaves were decently housed, clothed, and fed. According to Moore, James Sr. saw to it that his slaves were sufficiently educated to read, write, cipher, and learn a craft.

His son anguished over how slavery was fostering sectionalism in a fledgling nation. However, he was not an advocate of emancipation because he thought freed slaves would not have the life management skills to live in a white man's society. Instead, James hoped for a national plan to send them back to Africa.

The start of a new century preceded the final weeks of James Madison Sr.'s life. On January 10, 1801, James Madison wrote Thomas Jefferson that "the age and very declining state of my father are making almost daily claims on my attention, and from appearances it may not be long before these claims may acquire their full force."

In February of 1801 the House of Representatives resolved a deadlocked electoral college vote by electing Thomas Jefferson as America's third president. Jefferson sent James Madison an urgent request to come to Washington at once to assume the office of secretary of state. As James prepared to leave, his gravely ill father suffered a relapse.

On February 28, 1801, James Madison wrote the president-elect: "Yesterday morning rather suddenly, tho very gently, the flame of life went out." James Madison Sr. was dead at the age of seventy-seven.

James Madison's move to Washington, D.C., was delayed for nearly two months while he settled his father's estate. Through what was termed "amicable negotiations, concessions, and adjustments," James Madison divided the estate to the satisfaction of the numerous heirs. Then, after fulfilling his final obligation to his father, James Sr.'s firstborn child left for Washington, D.C.

Bibliography

Brant, Irving. *The Fourth President: A Life of James Madison*. Indianapolis: Bobbs-Merrill, 1970.

———. *James Madison: The Virginia Revolutionist, 1751–1780*. Indianapolis: Bobbs-Merrill, 1941.

———. *James Madison: The Nationalist, 1780–1787*. Indianapolis: Bobbs-Merrill, 1948.

Ketcham, Ralph. *James Madison: A Biography*. New York: Macmillan, 1971.

McCoy, Drew R. *The Last of the Fathers: James Madison and the Republican Legacy.* Cambridge, Great Britain: Cambridge University Press, 1989.
Moore, Virginia. *The Madisons: A Biography.* New York: McGraw-Hill, 1979.
Peterson, Merrill D., editor. *James Madison: A Biography in His Own Words.* New York: Harper, 1974.
Polikoff, Barbara G. *James Madison: Fourth President of the United States.* Ada, Okla.: Garrett Educational Corporation, 1989.
Rakove, Jack N. *James Madison and the Creation of the American Republic.* Glenview, Il.: Scott, Foresman, 1990.
Rives, William C. *History of the Life and Times of James Madison.* Freeport, N.Y.: Books for Libraries Press, 1970.
Rutland, Robert Allen. *James Madison: The Founding Father.* New York: Macmillan, 1987.
Steinberg, Alfred. *James Madison.* New York: Putnam's, 1965.

Spence Monroe
(?–1774)

*Circuit judge, farmer, carpenter, and father of
President James Monroe*

Spence Monroe is one of the most obscure fathers of an American president. There are no existing records of where and when the father of America's fifth president was born. James Monroe described his father in his *Autobiography* simply as a "worthy and respectable citizen possessed of good land and other property."

According to the lore of the Monroe family, Spence was a direct descendant of Andrew Monroe. Andrew, who was Spence's grandfather, was an officer in the army of King Charles I. Probably sometime after Oliver Cromwell's forces won the Battle of Preston in 1648, Andrew was exiled to the Virginia colony. There he settled on two hundred acres of land by a small stream that became known as Monroe's Creek. When James Monroe was born in 1758, the descendants of Andrew Monroe had expanded the land holdings to 1,100 acres on both sides of the creek. The larger portion of the holdings belonged to the elder branch of the family. The remainder, which amounted to around five hundred acres, belonged to Spence Monroe. Spence's five hundred acres were enough to qualify him as a minor landholder among the members of colonial Virginia's landed gentry.

It is not known how much schooling Spence Monroe received, but it is acknowledged that his family did not have the financial means to send him to college. In 1752 Spence Monroe married Elizabeth Jones, the daughter of a Welsh emigrant who had acquired a large amount of property in King George County. There is even less information available on Elizabeth Jones Monroe than on Spence. The dates of her birth and death are unrecorded, and James simply described her as "a very amiable and respectable woman possessing the best domestic qualities of a good wife, and a good parent."

Their first son, James, was born at the Monroe's home in Westmoreland County, Virginia, on April 28, 1758. After James's birth, they had four more children, three boys and a girl. In addition to his work as a farmer, Spence Monroe was also a carpenter and a circuit judge. Records show that Spence Monroe was apprenticed to a carpenter named Robert Walker in 1743. In colonial Virginia a man could perform the manual labor of carpentry and still be considered a landed gentleman because the trades were held in high esteem. None of James Monroe's biographies provide any specific dates for Spence Monroe's terms as judge. Where, when, and how Spence Monroe received whatever legal education he had is also unrecorded.

After the birth of James, the next significant event in the life of Spence Monroe was the passing of the Stamp Act by the English Parliament in 1765. British Prime Minister George Grenville believed that levying a tax on colonial legal documents, playing cards, newspapers, and other printed materials would be an acceptable way to meet "the expenses of defending, protecting and securing" the American colonies. Spence Monroe, and many other colonists, were in complete disagreement.

James was just eight years old when his father left home to attend a meeting of anti–Stamp Act activists in Leeds. Spence Monroe became one of the 115 signers of the anti–Stamp Act resolutions. He was also actively involved in an economic boycott of imported English goods in an attempt to pressure Parliament into repealing the Stamp Act. Other prominent early American patriots who joined Spence Monroe in the boycott were George Washington, Richard Henry Lee, and Archibald Cary (a cousin of Thomas Jefferson).

Spence Monroe died in 1774 when James was around sixteen. Since James was the oldest son, he inherited Spence's estate and became responsible for the welfare of his siblings. According to Harry Ammon's biography, *James Monroe: The Quest for National Identity*, caring for his brothers became a lifetime responsibility for James, "for neither of his brothers were successful." Joseph Jones, who was James's maternal uncle and a member of the Continental Congress, was the executor of Spence's estate. Jones also became James Monroe's guardian, benefactor, and surrogate father.

Since Spence Monroe is such a shadowy figure, it is difficult to say how he influenced James. Spence's prominent opposition to the Stamp Act and his espousal of the revolutionary ideal of "no taxation without representation" likely influenced James. It is reasonable to assume that some of the father's political beliefs and sympathies were passed on to his oldest son. James must have shared some of his father's revolutionary fervor, because he dropped out of William and Mary College in 1776 to join the Continental Army. James saw action in several battles, crossed the Delaware with Washington, and endured the extremely harsh winter at Valley Forge in 1777–1778.

Spence apparently wanted James to be better educated than he had been. From ages eleven to sixteen, James was a student at Campbelltown Academy, which was regarded as the finest school in the colony. When James attended, the enrollment was limited to twenty-five students. The academy prepared James for admission to William and Mary College. According to Stuart Gerry Brown, editor of *The Autobiography of James Monroe*, both Spence and Uncle Joseph "had intended him [James] for the bar which his mind by preference had been directed."

James fulfilled his father's intentions and then some. He not only was admitted to the bar, James Monroe served as a member of the Virginia Assembly, the Continental Congress, and the U.S. Senate. He also served as secretary of state, governor of Virginia, and two terms as president of the United States. Spence would have been proud.

Bibliography

Ammon, Harry. *James Monroe: The Quest for National Identity.* New York: McGraw-Hill, 1971.
Brown, Stuart Gerry, editor. *The Autobiography of James Monroe.* Syracuse, N.Y.: Syracuse University Press, 1959.
Cresson, W. P. *James Monroe.* Chapel Hill, N.C.: University of North Carolina Press, 1946.
Gilman, Daniel C. *James Monroe.* Boston & New York: Houghton Mifflin, 1883.
Morgan, George. *The Life of James Monroe.* Boston: Small, Maynard, 1921.
Styron, Arthur. *The Last of the Cocked Hats: James Monroe and the Virginia Dynasty.* Norman, Okla.: University of Oklahoma Press, 1945.
Wetzel, Charles. *James Monroe.* New York: Chelsea House, 1989.

John Adams
(1735–1826)

Teacher, attorney, politician, public official, legislator, diplomat, vice president of the United States, president of the United States, and father of President John Quincy Adams

The next father in this series needs no introduction, since John Adams is the only father of an American president to also serve as president of the United States. The father of America's sixth president was born on October 30, 1735, at the Adams family homestead in Braintree (now called Quincy), Massachusetts. John was the first of three sons born to Deacon John and Susanna Boylston Adams.

Despite a professed interest in farming as a career, John's parents insisted that their oldest son go to college. John was an underachieving and indifferent student until he came under the tutelage of a teacher named Joseph Marsh. Because of Marsh's energetic and inspired teaching, John began to develop his intellect and acquire a respect for knowledge. After being taught by Marsh for about one year, John Adams was admitted to Harvard College.

In 1755 John received a B.A. degree from Harvard. His class rank was fifteenth of twenty-four, but that is a bit misleading. At that time, class standing was based on the family's social status rather than on academic achievement. After graduation, John found employment as master of the grammar school in Worcester, Massachusetts. John never liked teaching and never pretended that he did. He was responsible for teaching fifty boys ranging in age from five to fifteen. John referred to his reluctant scholars as "little runtlings; just capable of lisping A, B, C, and troubling their master."

John found escape, solace, and satisfaction by spending his time outside of school in the law office of James Putnam. Adams learned and absorbed enough from Putnam to be admitted to the Massachusetts bar in 1758. He began practicing law in Braintree.

Sometime in 1762 John accompanied his friend, Richard Cranch, to Weymouth, Massachusetts. Cranch went there to visit his fiancée, Mary Smith. To his delight John discovered that Mary had an attractive, petite, teenaged sister named

Abigail. Abigail Smith was a feminist before the term was coined. She read then more than a woman was expected to read. She was outspoken in social situations where women were expected to maintain a ladylike silence. Biographers of Adams write that John easily fell in and out of love, but Abigail is the only woman he ever proposed to. They were married in Weymouth on October 25, 1764, when she was nineteen and John was twenty-nine.

John and Abigail had five children (two girls and three boys). Four of their children lived to maturity. John Quincy Adams was their second child and first son. He was born at the family home in Braintree on July 11, 1767. When John Quincy was three, his father temporarily retired from politics. John's brief departure from the political arena allowed him to spend more time with John Quincy. As David Jacobs writes in *The American Heritage Book of the Presidents and Famous People*, John was able "to establish an extremely close if not demonstrative relationship with his son."

As John became increasingly involved in the American Revolution, his precocious son began adopting John's anti–British sentiments. By the time he was seven, John Quincy was an avid reader of the patriot press. Less than a month before his eighth birthday, John Quincy sat on a hilltop with Abigail and watched the Battle of Bunker Hill.

While John Quincy was embracing and advocating his father's political beliefs, John and Abigail were incessantly goading their oldest son to read, study, and make more productive use of his time. In a letter to his father written at age nine, John Quincy apologizes for not being more studious:

> I love to receive letters very well; much better than I love to write them. I make but a poor figure at composition. My head is much too fickle. My thoughts are running after bird's eggs, play and trifles, till I get vexed with myself. Mamma has a troublesome task to keep me studying. I own that I am ashamed of myself. . . . I am determined this week to be more diligent. . . . I wish sir, you would give me in writing some instructions with regard to the use of my time, and advise me how to proportion my studies and play, and I will keep them by me, and endeavor to follow them. With the present determination of growing better, I am dear sir, your son.

In February of 1778 John Quincy made his first trip to Europe, accompanying his father to Paris. John was sent by the Continental Congress to lobby the French to intervene and side with the colonies during the Revolutionary War. John and Abigail saw the journey as an opportunity to give John Quincy a superior European education.

During the ship's first morning out of harbor, it was spotted by British warships who pursued the craft for two days. That adventure was followed by a three-day winter storm. After the stormy weather cleared, they were fired upon by an English pirate ship. In his diary, John made note of his son's courage: "Mr. Johnny's behavior gave me a satisfaction that I cannot express, fully aware of our danger, he was constantly endeavoring to bear it with manly patience."

John Adams. Courtesy of U.S. Department of the Interior, National Park Service, Adams National Historic Site, Quincy, Massachusetts.

Upon arriving in France, John and John Quincy moved in with Benjamin Franklin at his residence in the Paris suburb of Passy. John Quincy was promptly enrolled in a private boarding school where he studied Latin, French, music, dancing, drawing, and fencing. In August 1779 John and John Quincy returned to America. Father and son barely had time to unpack before they were preparing for another trip to Europe. John had been appointed minister plenipotentiary to negotiate a peace treaty with England. John Quincy wanted to stay at home. He had hopes of enrolling in Andover Academy to prepare himself for admission to Harvard. However, Abigail persuaded him to accompany his father and younger brother, Charles, to France. John Quincy reluctantly but obediently acquiesced.

On December 18, 1779, the three Adamses landed in Spain. They traveled on to Paris, and John Quincy was reenrolled in the boarding school at Passy. Early in 1781 a new diplomatic assignment moved John and his sons to Amsterdam. While in the Netherlands, John Quincy attended the Amsterdam Latin School and the University of Leyden. In a letter to his father, John Quincy describes his journey to the university and the lectures he and Charles attended as well as their lodgings. Finally, he gets to the true purpose of the communiqué by asking his father for money to buy a pair of ice skates: "They are of various prices from 3 Guilders to 3 Ducats those of a ducat are as good as need to but I would like to know whether you would chuse to have me give so much."

One week later, John answered his son's request. He agreed to give him the money but not without first telling his son: "Do not conclude from this that I advise you to spend much of your time or Thoughts upon these Exercises or Diversions.... But, as your Constitution requires vigorous Exercise, it will not be amiss, to spend some of your Time in swimming, Riding, Dancing, Fencing and Skating. ... Every Thing in Life should be done with Reflection, and Judgement, even the most insignificant Amusements."

In 1781 John procured for John Quincy his first job in the field of diplomacy. John's friend, Francis Dana, was sent by Congress to Russia with the diplomatic mission of persuading Catherine the Great to recognize the United States of America as an independent nation. French was the language of diplomacy, and Dana needed an interpreter and translator. John Quincy served as Dana's private secretary for about eighteen months.

After the completion of his work in Russia, John Quincy took a leisurely six months to travel back to the Netherlands. Upon arriving there, he became the secretary to the American delegation of John Adams, Ben Franklin, and John Jay, who were negotiating the Treaty of Paris, officially ending the Revolutionary War. According to Fred G. Clarke's biography, *John Quincy Adams*, during those peace negotiations "young Adams acquired most of the qualities, the strong sides and the weak, of his father — his brilliance, courage and integrity, as well as his inflexibility and his obtuseness about human nature."

In February of 1785 John Adams was appointed minister to England. Once again he requested his oldest son to make a trip to Europe with him. He offered

John Quincy the position of private secretary. John Quincy declined because he still desired to attend Harvard. This time, John and Abigail let their son have his way. John Quincy Adams entered Harvard as a junior. He graduated second among the fifty-one students in the class of 1787. He spent the next three years studying law in the office of Theophilius Parsons in Newburyport, Massachusetts. In July of 1790 John Quincy passed the bar exam and set up practice in Boston.

On a spring day in 1794 John Quincy made the mistake of telling his father that the fires of youthful ambition that had once blazed within him were now nearly extinguished. "I find myself contented with my state as it is," John Quincy told his father. "I see very few things in this life beyond the wants of nature that I desire."

Those candid remarks earned him a stinging rebuke from his father, who was then serving a second term as President George Washington's vice president. John let his unambitious son know that he expected him to someday be president. John wrote: "You come into life with advantages which will disgrace you if your success is mediocre. And if you do not rise to the head not only of your Profession but of your Country, it will be owing to your own Lasiness, Slovenliness and Obstinancy."

Shortly after receiving that highly critical letter, John Quincy Adams was appointed minister to the Netherlands by President Washington. He had not sought the appointment, and he was extremely sensitive to the charges of nepotism the appointment would invariably bring. However, John Quincy would soon discover that the office was a minor, boring, and unimportant diplomatic post. Biographers of Adams write that John and Abigail were much more excited about the appointment than John Quincy was. Once again, John Quincy was being the dutiful son by embarking upon the career path his parents had chosen for him. John Quincy made note of this by writing: "I have indeed long known that my father is far more ambitious for my advancement, far more solicitous for the extension of my fame, than I have ever been, or ever shall be."

Before leaving for his new post, John Quincy unexpectedly received a generous gift from his father, an order on Dutch bankers for the large sum of five thousand guilders. That was John Quincy's financial reward for going along with his parents' wishes. John Quincy gave part of the money to his Aunt Eliza, and he gave the rest to his brother, Charles, to invest. Unfortunately, Charles squandered the money, and John Quincy spent the rest of his life devoid of the financial security his father's gift would have provided.

Once he assumed his diplomatic post, John Quincy found that there was little to do besides processing American loans made to Dutch bankers. In a letter to his father he complained, "An American Minister at the Hague is one of the most useless beings in creation." John tried to buoy his son's sagging spirits by pointing out, "the pleasure that I have received from the satisfaction you have given the President and the Secretary of State . . . from the clear, comprehensive and masterly accounts . . . of the public affairs of the nations in Europe, whose situations and politics it most concerns us to know. Go on, my dear son . . . continue to deserve well of your father, but especially of your country."

Despite initial objections from his parents, John Quincy Adams married Louisa Catherine Johnson in London, England, on July 26, 1797. The groom was thirty and the bride was twenty-two. Abigail and John had thwarted an earlier romance. When he was a twenty-two-year-old law student, John Quincy had fallen deeply in love with eighteen-year-old Mary Frazier. His parents conspired to convince John Quincy that a fledgling lawyer did not have the financial resources to support a wife.

Shortly before his wedding, John Quincy had been appointed minister to Portugal by outgoing President George Washington. John Quincy was prepared to accept the post, but everything changed when his father was elected president in 1796. After consulting with Washington, President John Adams appointed John Quincy Adams minister to Prussia. John Quincy vehemently objected to his latest appointment. In a letter to Abigail, he wrote that he would rather have no position if it would shield his father from charges of nepotism. John admonished John Quincy for worrying about nepotism: "It is the worst found opinion I have ever known you to conceive." Abigail settled the matter by forwarding a letter from ex-President Washington to her highly principled son. Washington wrote: "there remains no doubt in my mind that he will prove himself the ablest of all our diplomatic corps. . . . The country would sustain a serious loss if [his talents and worth] were to be checked by over-delicacy on your [John Adams's] part."

John Quincy Adams served as minister to Prussia for four years before being recalled by his father in 1801. John's motives for the recall remain unclear. Some historians say that President John Adams wanted to spare Thomas Jefferson the embarrassment of having an Adams serving in his administration. Others claim that President John Adams knew that Jefferson would retain John Quincy's services and President John Adams did not want to be beholden to President-elect Jefferson.

After his defeat by Jefferson in the 1800 presidential election, John Adams permanently retired from politics. All through his postpresidential years, John Adams took an avid interest in John Quincy's political career. The recalled diplomat won election to the Massachusetts State Senate in 1802. That same year, John Quincy unsuccessfully ran as a Federalist candidate for the U.S. House of Representatives. One year later, John Quincy Adams was elected to the legislature his father had once presided over, the United States Senate.

As a senator, John Quincy Adams showed a remarkable degree of independence by supporting the Jefferson administration. Ultimately he showed more independence than the legislature that elected him could tolerate. In 1808 the Massachusetts Legislature voted to replace him before his senatorial term expired. The Federalist-dominated legislature elected James Lloyd Jr. as U.S. Senator. John Quincy resigned his senate seat in June of 1808.

Apparently, John Adams had expected that his son's stubborn independence would lead to such a course of events. In January of 1808 he had written to John Quincy: "You are supported by no party; you have too honest a heart, too independent a mind, and too brilliant talents, to be sincerely and confidentially trusted by any man who is under the domination of party maxims or party feelings. . . .

You may depend upon it then that your fate is decided.... You ought to know and expect this, and by no means to regret it." In his biography, *Passionate Sage: The Character and Legacy of John Adams*, Joseph J. Ellis notes the influence of the father upon the son: "The correspondence between the father and son continued the tradition of paternal advice and patriarchal supervision begun when John Quincy was a boy."

John Adams seems to have viewed his son's ascendancy in national politics with mixed emotions. In an 1813 letter he sounded as though having a son near would be preferable to having a son in the White House: "I should not much care if, like Mr. Jay, you should retire and study prophecies or translate Demosthenes provided that you are so near me that I would see you once a day or even once a week." A few years later, John bluntly told John Quincy that it would be good for him to get out of government service altogether. The news that President James Monroe was considering John Quincy for secretary of state caused John to write that he would "rather have you retire to Montizillo, renounce all public employment forever, and lay your bones here with your Ancestors than remain where you are [in Washington], annihilating yourself and ruining your children."

In 1824 John Quincy Adams fulfilled his father's paternal prophecy by being elected president of the United States. John Adams became the first presidential father to see his son elected to that exalted office. Oddly enough there was no celebrating or rejoicing by John Adams. When friends offered their congratulations, John Adams said, "No man who ever held the office of President would congratulate a friend on attaining it."

John Adams died at his home in Quincy, Massachusetts, on July 4, 1826. He was ninety. John Quincy Adams did not learn of his father's death until July 9. On July 8, while en route from Washington to Quincy, President John Quincy Adams (who had been warned that his father's death was imminent) wrote in his *Diary*, "my intention had been to visit him about the beginning of next month. I had flattered myself that he would survive this summer, and even other years."

After receiving news of his father's death, President John Quincy Adams wrote in his *Diary*, "For myself, all that I dare to ask is, that I may live the remnant of my days in a manner worthy of him from whom I came, and at the appointed hour of my Maker, die as my father had died, in peace with God, and man, sped to the regions of futurity with the blessings of my fellow-men."

Although he described himself as "a man of reserved, cold, austere and forbidding manners," John Quincy Adams evidently had feelings of profound anguish and grief when his beloved father died. The *Diary* entry of July 13, 1826, eloquently describes the pain, sorrow, and heightened sense of his mortality brought about by a visit to his father's home. America's sixth president wrote:

> Everything about the house is the same. I was not fully sensible of the change till I entered his bed-chamber, the place where I had last taken leave of him, and where I had most sat with him at my last two yearly visits to this place.

The moment was inexpressibly painful, and struck me as if it had been an arrow to the heart. My father and my mother have departed. The charm which has always made this house to me an abode of enchantment is dissolved; and yet my attachment to it, and to the whole region round, is stronger than I ever felt it before. I feel that it is time for me to begin to set my house in order, and to prepare for the church-yard myself.

Bibliography

Bemis, Samuel Flagg. *John Quincy Adams and the Foundations of American Foreign Policy.* New York: Norton, 1973.

Butterfield, L. H., Marc Fridlaender, and Mary Jo Kline, editors. *The Book of Abigail and John: Selected Letters of the Adams Family.* Cambridge, Mass.: Harvard University Press, 1975.

Clarke, Fred G. *John Quincy Adams.* New York: Collier, 1966.

East, Robert A. *John Quincy Adams: The Critical Years, 1785–1794.* New York: Bookman Associates, 1962.

Ellis, Joseph J. *Passionate Sage: The Character and Legacy of John Adams.* New York: Norton, 1993.

Greenblatt, Miriam. *John Quincy Adams: Sixth President of the United States.* Ada, Okla.: Garrett Educational Corporation, 1990.

Hecht, Marie B. *John Quincy Adams: A Personal History of an Independent Man.* New York: Macmillan, 1972.

Hess, Stephen. *American Political Dynasties: From Adams to Kennedy.* Garden City, N.Y.: Doubleday, 1967.

Jacobs, David. "John Adams" and "John Quincy Adams." In *The American Heritage Book of the Presidents and Famous People.* New York: Dell, 1967, pp. 60–89, 184–200, 202–205.

Kennedy, John F. *Profiles in Courage.* New York: Harper & Row, 1956.

Morse, John T., Jr. *John Adams.* New Rochelle, N.Y.: Arlington House, 1970.

Nagel, Paul C. *Descent From Glory: Four Generations of the John Adams Family.* New York: Oxford University Press, 1983.

Nevins, Allan. *The Diary of John Quincy Adams, 1794–1845.* New York: Ungar, 1969.

Shepherd, Jack. *Cannibals of the Heart: A Personal Biography of Louisa Catherine and John Quincy Adams.* New York: McGraw Hill, 1980.

Andrew Jackson Sr. (?–1767)

*Linen weaver, farmer, and father of
President Andrew Jackson*

Any influences that Andrew Jackson had on his famous namesake son were merely biological. The father of America's seventh president was the first of three presidential fathers to die before their future chief executive sons were born (the fathers of Rutherford Hayes and Bill Clinton are the other two).

Andrew Jackson (hereafter called Andrew Sr. to distinguish him from his son) was born in Ireland, the son of a well-to-do merchant and linen weaver in the town of Carrickfergus. The date and year of his birth are not known. The sparse records of his ancestors indicate only that they had emigrated to northern Ireland from Scotland sometime after 1690. According to some sources, Andrew Sr. worked as a linen weaver before turning to tenant farming. Other biographies of Old Hickory claim that Andrew Sr. rejected an apprenticeship in that trade to become a farmer.

It is believed that Andrew Sr. was working as a tenant farmer in or around Carrickfergus when he met and married Elizabeth Hutchinson, who was working as a weaver. Elizabeth Hutchinson Jackson's birthdate is not known; neither is the date of their wedding. Andrew Sr. and Elizabeth had two sons before Andrew was born in 1767. Their first son, Hugh, was born in 1762, and their second son, Robert, was born in 1765.

The Jacksons were of necessity a two-income family. Andrew Sr. farmed by day and Elizabeth wove flax by night. Together, they saved what money they could in hopes of becoming part of the mass movement of Irish immigrants coming to America. It was impossible for the Jacksons to remain untouched by the great migration from Ireland to America occurring in the latter half of the eighteenth century. Four of Elizabeth's sisters and one of Andrew Sr.'s brothers had journeyed to America before Andrew, Elizabeth, and their two sons sailed out of Ireland in 1765.

Originally the Jacksons were to sail from Larne, Ireland, with nineteen other families. Andrew Sr.'s brother, Hugh, had lined up twenty families for this great adventure. Hugh Jackson had already seen America. He had fought with General

Edward Braddock's army during the French and Indian Wars. Hugh Jackson had fought Indians from Canada to the Carolinas. When he returned to Ireland, Hugh Jackson regaled his friends and neighbors with tales of a vast land of opportunity across the Atlantic.

However, Hugh Jackson's willful, stubborn Irish wife accomplished what all the Indian wars, battles, and skirmishes could not. She kept Hugh Jackson out of America. Mrs. Hugh Jackson forbade her husband to return to America. She refused to leave Ireland, and she also deterred most of Hugh's recruits from leaving the Emerald Isle. But she could not stop Andrew Sr. and Elizabeth.

In the spring of 1765 Andrew Sr., Elizabeth, Hugh (age two), and Robert (six months old), and two of the original twenty families set sail for a new life in a new land. Since there is a lack of documentary evidence, it is not certain exactly where and when the Jacksons landed in America. It is generally assumed that they landed in Pennsylvania and headed south after Andrew Sr. acquired the wagons, horses, and other needed provisions for the journey.

The Jacksons presumably traveled through Pennsylvania, Maryland, and the Virginia settlements before reaching the Carolina frontier. Andrew Sr. took his family on a well-traveled route; more than 1,000 wagons passed through the North Carolina village of Hillsboro in 1765. Continuing south from Hillsboro, Andrew Sr. ended the trek in a settlement called Waxhaw on the border of North and South Carolina. Waxhaw was chosen because four of Elizabeth's sisters and their families had already settled in that area. Friends and relatives helped Andrew Sr. build a crude cabin near the head of Liggett's branch, a tributary of the Twelve-Mile Creek on the watershed of the Catawba River.

It is generally assumed that Andrew Sr. was a squatter. Like so many other details of his life, this one also cannot be verified by records or documents. Biographies of Andrew Jackson usually indicate that his father never owned any land in America. What is known and agreed on is that Andrew Sr. spent the last months of his life in hard, manual labor. Andrew Sr. worked long and hard trying to establish himself as a self-sufficient farmer and was doing his best to provide for his family.

By the spring of 1766, Andrew Sr. had cleared about five or six acres and had begun growing corn and other vegetable crops. The following winter, Andrew Sr. had cleared some more land and his family's economic situation was gradually improving. That suddenly changed sometime in early March of 1767. Andrew Sr. attempted to move a log by himself. In all probability, the exertion caused an internal blood vessel to rupture. Death came rather quickly. Andrew Jackson once recalled his mother telling him that Andrew Sr. was ill for only about forty-eight hours. When Andrew Sr. was stricken, the nearest physician was twelve miles away. The nearest road was four miles from the Jackson cabin, and the nearest neighbor was a mile away. Elizabeth was essentially helpless. She was well into her last pregnancy, and she could not leave two young children home alone while she fetched a doctor.

According to Burke Davis's book, *Old Hickory: A Life of Andrew Jackson,* an old-fashioned Irish wake was held in the Jacksons' cabin. Mourners sipped whiskey from a gourd, mirrors were turned to the wall, and the clock was stopped with its face covered. The mourners attempted to console the widow and orphans by chanting psalms and reading Bible verses. On the morning after the wake, Andrew Jackson Sr. was buried in the churchyard of the Waxhaw Presbyterian Church. Legend has it that during the funeral procession, the coffin fell off the sled it was on. The pallbearers had been imbibing whiskey and did not notice the missing coffin until they arrived at the burial site. They retraced their steps and found it in the underbrush of the last creek they had crossed. The Reverend William Richardson eulogized Andrew Sr. while cold winds and sleet chilled the pallbearers and mourners.

Less than two weeks later, Elizabeth gave birth to her third son and last child. She named him Andrew in memory of her late husband. She abandoned the small cabin and moved in with her sister, Jane Crawford, and her in-laws.

According to Augustus C. Buell's biography of Andrew Jackson, *History of Andrew Jackson*, Jackson was never able to speak about his father without struggling to maintain his composure. Buell wrote that Jackson tried to locate his father's grave so that he could leave a suitable memento. Unfortunately, all the graves in the churchyard were unmarked. Francis P. Blair, a longtime Jackson friend and political advisor, recalled Andrew Jackson telling him that "his father died like a hero in battle fighting for his wife and babes; fighting an uphill battle against poverty and adversity such as no one in our time could comprehend."

Andrew Jackson Sr. had a hard life, a short life, and a simple life. But in the eyes of the son who never knew him, he was a hero.

Bibliography

Bassett, John Spencer. *The Life of Andrew Jackson*. New York: Macmillan, 1931.
Buell, Augustus C. *History of Andrew Jackson*. New York: Scribners, 1904.
Chidsey, Donald Barr. *Andrew Jackson: Hero*. Nashville: Thomas Nelson, 1976.
Curtis, James C. *Andrew Jackson and the Search for Vindication*. Boston: Little, Brown, 1976.
Davis, Burke. *Old Hickory: A Life of Andrew Jackson*. New York: Dial Press, 1977.
James, Marquis. *Andrew Jackson: The Border Captain*. Gloucester, Mass.: Smith, 1977.
Remini, Robert. *The Life of Andrew Jackson*. New York: Harper, 1988.
Sumner, William Graham. *Andrew Jackson as a Public Man*. Westport, Conn.: Greenwood Press, 1970.

Abraham Van Buren
(1737–1817)

*Town clerk, farmer, soldier, inn and tavern owner, and father of
President Martin Van Buren*

In his *Autobiography*, Martin Van Buren mentioned his father only once. America's eighth president used a mere sixty-one words to describe Abraham Van Buren and his paternal influence: "My father was an unassuming amiable man who was never known to have an enemy. Utterly devoid of any spirit of accumulation, his property, originally moderate, was gradually reduced until he could ill afford to bestow the necessary means upon the education of his children. My advantages, in that respect, were therefore limited to those offered by the Village academy."

Reading between the lines, one gets the impression that the son had some ambivalent feelings toward his father. Martin respected, maybe even envied, Abraham for having no enemies, a feeling that is only natural for a politician. However, he also felt some resentment because his father's improvident ways kept Martin out of the private schools.

Abraham Van Buren was the fifth of nine children born to Martin Van Buren and Dirckie Van Aelstyne. Abraham was born in Albany, New York. It is assumed that his date of birth was February 17, 1737. Abraham was baptized on February 27, 1737, and the custom of the Dutch Reformed Church his family belonged to was to christen a child ten days after birth. Abraham was born in his parents' home, which is described as a one-and-a-half story clapboard farmhouse with a brick chimney at each end. The house was located on the post road connecting Albany and New York City.

When his father died, Abraham inherited the family farm, the family's inn and tavern, and an unknown number of slaves. Why Abraham inherited most of his father's estate is not clear. Abraham was not the oldest child, but he may have been the oldest son. Under the then prevailing legal practice of primogeniture, Abraham would have inherited all the land for being the firstborn son. If he was not the oldest son, then Abraham must have been the favorite of the nine children.

The Van Buren farm and business were located in the village of Kinderhook.

The village was settled by Dutch immigrants in the early 1600s and had remained exclusively Dutch. Five generations of Van Burens had lived and died in Kinderhook by the time Martin Van Buren was born. Martin Van Buren once said that in Kinderhook there had not been "a single intermarriage with one of different extraction from the time of the arrival of the first immigrant to that of the marriage of my eldest son." While there was no intermarriage with outsiders, there appears to have been intermarriage within Kinderhook. According to research by Frank J. Conkling in the *New York Genealogical and Biographical Record,* Abraham Van Buren and Martin's grandfather both married women with Van Buren blood.

The bounty from the Van Buren farm was plentiful, but the profits were not. Abraham would "sell" the surplus to friends and neighbors who would neglect to pay, and Abraham Van Buren was never known to dun anyone over a debt. Abraham's generosity reportedly interfered with his social life. The mothers of Kinderhook warned their daughters to shun the romantic overtures of the improvident innkeeper. When he was still a bachelor at thirty-nine, Abraham Van Buren found a woman who consented to spend the rest of her life with him. Maria Hoes Van Alen was a widow with three dependent children when she married Abraham Van Buren in 1776. Maria was described as "good to look upon," but she had no dowry and three mouths to feed. Those circumstances made her unattractive to most of the single men in Kinderhook.

There seemed to be a pattern in the Van Buren family that the men would wait a while before marrying, and when they did get married, it would be to women significantly younger. Abraham's father married at thirty-three a lady thirteen years younger. Maria was ten years younger than Abraham when they wed. Martin Van Buren changed that by marrying a twenty-three-year-old lady when he was twenty-four. According to John Niven's biography, *Martin Van Buren: The Romantic Age of American Politics,* Maria, struggling to provide a home for three fatherless children, appealed to Abraham's sentimental side. Another likely reason for the marriage was the fact that Abraham was almost forty. Abraham certainly realized that if he wanted to start a family, time was running out.

The union of Abraham and Maria produced two daughters, Dirckie and Jannetje, before Martin was born on December 5, 1782. Martin Van Buren was christened at the Dutch Reformed Church in Kinderhook on December 15, 1782. His birth was followed by two younger brothers, Lawrence in 1786 and Abraham in 1788.

It is doubtful that Abraham was able to give young Martin much time or attention. By the time Martin was ten, he had seven siblings ranging in age from four to twenty-four. Besides his many family and business obligations, Abraham had six slaves to clothe, feed, and supervise. With Maria there was a total of fourteen people competing for a piece of Abraham's time, along with the customers at the inn and tavern.

While the Van Burens were not indigent, they certainly were not well-to-do. Abraham's generous nature, his practice of borrowing money on anything he owned, and his reluctance to pester his debtors made their financial situation even worse. In a small community like Kinderhook, it soon became known that Abraham Van Buren was an easy mark. Virtually any neighbor, acquaintance, or traveler with a hard luck story could get Abraham Van Buren to "lend" him a shilling or two.

Abraham was able to provide his family with some sporadic additional income by working as town clerk of Kinderhook for about ten years. When he left that office, he was able to pass it on to his stepson. Abraham also rented out space in the tavern as a meeting hall for various political and social organizations in the village. Although Abraham Van Buren also had a brief and undistinguished military career, there is no record indicating if he received a stipend for his military services. After the Treaty of Paris ended the Revolutionary War in 1783, New York Governor George Clinton (who would later serve as vice president of the United States under Jefferson and Madison) appointed Abraham a captain in the Seventh Regiment of the Albany County militia. Apparently, Abraham had no affinity for warfare or knowledge of military tactics and soon afterward resigned his commission.

One of the most important influences Abraham had on the life of Martin Van Buren was that he provided his son with an environment where he could cultivate his passion for politics. The Van Buren tavern was a favorite stop for lawyers and politicians traveling between the state capitol in Albany and New York City. John Jay, Aaron Burr, and Alexander Hamilton are three of the more prominent New York politicians known to have patronized Abraham's establishment. Village politicians would also gather at the tavern to discuss local, state, and national issues, and during elections the tavern also served as the village's polling place. The keenly observant Martin absorbed the political discussions, banter, and arguments while sweeping the floor or washing tankards. He learned to emulate his father's practice of being neutral on controversial issues so as not to antagonize any customers.

Other influences of Abraham on Martin are a matter of speculation. Donald B. Cole surmises in his book, *Martin Van Buren and the American Political System,* that Martin inherited Abraham's amiability and that Abraham taught him how to get along with people. Growing up with an extended family in crowded living quarters must have made Martin acutely aware of other people's sensibilities. Martin learned how to be alternately accommodating and manipulating. He learned how to compromise.

When he did let his guard down long enough to reveal his political beliefs, Abraham Van Buren was an ardent supporter of Thomas Jefferson. Martin Van Buren was elected president of the United States as the nominee of the Democratic party Jefferson had helped to found.

Fortunately, Abraham did not pass on his spendthrift ways to his son. After he left the presidency in 1841, Martin Van Buren retired to a thirty-room brick mansion on a two-hundred-acre farm in Kinderhook. When he died in 1862, Martin Van Buren left an estate valued at $225,000.

Abraham Van Buren died, presumably at his home in Kinderhook, on April 8, 1817, at the age of eighty. He lived long enough to see Martin take the first steps of a long political career by being admitted to the New York bar and later being elected to the New York State Senate.

An examination of the correspondence of Martin Van Buren reveals that he never wrote anything about his father being a tavern keeper. Perhaps Martin felt some shame or embarrassment that his father occupied what he perceived to be a lowly station in life.

The epitaph on Abraham Van Buren's tombstone describes him as "tender and indulgent . . . benevolent and charitable, a good man (of) mild temper and conciliatory manners." Martin certainly had nothing to be ashamed of.

Bibliography

Cole, Donald B. *Martin Van Buren and the American Political System*. Princeton, N.J.: Princeton University Press, c. 1984.

Ellis, Rafaela. *Martin Van Buren: Eighth President of the United States*. Ada, Okla.: Garrett Educational Corporation, 1989.

Fitzpatrick, John C., editor. *The Autobiography of Martin Van Buren*. Washington, D.C.: U.S. Government Printing Office, 1920.

Hoyt, Edwin P. *Martin Van Buren*. Chicago: Reilly & Lee, 1964.

Lynch, Denis Tilden. *An Epoch and a Man: Martin Van Buren and His Times*. Port Washington, N.Y.: Kennikat Press, 1929.

Mackenzie, William L. *The Life and Times of Martin Van Buren*. Boston: Cooke & Co., 1846.

Niven, John. *Martin Van Buren: The Romantic Age of American Politics*. New York, Oxford: Oxford University Press, 1983.

Shepard, Edward M. *Martin Van Buren*. New York: AMS Press, 1972.

Benjamin Harrison V
(1726–1791)

*Planter, politician, legislator, governor of Virginia, and father of
President William Henry Harrison*

Benjamin Harrison V was a most unlikely revolutionary. The father of America's ninth president was a wealthy man who reveled in his wealth. He was well known in colonial Virginia for entertaining lavishly, enjoying good food, and being a fashion plate with a penchant for blue tinted wigs and brightly colored silk coats with silver buttons. However, when Benjamin V aligned himself with the movement for American independence, he did so with courage, conviction, and an unwavering belief that the cause was just.

Benjamin Harrison V was born on April 5, 1726, at the Harrison plantation in Charles City County, Virginia. His father, Benjamin IV, was already a well-to-do owner of a dozen plantations along the James and Nottoway Rivers. The family's net worth increased when Benjamin IV married Anne Carter. In *Old Tippecanoe: William Henry Harrison and His Time*, Freeman Cleaves describes Anne's father, Robert (King) Carter, as the "richest native-born American of his day."

Prior to his marriage to Elizabeth Bassett in 1748, Benjamin V was a student at William and Mary College, but he left the college without graduating. Various Harrison biographers cite two different reasons. Some report a disagreement with a member of the faculty; others indicate that he left because of his father's death and the need to take over the administration of the family plantations.

In 1749 Benjamin V embarked upon his long political career when he was elected to the Virginia House of Burgesses. He served continuously for over a quarter of a century and acted as its speaker from 1778 to 1781. After three years of overseeing the family's vast landholdings, Benjamin V married Elizabeth Bassett in 1748. They had seven children over a period of twenty-two years. William Henry Harrison was the seventh of seven (four girls and three boys). He was born at the family's Berkeley plantation on February 9, 1773.

In the early 1760s, Benjamin V was one of the conservative members of the House of Burgesses who were cautious about opposing parliamentary measures and the power of the crown. By 1764 Benjamin V had become a bit bolder after serving on a legislative committee that wrote a petition formally protesting the Stamp Act. One year later, Benjamin V was once again exercising caution and restraint when he joined the conservative minority in the House of Burgesses in opposing Patrick Henry's anti–Stamp Act resolutions. However, by 1773 Benjamin V was fully committed to the cause of independence. He was a member of the Virginia committee of correspondence, which mapped out the plan of resistance and revolution. Benjamin V also served in the First Continental Congress after Virginia's Governor Dunmore had dissolved the rebellious House of Burgesses.

Although he was usually silent during the debates, Benjamin V is credited with making important contributions when he served on the marine, military, financial, and foreign affairs committees. Serving as chairman of the committee on the whole, Harrison chaired the deliberations that led to the adoption of the Declaration of Independence. In 1776 Benjamin V unequivocally cast his lot with the revolutionaries when he became one of the fifty-six signers of the Declaration of Independence who "mutually pledge to each other our Lives, our Fortunes and our Sacred Honor." By doing so, Benjamin V became one of the two fathers of an American president to sign that landmark document (John Adams is the other).

Benjamin V's youngest child, William Henry, experienced the American Revolution firsthand when his family abandoned Berkeley because of the threat of approaching British troops. It was a wise decision. Shortly after the family had left, the British ransacked the mansion, burning all furniture, clothes, and portraits the Harrisons had left behind. All of their horses and cattle were either commandeered or slaughtered. Years later, William Henry Harrison told an anecdote about a British nobleman who visited Berkeley after the American Revolution. The nobleman told Benjamin V that the exteriors of the great Virginia mansions compared favorably to their English counterparts, but the interiors were devoid of paintings, portraits, and other decorations. Benjamin V answered, "I can account for my paintings and decorations, sir — your soldiers burned them in my back yard."

Harrison biographers mention that the cheerful, optimistic personality of Benjamin V helped lift the spirits of other revolutionaries during the American Revolution's darkest days. When one of his colleagues in the Continental Congress suggested that they could be hanged for their activities, Benjamin V made light of the situation. He said that because of his size and weight, it would be over for him rather quickly. His thinner cohorts, he pointed out, might have to dangle at the end of the rope for an hour.

In October 1777 Benjamin V retired from the Continental Congress and took a seat in the Virginia House of Delegates. Seven months later, he was elected speaker, an office he held until 1781 when he was elected governor of Virginia. Benjamin V was elected to three consecutive one-year terms as governor, serving in that office from 1781 to 1784. John W. Raimo's book, *Biographical Directory of American Colonial and Revolutionary Governors, 1607–1789,* characterizes Harrison's administration as "marked by an easing of the legal restrictions which had been imposed

Benjamin Harrison V. Courtesy of The Library of Virginia.

on Loyalists during the Revolution." All Loyalists, except those who had actually taken up arms against American troops, were now free to return to their homes in Virginia.

While Benjamin V was governor, Virginia also relinquished its claims to lands north and west of the Ohio River. Ironically, that action made it possible for William Henry Harrison to later serve as secretary of the Northwest Territory. After leaving the governorship, Benjamin V was once again elected to the House of Delegates. He served there until his death at the Berkeley plantation on April 24, 1791. Harrison biographers agree that gout was the most likely cause of Benjamin V's death. A lifelong affinity for good food and fine wine put an end to the life of the portly patriot.

Biographies of William Henry Harrison provide scant information on the father-son relationship between Benjamin V and William Henry. It is believed that Benjamin V pulled William Henry out of Hampden-Sydney College because the school's emphasis on religion annoyed Benjamin V.

Before becoming a soldier/politician, William Henry Harrison studied medicine. It is not clear if that is what William Henry had wanted or what Benjamin V had wanted him to do. However, it is believed that Benjamin V terminated William Henry's apprenticeship to a Richmond physician because of his son's membership in an abolition society and William Henry's growing friendship with abolitionists. Despite having signed the Declaration of Independence, Benjamin V was an implacable foe of abolition. Dorothy Burne Goebel describes Benjamin V in her *William Henry Harrison: A Political Biography* as "a violent opponent of any scheme of Negro emancipation."

Stanley Young in his juvenile Harrison biography, *Tippecanoe and Tyler, Too!*, quotes two letters written by William Henry Harrison. In the first, Harrison wrote: "All during my youth, my father admonished me about my studies," and added, "Father also spoke long and frequently of our family background." In a second letter, Harrison sighed, "How I wished, at that moment, my father were alive to be with me." The letter refers to a meeting William Henry had with President George Washington around 1792 when he asked Washington for a military commission.

There was reportedly no strong physical resemblance between Benjamin V and his son. Benjamin V was described as six feet, four inches tall and weighing 249 pounds. William Henry did not inherit his build or dietary habits; his biographers usually portray him as thin, five feet, eight inches tall with a thin, angular face.

The character and personality of Benjamin V is summed up in a biographical sketch from the 1888 edition of *Appleton's Cyclopedia of American Biography:*

> In person Benjamin was large and fleshy; in spite of suffering from gout, his good humor was unfailing. Although without conspicuous intellectual endowments, he was a man of excellent judgement and the highest sense of honor, with a courage and cheerfullness that never faltered and a "downright candor" and sincerity of character which conciliated the affection and respect of all who knew him.

Bibliography

Bakeless, John and Katherine. *Signers of the Declaration.* Boston: Houghton Mifflin, 1969.

Cleaves, Freeman. *Old Tippecanoe: William Henry Harrison and His Time.* New York: Scribners, 1939.

Ferris, Robert G., editor. *Signers of the Declaration.* Washington, D.C.: U.S. Government Printing Office, 1973.

Fitz-Gerald, Christine Maloney. *William Henry Harrison.* Chicago: Children's Press, 1987.

Goebel, Dorothy Burne. *William Henry Harrison: A Political Biography.* Indianapolis: Indiana Library and Historical Department, 1926.

Goodrich, Rev. Charles A. *Lives of the Signers of the Declaration of Independence.* New York: William Reed, 1829.

Green, James A. *William Henry Harrison: His Life and Times.* Richmond, Va.: Garrett and Massie, 1941.

Hess, Stephen. *America's Political Dynasties: From Adams to Kennedy.* Garden City, N.Y.: Doubleday, 1966.

Johnson, Allen, and Dumas Malone, editors. *Dictionary of American Biography.* New York: Scribners, 1936.

Lossing, B. J. *Biographical Sketches of the Signers of the Declaration of Independence.* New York: Derby and Jackson, 1858.

Raimo, John W. *Biographical Directory of American Colonial and Revolutionary Governors, 1607–1789.* Westport, Ct.: Meckler, 1980.

Wilson, James Grant, and John Fiske, editors. *Appleton's Cyclopedia of American Biography.* New York: Appleton, 1888.

Young, Stanley. *Tippecanoe and Tyler, Too!* New York: Random House, 1957.

John Tyler Sr. (1747–1813)

Planter, soldier, attorney, public official, federal judge, governor of Virginia, and father of President John Tyler

John Tyler Sr. was born and bred a member of the colonial Virginia aristocracy, but he became an ardent revolutionary when he heard Patrick Henry speak. The father of America's tenth president was an eighteen-year-old law student at William and Mary College when he and his good friend Thomas Jefferson heard Henry speak at Williamsburg, Virginia, in the spring of 1765. Henry delivered an impassioned denunciation of King George III and the Stamp Act. Henry's electrifying oratory made John Sr. an unwavering advocate for the cause of American independence. John Sr.'s father, Henry, warned his headstrong son in vain about the dangers of defying the all-powerful British, telling him, "Ah! John, they will hang you for a rebel. They will hang you yet."

John Tyler Sr. was born in James City County, Virginia, on February 28, 1747. John Sr. was of the fourth generation of Tylers in America. The first was Henry Tyler, who left England at about the time the Puritans defeated King Charles I and took control of the country in the mid–1600s. Henry obtained a grant for 254 acres of land in what later became Williamsburg, Virginia.

Among the heirs of Henry Tyler were a son, grandson, and great-grandson all named John. In his book, *John Tyler: Champion of the Old South*, Oliver Perry Chitwood writes:

> Of these three Johns the most prominent was the third — the father of the President. He was a man of strong convictions and prejudices, both of which he expressed with utter fearlessness. In giving vent to his feelings regarding public questions he was not restrained by considerations of diplomacy to the same extent as was the younger Tyler. For this reason he leaves the impression of having had a more vigorous and picturesque personality than that possessed by his distinguished son.

After completing his law studies at William and Mary, John Sr. began prac-

John Tyler Sr. Courtesy of Virginia Historical Society.

ticing law in Charles City County around 1770. That same year he held his first public office when he was appointed to the Charles City County committee of safety. In 1776 John Sr. married Mary Armistead, the only daughter of a prominent planter in Elizabeth City County, Virginia. Shortly after the wedding, the couple moved to "Greenaway," the Tyler family plantation. John Sr. and Mary had eight children (five girls and three boys). John was their sixth child; he was born on March 29,

1790, at Greenaway. Mary Tyler died when John Sr. was fifty and John was only seven. John Sr. never remarried, and he is credited with being the parent who raised John and exerted the strongest influence on his life.

As part of his Revolutionary War activities, John Sr. raised a company of volunteers and joined his revolutionary mentor, Patrick Henry, in a march against Lord Dunmore to recapture munitions Dunmore had seized from a magazine in Williamsburg. Tyler biographers mention that John Sr. freely risked his life and everything he owned for the cause of American independence.

In 1777 John Sr. and his fellow presidential father, Benjamin Harrison V, were both elected to represent Charles City County in the Virginia House of Delegates. Four years later, Harrison was elected governor of Virginia and John Sr. succeeded him as Speaker of the House. In 1784 the two presidential fathers became political rivals when they ran for the same seat in the House of Delegates. John Sr. won that election, but Harrison later evened the score by getting elected from another county and subsequently defeating John Sr. in a race for the position of Speaker of the House.

John Tyler Sr. had an eight-year tenure in the Virginia House of Delegates (1778–1786). For four of those eight years, he served as Speaker of the House (1781–1785). Obviously his colleagues regarded him as an able and effective legislator. As a member of the House of Delegates, John Sr. helped draft the resolutions appointing Virginia's delegates to the Annapolis Convention, the first of two conventions held to draft a federal constitution. John Sr. ultimately became an outspoken opponent of ratification of the constitution drafted in Philadelphia. He voiced his opposition by saying, "When I consider the constitution in all its parts, I cannot but dread its operation. It contains a variety of powers too dangerous to be vested in any set of men whatsoever." Fifty-four years later, the constitution John Sr. had so vigorously opposed would make his son the president of the United States.

Other offices held by John Sr. during his lengthy political career include judge of the state admiralty court (1785–1788), vice president of the Virginia Convention considering the adoption of the federal Constitution (1788), judge of the General Court of Virginia (1788–1808), and governor of Virginia (1808–1811).

Like his friend, Thomas Jefferson, John Tyler Sr. was a member of the Democratic-Republican Party. John Sr. was elected governor by the state legislature for three consecutive terms. During his administration, the number of state Supreme Court judges was increased from three to five and the state's Literary Fund was established as a result of Tyler's advocacy. As governor, John Sr. also voiced opposition to England's maritime policies. Lyon Gardiner Tyler summed up John Sr.'s political beliefs in his book, *The Letters and Times of the Tylers,* as follows: "Schools for the people, funds for the army and taxes for the just creditors of the state, were the themes of his oratory on every occasion."

The most commonly told anecdote regarding John Sr. and his most famous son is the story of a ten- or eleven-year-old John Tyler being a ringleader in a classroom revolt against a tyrannical teacher named William McMurdo. McMurdo was fond of administering corporal punishment. One day his students rebelled by physically overpowering him, tying him up, and locking the deposed teacher in the schoolhouse. After a traveler found and released him, McMurdo went to Tyler Sr. and demanded that he punish his son for his part in the schoolhouse mutiny. John Sr. responded by reciting the Virginia state motto: "Sic semper tyrannis" (ever thus to tyrants) and sent McMurdo on his way. Never depend on a revolutionary to punish a mutineer.

Biographers of John Tyler characterize the tenth president's relationship with his father as excellent. To compensate for the loss of their mother, John Sr. lavished attention upon John and his siblings. Tyler biographers also describe John spending hours sitting under a large willow tree listening to John Sr. play his fiddle and regale listeners with tales of the Revolutionary War.

John Tyler emulated his father in several ways. Like his father, he played the fiddle and wrote poetry. Like his father, he pursued a career in law and politics. When John Tyler began the study of law, John Sr. was his first mentor. John Tyler and his father also shared the same proslavery views. As wealthy, slave-owning, white property owners, they fervently believed that states' rights superseded the powers of a federal government. Both father and son were slave owners for all of their adult lives.

In his biography, *And Tyler Too,* Robert Seager II sums up the father's influence on the son: "The most important single fact that can be derived from John Tyler's formative years is that he absorbed the political, social and economic views of his distinguished father." Along with the shared political views, John Tyler Sr. and John Tyler shared some of the same physical attributes. They had the same prominent forehead, large Roman nose, and thin build.

John Tyler Sr. died in Charles City County, Virginia, on January 6, 1813, at the age of sixty-five. He had spent the last two years of his life as judge of the U.S. District Court of Virginia. He lived long enough to see his son John start his political career by being elected to the Virginia House of Delegates. When John Tyler Sr. died, the United States and England were engaged in the War of 1812. Before he died, the old revolutionary declared that his only regret was that he "could not live long enough to see that proud British nation once more humbled by American arms."

Bibliography

Chitwood, Oliver Perry. *John Tyler: Champion of the Old South.* New York: Russell & Russell, 1964.
Dodson, E. Griffith. *Speakers and Clerks of the Virginia House of Delegates.* Richmond, Va., 1956.
Falkoff, Lucille. *John Tyler: Tenth President of the United States.* Ada, Okla.: Garrett Educational Corporation, 1990.
Hoyt, Edwin P. *John Tyler the Tenth President.* New York: Abelard-Schuman, 1969.

Malone, Dumas, editor. *Dictionary of American Biography.* Vol. 10, pp. 87–88. New York: Scribners, 1936.
The National Cyclopedia of American Biography. New York: White, 1894.
Seager, Robert II. *And Tyler Too: A Biography of John and Julia Gardiner.* New York: McGraw-Hill, 1963.
Sobel, Robert, and John Raimo, editors. *Biographical Directory of the Governors of the United States, 1789–1978.* Vol. 1, pp. 1628–1629. Westport, Ct.: Meckler, 1978.
Tyler, Lyon Gardiner. *The Letters and Times of the Tylers.* Vol. 3. Williamsburg, Va., 1896.

Samuel Polk
(1772–1827)

Surveyor, planter, land speculator, businessman, magistrate, and father of President James K. Polk.

Because of his father, Samuel, James K. Polk was not baptized until he was fifty-four years old and on his deathbed. Samuel Polk did not have anything against religion; the father of America's eleventh president just did not compromise when he thought he was right. When the infant James K. Polk was taken by his parents to be baptized, the Presbyterian clergyman refused to perform the sacrament until both parents had observed the custom of professing their faith. Mrs. Polk obliged, but Mr. Polk refused. Apparently, Samuel Polk did not feel that was necessary. He left with his wife and unbaptized son.

The first Polks to come to America had emigrated from Scotland in 1680. They settled in Somerset County, Maryland. Samuel's father, Ezekiel, was a restless and enterprising man whose work as a surveyor had gained him title to large amounts of land in Tennessee. Samuel Polk was born on July 5, 1772, in Tyron, North Carolina. He was the third child and second son of Ezekiel Polk. Charles Sellers's biography, *James K. Polk, Jacksonian,* describes Samuel Polk as "one of the sober, conventional Polks, though his conventionality took the form of a passion for the world's goods rather than his neighbor's zeal for the Presbyterian God." Seller adds that Samuel was better educated than most of his peers and that his education and levelheaded sobriety were an asset when he began courting Jane Knox.

Samuel's impending marriage to Jane was hastened by the death of her father in October of 1794. Samuel Polk and Jane Knox were married in a double wedding with Samuel's brother, Thomas, and his bride on Christmas evening in 1794. Because of their parent's largesse, Samuel and Jane Polk were able to begin their married life with an abundance of material goods. Ezekiel presented Samuel with a 250-acre farm. From her father's estate, Jane received two slaves, a horse with a saddle and bridle, three cows, one-third of her father's furniture, and one-fifth of his undivided estate.

The Polks had been married just over ten months when the future president,

James Knox Polk, was born at their home in Mecklenberg County, North Carolina, on November 2, 1795. James was the first of ten children (six boys and four girls) born to Samuel and Jane.

In 1806 Samuel gave in to his father's persistent urgings and moved his family to Tennessee. Ezekiel had made the move west several years earlier and had settled in Carter's Creek, a few miles south of Franklin, Tennessee, with members of his immediate family. It took the Polks about a month and a half to make the 500-mile journey.

Ezekiel gave Samuel a large portion of his landholdings. Samuel and his family settled on a site about six miles north of the Duck River. The tract Samuel chose was on a trail that was soon to become the main road from the Duck River to Franklin and Nashville. Samuel and his family produced their own food and clothes and likely bartered for their other necessities. That meant that James and the other children worked long and hard to meet their family obligations.

Shortly after settling in the Duck River area, Samuel became actively involved in local politics. In the summer of 1807 Samuel was one of over one hundred signers of a petition to create a new county. Their petition was favorably received, and in 1807 Maury County, Tennessee, was created. Samuel Polk was one of the first jurors to try a case in the newly created county court, and he later served as a county magistrate. However, Samuel's true interests were surveying and land speculation, not law and politics. William Polk, one of Samuel's cousins, had inherited the major share of their Uncle Thomas's ample landholdings in Tennessee. Samuel became William's agent for renting and selling land. Samuel's compensation for surveying often was a large portion of the land he had surveyed.

When Samuel took James on his surveying trips, he began to notice that his oldest son lacked the aptitude and physical stamina needed by a surveyor. While Samuel and other members of the surveying party were making their way through the wilderness and running lines through the thick foliage, James was left behind at the campsite to tend the horses and cook the evening meal. Samuel also noticed that James was usually too weak to compete with boys his own age in athletic competitions and in their rough horseplay. James's lack of strength and energy was diagnosed as gallstones. Samuel had heard of a doctor in Danville, Kentucky, named Ephraim McDowell who was renowned for his pioneering work in abdominal surgery. In the fall of 1812 the concerned father and sickly son embarked on a 230-mile horseback trip to Danville.

When the Polks arrived at Doctor McDowell's office, McDowell examined James and ordered him to get several weeks of rest before he would operate on him. The constant jostling of horseback riding and the other hardships of the journey had made James too weak for an immediate operation. On the day of the operation, James was ordered to drink enough brandy to dull his senses. That was the only anesthetic available at the time. James was strapped to a wooden table and further restrained by the doctor's assistants. An incision was made and the gallstone was removed.

The operation's success was a testimony to Dr. McDowell's surgical skill. James Polk could have suffered severe shock, bled to death, or contracted a deadly infection. The courage and stoicism James showed when undergoing a life-threatening operation certainly impressed his father. After the operation, Samuel accepted the reality that James would never be hardy enough to work as a surveyor or farmer. Samuel decided that merchandising would be a good career for his son. He got James a job in a Columbia, Tennessee, store. However, James did not like merchandising, and he kept the job for only a few weeks before convincing his father to send him to school.

In July of 1813 James enrolled at a Presbyterian academy outside Columbia. Samuel was so pleased with James's work there that after one year he had James transfer to an academically more challenging school in Murfreesboro. James attended that school for two years before starting college.

James Polk entered the University of North Carolina in 1816 and graduated with honors two years later. The honors came with a price. When Samuel came to take James home in July of 1818, his son was too weak to make the trip back to Columbia. In his relentless pursuit of academic excellence, James had worked himself to the point of exhaustion. By October of 1818 James was strong enough to move to the lavish, new two-story home Samuel had built in Columbia.

Samuel's growing affluence was a direct result of his entrepreneurial spirit. In addition to his land business and merchandising ventures, Samuel and his business partner, James Walker, engaged in other enterprises. They founded the first newspaper in Columbia. They also worked as contractors for the U.S. War Department and Post Office Department. Samuel was also a director of the first bank established in Columbia. Not all of Polk and Walker's ventures were profitable. Sellers reports that Polk and Walker spent $40,000 to build a steamboat and later sold it for $7,000.

With Samuel footing the bills, James studied law in Nashville after graduating from college. His instructor was Felix Grundy, who would later serve as a U.S. senator and as attorney general in the Van Buren administration. James Polk was admitted to the bar in 1820. When James began practicing law in Columbia, Samuel was there to help him get started. Samuel spent $220 to build James a one-room law office. He also spent another $140 to help James buy a law library. Samuel also became his son's first client. Reportedly, Samuel lost his temper during an argument. The judge let Samuel off with a one-dollar fine.

By 1821 Samuel Polk was in failing health. Recurrent rheumatism kept him confined to his home for months at a time. In a letter dated 1822 to William Polk, Samuel wrote, "my days of active service are ended."

In the last months of his life, Samuel Polk was failing mentally as well as physically. According to Sellers, Samuel's mind was wandering and he was receiving regular doses of laudanum. Samuel Polk died at the age of fifty-five on November 5, 1827. A vault erected over his remains pays homage to his entrepreneurial spirit with the inscription: "Men of enterprise, here Moulder the Mortal Remains of a kindred spirit."

James K. Polk never wrote an autobiography that would provide any insights into his feelings about his father. In the multivolume *Correspondence of James K. Polk*, Polk does not mention his father. The known facts about Samuel Polk's life show him to be a father who listened to his son James. Samuel found out what James wanted to do with his life, and he did all he could to help him achieve his goals. Polk biographers concur that James shared many of his father's political beliefs. As Eugene McCormac sums it up in his book, *James K. Polk: A Political Biography*, "He [Samuel] was an ardent supporter of Jefferson, and his faith in the soundness of Republican doctrines was shared by his son James."

Bibliography

Braun, Saul. "James Knox Polk." *The American Heritage Pictorial History of the Presidents of the United States*. New York: Simon & Schuster, 1968.

Claxton, Jimmie Lou Sparkman. *Eighty-Eight Years with Sarah Polk*. New York: Vantage Press, 1972.

Elder, Betty Doak. *A Special House*. Columbia, Tenn., 1980.

Greenblatt, Miriam. *James K. Polk: Eleventh President of the United States*. Ada, Okla.: Garrett Educational Corporation, 1988.

McCormac, Eugene Irving. *James K. Polk: A Political Biography*. New York: Russell, 1922.

Morrell, Martha McBride. *Young Hickory: The Life and Times of President James K. Polk*. New York: Dutton, 1949.

Sellers, Charles. *James K. Polk, Jacksonian*. Princeton, New Jersey: Princeton University Press, 1957.

Richard Taylor
(1744–1829)

*Farmer, soldier, magistrate, politician, and father of
President Zachary Taylor*

Zachary Taylor never had much to say about his father, Richard. So little in fact, that the extent of his father's influence on America's twelfth president is largely a matter of speculation and conjecture. Both Richard and Zachary were soldiers, politicians, and slave owners. However, Zachary was opposed to the extension of slavery, and he took no apparent interest in politics prior to being elected president in 1848.

In a fifteen-page *Autobiography* he wrote in 1826, Zachary devoted these two sentences to his father: "My father, Richard Taylor, was appointed an officer in the first Regiment of the continental troops raised by the state of Virginia to oppose the British at the commencement of the Revolution & remained in the service in the Continental Line until the close of the war & quit the Service as a Lt. Colonel. In the Spring of '85 he emigrated to this state, settled in the neighborhood of Louisville where I was raised."

The first Taylors to come to America had settled in Virginia in the first half of the seventeenth century. Richard's great-grandfather, James, had emigrated from Carlisle, England, and acquired land around the Mattaponi River in what is now Caroline County, Virginia. Richard Taylor was born on April 3, 1744, in Orange County, Virginia. Richard was one of four children born to Zachary and Elizabeth Lee Taylor. Elizabeth was a first cousin of famed Revolutionary War General Henry Lee.

Richard grew up on Meadow Farm, the Taylor family plantation. The plantation was tended by the family's twenty-six slaves. According to Holman Hamilton's biography, *Zachary Taylor: Soldier of the Republic,* the Taylors of Virginia were "a family high on the colonial social scale." According to K. Jack Bauer's biography, *Zachary Taylor: Soldier, Planter, Statesman of the Old Southwest,* Richard was a graduate of William and Mary College. However, none of the Taylor biographies record the dates when Richard attended college.

Apparently, Richard had a strong feeling of wanderlust and a craving for adventure. In 1769 Richard, his older brother Hancock, and a companion named Abraham Haptonstall explored the Mississippi and Ohio Rivers. The adventuresome trio began the river journey in Pittsburgh after acquiring a boat there. After traveling down the Ohio to the Mississippi River, the three men wandered one hundred miles up the Mississippi before descending to the mouth of the Arkansas River. One hundred miles later, they stopped at a small French settlement on the Arkansas to camp, hunt, and fish. In the spring, the threesome separated. Hancock and Abraham went to New Orleans. Richard, accompanied by an Indian trader, traveled through the Creek, Choctaw, and Chickasaw Indian nations of Georgia.

While in Georgia, Richard examined a tract of land the Georgia colony had recently acquired from the Creeks. Then Richard set off through the Carolinas before returning to his Virginia home after an absence of more than one year.

In 1775 Richard enlisted as a lieutenant in the First Virginia Regiment commanded by Patrick Henry. He fought in the battles of Brandywine, Monmouth, and White Plains as well as in several lesser engagements. By the end of the war, Richard had advanced to the rank of colonel. In the midst of the Revolutionary War, Richard took a respite from the fighting to marry Sarah Dabney Strother. They were wed on August 20, 1779. She was eighteen and he was thirty-five.

The first home of Richard and Sarah was a family plantation called Hare Forest. Their first two children were born there, Hancock in 1781 and William in 1782. Zachary Taylor was born on November 24, 1784, in Orange County, Virginia. Most historians agree that Zachary's birthplace was at Montebello, the home of Richard's cousin, Valentine Johnson. From accounts of their physical characteristics, the resemblance between Richard and Zachary must have been faint. Hamilton describes Richard as "six feet two inches of height, clear complexion, blue eyes and strong features." Zachary has been described as five foot eight inches tall with brown hair, hazel eyes, and a long, thin face.

Prior to Zachary's birth, Richard had decided to move his family to Kentucky. The Hare Forest plantation was not generating sufficient income to support his family and the State of Virginia had offered Richard a tract of six thousand acres of western lands as a bonus for his wartime service. Richard may also have wanted to join his brother, Hancock, who had already moved to the village of Louisville.

In the spring of 1785 the Taylors began traveling westward. There is no record of the route they took. Since they were probably traveling with household goods and heavy items, the Taylors likely crossed the Blue Ridge mountains and used the Shenandoah, Potomac, and Ohio Rivers to reach Louisville. The Taylors settled in Kentucky when Zachary was about eight months old. Richard established his new domicile on a four-hundred-acre tract about five miles east of Louisville. His property fronted the Muddy Fork of the Beargrass Creek. Richard built a log house and named his estate Springfield. That would be his home for the rest of his life.

As the village of Louisville grew and prospered, so did the estate of Richard

Taylor. Richard would eventually own over eleven thousand acres in Kentucky. His tax returns indicate that he also acquired more slaves as his landholdings grew. In 1790 Richard Taylor owned seven slaves. By 1800 he owned twenty-six. Ten years later, the number was thirty-seven. Richard Taylor also became a public official of some prominence. At various times Richard Taylor was a justice of the peace, Jefferson County magistrate, delegate to Kentucky's first two constitutional conventions, and a state legislator in Kentucky. He also served as the collector of the port of Louisville after being appointed to that post by President George Washington. In 1812, 1816, 1820, and 1824 Richard also held the office of presidential elector. He voted for Madison, Monroe (twice), and Henry Clay.

Biographies of Zachary Taylor uniformly portray the twelfth president as apolitical prior to his election in 1848. Until that time Zachary had never held political office or voted in a presidential election. Still, it is hard to imagine that he could have been totally uninterested in politics when his father was so actively involved in public affairs. Undoubtedly, politics was a frequent topic of conversation at the dinner table during Zachary's formative years.

Richard Taylor's distinguished Revolutionary War record influenced Zachary's decision to become a career military officer. When Zachary was commissioned as a first lieutenant in the Seventh Infantry in 1808, his father's political connections may have helped him to secure the commission. Richard's status as a Revolutionary War hero must have affected all his sons. All four of Richard's sons who were eligible served in the War of 1812.

When Zachary Taylor married Margaret Mackall Smith in 1810, Richard gave them 324 acres of land as a wedding gift. When the land was given, the tax rolls of Jefferson County rated the acreage as second-class land. Today that land is located in downtown Louisville. Zachary later sold the land at a handsome profit.

The only insight we have into the relationship between the adult Zachary and his father comes from Hamilton's biography. Hamilton describes Zachary as concerned about his father's "senile stubborness" when Richard was in his eighties. In a letter to his sister, Elizabeth, Zachary wrote,

> Indeed I should not be at all astonished . . . (if) some person or other will cheat him out of his plantation one of these days. . . . It is perhaps father's weakest point that he has no confidence in his children who . . . are all interested in his welfare; but this should in no wise alter our deportment to him . . . , and I am truly sorry that it is not in my power to visit him frequently.

Richard Taylor died on January 19, 1829, at the age of eighty-four. Zachary was then a lieutenant colonel serving as commandant of Fort Snelling, Minnesota. Richard left Zachary a small farm outside of Louisville. Zachary sold the property the following summer for $2,000.

In a letter to John Gibson, Zachary wrote, "I need not say how much his loss has distressed us all." Apparently Zachary felt that the love he felt for his father and his sense of loss was understood and did not have to be expressed in more detail.

Bibliography

Bauer, K. Jack. *Zachary Taylor: Soldier, Planter, Statesman of the Old Southwest.* Baton Rouge: Louisiana State University Press, 1985.
Dyer, Brainerd. *Zachary Taylor.* Baton Rouge: Louisiana State University Press, 1946.
Faber, Doris. *The Mothers of American Presidents.* New York: New American Library, 1968.
Hamilton, Holman. *Zachary Taylor: Soldier of the Republic.* Indianapolis: Bobbs-Merrill, 1941.
Howard, Oliver Otis. *General Taylor.* New York: Appleton, 1892.
Hoyt, Edwin P. *Zachary Taylor.* Chicago: Reilly & Lee, 1966.
McKinley, Silas Bent and Silas Bent. *Old Rough and Ready: The Life and Times of Zachary Taylor.* New York: Vanguard Press, 1946.

Nathaniel Fillmore
(1771–1863)

*Tenant farmer, magistrate, and father of
President Millard Fillmore*

Nathaniel Fillmore did the best he could so that his oldest son, Millard, and his eight other children could enjoy a better life than he had had. Nathaniel spent his working life engaged in the physically demanding toil and unrelenting drudgery of tenant farming. Perhaps his great reward for a lifetime of hard labor was that he became the first father of an American president to be entertained by his son at the White House.

Nathaniel Fillmore was born in Bennington, Vermont, on April 19, 1771. He was named for his father, who was one of Bennington's earliest settlers and a veteran of the Revolutionary War. Millard Fillmore's biographers do not provide any information or insights into the early life of the father of America's thirteenth president. It is known that in or around 1796 Nathaniel married a sixteen-year-old physician's daughter named Phoebe Millard. Phoebe fell in love with an ambitious farmer who was long on energy, hopes, and dreams, but woefully short on luck and acumen.

In 1799 the bleak prospects of trying to eke out an existence by tenant farming the stone-strewn soils of Bennington caused the Fillmore family to fall prey to some slick salesmanship.

During the Revolutionary War, New York had set aside almost 1.5 million acres of land in the central part of the state. The state's original plan had been to give land parcels to qualified war veterans as a bonus for their military service. This area was commonly known as the Military Tract. However, few war veterans chose to settle there. As a result, real estate entrepreneurs who were in partnership with corrupt government officials were able to gain title to most of the land. Sales agents roamed the countryside looking for potential buyers. A crooked land agent's sales pitch of rich, fertile loam soil in the Military Tract convinced Nathaniel and his brother, Calvin, to purchase land located in Locke Township in Cayuga County without first inspecting the property. After clearing the land and building a cabin, they found rock-hard, infertile clay soil. They had hoped for prosperity and had found poverty instead.

The birth of their first son on the morning of January 7, 1800, gave Nathaniel and Phoebe a brief respite from their worries and woes. After much deliberation, the Fillmores chose a name for their son that expressed their faith in each other — Millard, the mother's maiden name. Their joy was short-lived. Along with the burdens of poor crops, poor weather, and cramped living quarters, the Fillmores suffered yet another setback; the state of New York determined that their title to the land was not valid. Faulty land surveys, claim jumping, dishonesty, and duplicity were common occurrences in the Military Tract. The state of New York sent a team of commissioners to review land claims there, and the Fillmores were unable to defend their ownership against the commission's findings.

The dejected settlers loaded their meager possessions onto a farm wagon and moved a few miles north to Sempronius (now called Niles). Instead of settling on their own land, the Fillmores took a perpetual lease on a 130-acre farm and became tenant farmers once again.

As soon as Millard was old enough, Nathaniel put him to work on the farm. Under his father's tutelage, Millard learned to reap wheat, hoe corn, and mow grass for hay. When he became big enough to handle the implement, Millard learned how to operate a wooden plow pulled by a mule. During the winter months, Nathaniel taught Millard how to chop wood, burn brush, and pull stumps. Millard's infrequent leisure periods when he would steal away to hunt or fish were invariably followed by a stern lecture from Nathaniel, who would somberly remind his son that "No man ever prospered from wasting his time in sporting." Fishing and hunting were suitable diversions only for Indians and ne'er-do-well whites. Civilized life was a very serious business.

Since he did not have the funds to send his son to school, Nathaniel apprenticed Millard to a cloth-dresser when the boy was just fourteen. Apparently the man Millard was apprenticed to was a harsh taskmaster. Millard tearfully returned home just four months after beginning his apprenticeship. Nathaniel could not afford to keep Millard at home, so he wasted little time in finding him another apprenticeship in the cloth-dressing industry. The second apprenticeship lasted about three years before Millard bought his freedom from indentured servitude for $30.

In or around 1818 Nathaniel decided that seventeen years of attempting to coax crops out of the infertile clay soil of Sempronius were enough. He sold his tenancy and moved his family twelve miles southwest to the town of Montville. While in Montville, Nathaniel became a tenant of Judge Walter Wood. Judge Wood, one of the wealthiest men in the region, would later have a strong influence on the fortunes of the Fillmores. Sensing a chance for his eldest son, Nathaniel paid the judge a visit and convinced him to give Millard a two-month tryout as a clerk in his law office. If Nathaniel Fillmore could not give his son an education, at least he would give him an opportunity.

Millard learned of his chance at a law career when his mother surprised him

Nathaniel Fillmore. Courtesy of the Buffalo and Erie County Historical Society.

by proudly announcing the news at the dinner table. Millard was so overcome with emotion, that he burst into tears of joy. Then he bolted from the table because he was embarrassed by such an unmanly display of emotion.

Millard's interest in law may have been a result of seeing Nathaniel serve as justice of the peace when he lived in Cayuga County. Nathaniel's fellow citizens thought he was worthy of that office despite his lack of formal education. They must have perceived Nathaniel as someone with a logical mind and a sense of justice.

At the time of his clerkship, Millard may have had roughly the equivalent of a high school education. Before his apprenticeships, his only formal schooling had taken place in the rare times when he could be spared from helping out on the family farm to attend whatever school was available. Millard's introduction to the world of ideas came when he was seventeen and joined a circulating library in his community. When the cloth mill had its slack season, Millard enrolled in an academy at New Hope, New York. At the academy, Millard was a favorite student of his teacher, Abigail Powers. Miss Powers later became Mrs. Millard Fillmore.

Nathaniel Fillmore was probably literate, but he had had little time for reading and self-education. Millard once described the family library as "a Bible, a hymn book, and an almanac." The lack of reading material in the home obviously had an effect on Millard. When he died, he had a personal library of around four thousand volumes.

The next time Nathaniel was able to intervene in Millard's life was in 1821 after he had once again moved his family. This time the Fillmores had settled on a farm in Aurora Township, eighteen miles east of Buffalo. Millard had successfully completed his two-month clerkship, but he later had a parting of the ways with Judge Wood because he had performed some legal work outside of Judge Wood's firm. Millard moved back in with his parents and began teaching school in East Aurora and also performing some minor justice of the peace work for friends and neighbors. Following his family to Aurora created some new opportunities for Millard. Buffalo had a booming economy, and Millard was able to find a teaching job there. The teaching job gave him the means to study law part-time in the office of attorneys Asa Rice and Joseph Clary. In 1823 Millard was admitted to the bar.

In 1831 Nathaniel became a widower when Phoebe passed away. Three years later, he married Eunice Love. His remarriage would make Millard Fillmore the first American president to have a stepmother. During the winter of 1851–52 Nathaniel made history by being the first father of an American president to have his son entertain him at the White House. The reception for the elder Fillmore had been well publicized. Both high government officials and ordinary citizens turned out in unexpectedly large numbers.

Father and son stood shoulder to shoulder in the reception line and many of the guests were impressed by the unmistakable resemblance between the gracious host and the proud father. Tall, straight, and rawboned, eighty-year-old Nathaniel showed none of the infirmities of age. When one guest asked Nathaniel how to raise a son to be president, he quickly replied, "Cradle him in a sap trough." After the last guest had left, Nathaniel confided to a friend, "If I could have the power of marking out the pathway in life for my son, it would never have lead to this place, but I cannot help feeling proud of it now that he is here."

In a letter written to the noted American reformer, Dorothea Dix, in 1857, ex-President Fillmore described a visit with his then eighty-six-year-old father and shared his concerns about Nathaniel's mortality:

> I visited my good old father yesterday — or rather on Saturday — and found him enjoying his usual good health, with the exception of a slight lameness

caused by being thrown from a carriage recently, and he was apparently as cheerful and happy as he was 40 years ago. But still I can see that he has nearly reached "that bourne whence no traveler returns," and I can only hope that the rest of his journey may be as happy as that has been which is passed; and that my life may be spared to perform the last sad offices of filial affection to his mortal remains when his immoral spirit shall seek its congenial resting place in the society of those who have gone before it.

Nathaniel Fillmore died on March 28, 1863, in East Aurora, New York, at 1 o'clock in the morning. He was ninety-two years old. No father of an American president had a longer life, and few, if any, had a harder one. Nathaniel Fillmore's death notice, identifying him as the father of Millard Fillmore, appeared on page two of the March 30 edition of the *Buffalo Morning Express*. His obituary appeared on page three, and a small headline simply read: "Death of Ex-President Fillmore's Father."

In part, his obituary read as follows:

We had the pleasure of knowing the deceased from our boyhood, and learned to respect his character and life as a man. He was possessed of an eminently social disposition — a clear, practical and vigorous mind — a high sense of honor and the most unswerving integrity — all of which framed the make-up of a character alike genial and admirable. He was a practical demonstration of temperance on resolution — never having indulged in spiritous liquors as a beverage — and holding to this principle under a determination formed long before temperance organizations had manifested themselves in this state.... When the hour of dissolution came, he passed away like a cloud without pain or struggle. His name and character will linger in the memory of a large circle of friends and relatives with peculiar satisfaction, for his life has thrown a grateful fragrance upon the recollection of both.

Bibliography

Barre, W. L. *The Life and Public Services of Millard Fillmore*. Buffalo: Wanzer, 1856.
Buffalo Morning Express. March 30, 1863, pp. 2–3.
Law, Kevin J. *Millard Fillmore: Thirteenth President of the United States*. Ada, Okla.: Garrett Educational Corporation, 1990.
Rayback, Robert J. *Millard Fillmore: Biography of a President*. Buffalo: Stewart, 1959.
Severance, Frank H., editor. *Millard Fillmore Papers*. Vol. 2. New York: Kraus, 1970.
Snyder, Charles M. *The Lady and the President: The Letters of Dorothea Dix and Millard Fillmore*. Lexington, Ky.: University Press of Kentucky, 1975.

Benjamin Pierce
(1757–1839)

Soldier, farmer, inn and tavern owner, public official, governor of New Hampshire, and father of President Franklin Pierce

Benjamin Pierce was a genuine American patriot even before the United States of America came into being. The father of America's fourteenth president was born on Christmas Day in Chelmsford, Massachusetts, in 1757. He was the seventh of ten children of Benjamin and Elizabeth Merrill Pierce. Benjamin Sr. died when young Benjamin was six, and young Benjamin was sent to stay with his uncle, Robert Pierce, also of Chelmsford.

According to information provided by the New Hampshire Historical Society, Benjamin Pierce received three weeks of schooling a year until he entered the army. When he joined the army he could "write and cypher." Benjamin Pierce abruptly left his uncle's custody in April of 1775 when the news of the Battle of Lexington reached him. In his brief *Autobiography*, Benjamin Pierce recalled:

> I was ploughing in the field when the news first came that the British had fired upon the Americans at Lexington and killed eight men. I stepped between the cattle, dropped the chains from the plough, and without any further ceremony, shouldered my uncle's fowling piece [shotgun] swung the bullet pouch and powder-horn and hastened to the place where the first blood had been spilled, but finding the enemy had retired, I pursued my way towards Boston, but was not able to overtake them till they had effected their retreat to the garrison.

Benjamin Pierce promptly enlisted in the Twenty-Seventh Massachusetts Regiment, which was commanded by Captain John Ford. Pierce proved himself to be a very good soldier and advanced to the rank of lieutenant before being mustered out of the Continental Army in 1784.

During the American Revolution, Benjamin Pierce participated in maneuvers around Boston and in the Saratoga Campaign. He also spent the winter of 1777–78 with Washington's troops at Valley Forge. Benjamin Pierce was cited for brav-

Benjamin Pierce. New Hampshire Historical Society, #4153.

ery in several engagements. It is also recorded that while he was a prisoner of war, Benjamin Pierce was "grossly insulted by a British officer whom he ran through the body in a duel."

In the spring of 1784 Benjamin Pierce returned to Chelmsford after almost nine years of soldiering. One year later, Pierce began working for Colonel Samson Stoddard of Chelmsford. Stoddard was a wealthy merchant with landholdings in Vermont and New Hampshire. Pierce explored a tract of land in what is now Cheshire County, New Hampshire, and appraised the land for its agricultural and timbering potential. After finishing his exploration and evaluations, Pierce purchased a farm in Hillsborough, New Hampshire, and settled there.

On May 24, 1787, Benjamin Pierce married for the first time. Pierce's bride, Elizabeth Andrews, was the daughter of Isaac Andrews of Hillsborough. They had been married for less than fifteen months when Elizabeth Andrews Pierce died on August 13, 1788. By his first wife, Pierce had one child, a daughter named Elizabeth. Benjamin Pierce remarried on February 1, 1790, when he wed Anna Kendrick. Benjamin and Anna had eight children; six of them lived to maturity. Franklin, the sixth child and fourth son, was born in a log cabin beside the Contoocook River in Hillsborough, New Hampshire, on November 23, 1804. Shortly after the birth of Franklin, the Pierces moved from their log cabin to a roomy house Benjamin had built in the Hillsborough Lower Village. The home was on the highway, and, like the Abraham Van Buren home, the domicile of Benjamin Pierce was also a tavern.

Before he had reached his teens, Franklin Pierce had seen his father persevere in the rough and tumble world of New Hampshire politics. Prior to Franklin's birth, Benjamin Pierce had served as Hillsborough's representative in the New Hampshire General Court (state legislature) and as a delegate to the state constitutional convention. From 1803 to 1809 Benjamin Pierce also served on the governor's council. Pierce was an anti–Federalist and a staunch supporter of Thomas Jefferson. Pierce's anti–Federalist sentiments were so strong that he turned down an appointment as a regimental commander in a standing army being raised by Federalist President John Adams. In his *Autobiography*, Benjamin Pierce recalled:

> Although arms was my profession, I could not consistently accept an appointment in an army which appeared to me to have been raised to subvert those principles for which I had fought in the revolution; that I was forbidden by the duty I owed to myself, my country and my God; and that although I was poor rather than be instrumental in rivetting upon the necks of my countrymen the chains which had been forced on them, I would retire to a cave and eat potatoes to the last day of my life.

Roy Frank Nichols, in his book, *Franklin Pierce: Young Hickory of the Granite Hills*, tells of a political plot to disgrace Benjamin Pierce and ruin his career in politics. In 1813 Pierce was serving as sheriff of Hillsborough County when a Federalist named John T. Gilman was elected governor of New Hampshire. Gilman dredged up some fraudulent charges against Pierce, which precipitated judicial proceedings and ultimately resulted in Pierce's removal from office by the state legislature. Some of Pierce's political opponents also filed suits against him, but the fortunate appointment of a judge favorable to Pierce apparently saved his political career.

In 1814 Pierce was elected to the governor's council and was thrust into the position of actively opposing the man who tried to ruin him. After serving a four-year term on the governor's council, Pierce served as sheriff of Hillsborough County for almost a decade (1818–1827). Benjamin Pierce ran for governor of New Hampshire four times and was elected twice. In 1826 Pierce ran for the office as a Jackson Democrat, but lost to David L. Morrill. One year later, Pierce was elected to the office by a landslide vote of 23,695 to 2,529. A reelection bid in 1828 was unsuccessful, but Pierce was able to defeat incumbent Governor John Bell in 1829 by a margin of 22,615 to 19,583. According to the *Biographical Directory of the Governors of the United States, 1789–1978*, Pierce was a staunch advocate of improved transportation facilities for New Hampshire, and during his administrations, the state began to develop mining and quarry industries.

After his second term as governor ended in 1830, Pierce left public life and retired to his farm in Hillsborough. His last public office was serving as a Democratic presidential elector in 1832. The father's political career was ending just when that of the son was beginning. Franklin Pierce's first elected office was to the New Hampshire General Court during his father's last term as governor.

The Nichols biography offers one significant anecdote about Benjamin's influence on Franklin. When Franklin Pierce was twelve, he decided to quit school. Franklin walked about seven or eight miles from the Hancock Academy to the Pierce farm to tell his father that he had all the education he was ever going to need. When Franklin arrived, his parents were at church. When Benjamin returned home, he listened without comment to Franklin's arguments that he was sufficiently educated. Since his father had had so little formal education himself, Franklin must have felt confident that silence implied consent. An invitation to the family's Sunday dinner made Franklin feel even more confident.

After dinner, however, Benjamin hitched up the wagon and took his son back to the road leading to the academy. After traveling for some distance, Benjamin turned the wagon around and ordered Franklin to walk back to school. Franklin got caught in a storm and arrived back at the academy defeated, dispirited, and drenched.

After returning to the academy, Franklin Pierce later went on to graduate from Bowdoin College and ultimately became an attorney. He might not have accomplished that if a firm, but loving father had not made him take that long, wet walk back to school when he was twelve.

Franklin Pierce's political views were certainly influenced by his father. Both father and son were Jacksonian Democrats and admirers of Andrew Jackson. When Franklin Pierce ran for president in 1852, he took on the nickname "Young Hickory of the Granite Hills." It is also likely that the life of Benjamin Pierce influenced the decision of Franklin Pierce to serve in the Mexican War. Growing up listening to tales about a father who was a Revolutionary War hero would make a son want to emulate his father. Together with a sense of patriotism this must have contributed to Franklin Pierce's decision to abandon a thriving law practice and enlist in the Concord volunteers when he was forty-one.

Like a good father, Benjamin helped Franklin get started in life. When Franklin began practicing law in Hillsborough, it was in an office his father had built for him. When Franklin needed a law library, Benjamin paid half the cost. When Franklin decided to enter politics, Benjamin's network of political supporters and cronies helped Franklin get elected to the state legislature and both houses of Congress.

Benjamin Pierce died at his farm in Hillsborough on April 1, 1839. He was eighty-one years old. His obituary notices lauded him as "a man of great native talent . . . a leader of men. . . . Without the advantages of early education, without opulent and powerful friends . . . he grew to be the most influential man in New Hampshire."

Bibliography

Brown, Fern G. *Franklin Pierce: Fourteenth President of the United States*. Ada, Okla.: Garrett Educational Corporation, 1989.

Burbey, Louis H. *Our Worthy Commander: The Life and Times of Benjamin K. Pierce in Whose Honor Fort Pierce Was Named*. Fort Pierce, Fl.: IRCC Pioneer Press, 1976.

Malone, Dumas, editor. *Dictionary of American Biography*. Vol. 7. New York: Scribners, 1934.

New Hampshire Historical Society, Manuscripts Division. Benjamin Pierce Papers. Biographical Sketch and Scope and Content Note.

Nichols, Roy Franklin. *Franklin Pierce: Young Hickory of the Granite Hills*. Philadelphia: University of Pennsylvania Press, 1958.

Sobel, Robert, and John Raimo, editors. *Biographical Directory of the Governors of the United States, 1789–1978*. Westport, Conn.: Meckler, 1978.

James Buchanan Sr. (1761–1821)

Merchant, farmer, magistrate, and father of President James Buchanan

James Buchanan's feelings about his father are revealed in a biographical sketch he wrote about the life and character of James Sr.: "He was a man of great native force of character. He was not only respected, but beloved by everybody that approached him. He was a kind father, a sincere friend and an honest and religious man. My father was a man of practical judgement and of great industry and perseverance."

James Buchanan Sr. was born in County Donegal, Ireland, in 1761. James Buchanan described his father's family as "respectable, but their pecuniary circumstances were limited." It is probably because of those pecuniary circumstances that James Sr. was raised by an uncle named Samuel Russell. There is a bit of a mystery about what happened to James Sr.'s parents. In his book, *President James Buchanan*, Philip Shriver Klein explains, "His father, John Buchanan, had married Jane Russell in 1750, and the couple had several children before James was born in 1761. There is some evidence that the mother died about that time and that the father then disappeared. After 1764, no trace of the parents can be found."

How much formal schooling James Sr. received and when and where he attended school is also a mystery. James Buchanan wrote that James Sr. "had received a good English education, and had that kind of Knowledge of mankind which prevented him from ever being deceived in his business." When he was twenty-two, James Sr. and his uncle agreed that it was time for him to go off on his own. Joshua Russell, a brother of Samuel, had written that he could meet James Sr. in Philadelphia and take him in until the young man found employment.

On July 4, 1783, James Buchanan Sr. boarded the brig *Providence* and emigrated to America. Joshua met James Sr. in Philadelphia and they traveled to Joshua's tavern in Gettysburg. While staying with Joshua, James Sr. met his future bride, Elizabeth Speer. She was the youngest child of the widower James Speer, who was Joshua's neighbor. They were married five years later, in 1788, when James Sr. was twenty-seven and she was twenty-one.

From travelers stopping at Joshua's tavern, James Sr. learned of a clerical position at a trading post in Cove Cap, about forty miles west of Philadelphia. The trading post was a major rest stop for travelers from Philadelphia and Baltimore en route to Pittsburgh. Since goods arrived faster than they could be shipped out, there was also a warehouse. James Sr. became the factotum and right-hand man of the post's owner, John Tom. In December of 1786 John Tom offered to sell his business and property to James Sr. for 200 pounds Pennsylvania currency. However, a lawsuit against John Tom forced a sheriff's sale of his assets before the deal could be completed. On June 23, 1787, James Sr. purchased John Tom's 100 acres for 142 pounds. Included with the land were a few log cabins, stables and barns, the warehouse and store, cleared fields, and an orchard.

About ten months after buying out John Tom, James Sr. married Elizabeth. They moved into a log cabin on the newly acquired property and started a family. Their first child, Mary, was born in 1789. James was their second child. He was born in his father's log cabin at Cove Gap on April 23, 1791. Eight of the eleven children born to James Sr. and Elizabeth lived to maturity.

By 1794 James Sr. was prosperous enough to buy a 300-acre farm near the village of Mercersburg, Pennsylvania. Two years later, he moved his family to Mercersburg after buying a large lot in the center of town and building a two-story combination house and store. James Sr. soon became one of the town's leading citizens. For a time, James Sr. served as Mercersburg's justice of the peace. James began working in his father's store as soon as he was tall enough to see over the counter. Customers were impressed by the polite and perceptive boy with a gift for gab and a head for figures, but James Sr. was usually prone to criticize his son. As Klein explains,

> James learned fast and outstripped those his own age in handling assigned work, but he rarely experienced the joyous sense of a task well done; it was never done well enough for the squire. The boy hungered for commendation, but he seldom got it. There was little friendly informality and playtime between father and son; it was a man-to-man relationship between man and boy, full of mutual reliance and respect, but without humor or comradeship.

When James was sixteen, his father decided to send him to college. Doctor John King, the Buchanans' minister, had been urging James Sr. to do so. James Sr. badly needed his oldest son to help with the business, but he realized the importance of higher education. Elizabeth wanted her son to enter the ministry, but James Sr. wanted James to study law. The father prevailed, and in the fall of 1807 father and son saddled up their horses and rode to Dickinson College in Carlisle, Pennsylvania.

James's prior studies at Old Stone Academy in Mercersburg qualified him to enter Dickinson as a junior. During his first year at Dickinson, James's academic work was quite satisfactory, but his extracurricular activities incurred the wrath of the school administration. James complained that "to be a sober, plodding industrious youth was to incur the ridicule of the mass of students." James found that drinking, smoking cigars, rowdiness, and carousing were the keys to social acceptance.

In the fall of 1808 James was lounging in the family sitting room while on break from school. James Sr. answered a knock at the front door and then returned clutching a letter. James described what happened next:

> He opened it, and read it, and I observed that his countenance fell. He then handed it to me and left the room and I do not recollect that he ever afterwards spoke to me on the subject of it. This showed his perfect knowledge of my character. It was from Dr. Davidson, the principal of Dickinson College. He stated that, but for the respect that the faculty entertained for my father, I would have been expelled from the college on account of disorderly conduct. That they had bourne with me as best they could until that period; but that they would not receive me again, and that the letter was written to save him the mortification of sending me back and having me rejected.

James believed he could rectify things by seeing Dr. John King. He knew his father was furious, and he was too scared to ask James Sr. for help. Fortunately, Dr. King had recently become president of the board of trustees at Dickinson College. Dr. King persuaded the school to rescind its expulsion by having James solemnly promise that there would be a marked improvement in his conduct.

In his senior year, James in fact showed significant improvement in both his grades and his behavior. The literary society he belonged to unanimously nominated him for the first honor award as the top scholar of the senior class. A vindictive faculty, however, had the last word. They rejected James for both first honor and second honor recognition. The faculty said that it would be bad for the school's morale to honor a student who had been a discipline problem and had shown very little respect for the faculty.

James was outraged. He wrote to his father and bitterly complained about the unfairness of their decision. The first honor should go to the best scholar. He was the best scholar and he had the grades to prove it. James Sr.'s response is quoted in George Ticknor Curtis's book, *Life of James Buchanan:*

> Dear Son:—I think that it was a very partial decision, and calculated to hurt your feelings. Be that as it will, I hope that you will have fortitude enough to surmount these things.... The more you know of mankind, the more you will distrust them. It is said that the knowledge of mankind and distrust of them are reciprocally connected.

In December of 1809 James began the study of law under the tutelage of James Hopkins in Lancaster, Pennsylvania. James Sr. picked Hopkins as his son's instructor because he had seen Hopkins try a case and had been very impressed with Hopkins's courtroom competency. Recalling his son's earlier behavior at Dickinson, James Sr. wrote James shortly after he began his law studies. At that time Lancaster was the state capital, and James Sr. must have regarded the city as a hotbed of sin. He admonished his son, "I hope that you will guard against the temptations that may offer themselves in this way, or any other, knowing that without religion all other things are trifles, and will soon pass away. . . . Go on with your studies and endeavor to be eminent in your profession."

The desire to see his son succeed was more than just fatherly pride. James Sr. was aware of his mortality. He knew that someday James might have to help support his siblings. As a businessman, James Sr. looked upon the education of James as an investment in the future. He reminded James of that when he wrote, "I hope that the privation I have suffered & will suffer in giving you a good education will be compensated by the station in society that you will occupy."

In November of 1812 James Buchanan was admitted to the bar. On February 20, 1813, he became a practicing attorney in Lancaster. One month later, James was appointed prosecutor for Lebanon County, Pennsylvania. The position provided a stipend that would at least pay for his office rent. After the appointment, James Sr. wrote his son a congratulatory letter, but he tempered the congratulations with a plea to act "with compassion and humanity for the poor creatures against whom you may be engaged."

In 1814 James went into partnership with John Passmore and purchased a tavern they had been using for their offices and living quarters. It is likely that James Sr. helped his son finance the transaction. The terms were $4,000 down and another $1,000 to be paid within one year. At the time, James Buchanan was making about $1,000 a year as a beginning lawyer. It was also in 1814 that James Buchanan entered politics against the wishes of his father. In October of 1814 James was elected to represent Lancaster in the Pennsylvania House of Representatives. He ran as a Federalist. James Sr. had written him and advised him to stick to practicing law. He told his son that career was preferable to being "partly a politician and partly a lawyer."

Even after James was elected, James Sr. expressed his misgivings about his son's political career. On October 21, 1814, he wrote James, "The feelings of parents are always alive to the welfare of their children, and I am fearful of this taking you from the bar at a time when perhaps you may feel it most. . . ."

By the time James ran for reelection in 1815, James Sr. had changed his mind about politics. James had let his father know that the contacts he had made in the state legislature had brought in new clients. He had made over $2,000 practicing law in 1815. James Sr. wrote his son, "If a man's work is a source of comfortable income and offers contentment as well, why would one wish to change?"

James Buchanan Sr. lived to see his son elected to the U.S. House of Representatives in October of 1820. His son had been a congressman just over three months when a tragic accident ended the life of James Sr. On June 11, 1821, James Sr. was entering the driveway of his home when the horse pulling his carriage bolted. James Sr. was thrown from the carriage and struck his head on an iron wheel. He died at the age of sixty.

When James returned to Mercersburg from Washington, he discovered that

James Sr. had not left a will. He spent his summer settling his father's estate and making sure that his siblings were provided for. That is why James Sr. had wanted him to become an attorney. Like a good son, James did what his father had wanted.

Bibliography

Curtis, George Ticknor. *Life of James Buchanan: Fifteenth President of the United States*. New York: Harper, 1883.

Collins, David R. *James Buchanan: Fifteenth President of the United States*. Ada, Okla.: Garrett Educational Corporation, 1990.

Hoyt, Edwin P. *James Buchanan*. Chicago: Reilly & Lee, 1966.

Klein, Philip Shriver. *President James Buchanan*. University Park, Pa.: Pennsylvania State University Press, 1962.

Moore, John Bassett, editor. *The Works of James Buchanan*. New York: Antiquarian Press, 1960.

Thomas Lincoln
(1778–1851)

*Soldier, farmer, laborer, carpenter, wood cutter,
temporary law officer, slave patroller, and father of
President Abraham Lincoln*

When his father, Thomas, died, Abraham Lincoln was living about seventy miles away. Abraham never visited his dying father and did not attend his funeral. That illustrates how distant and estranged father and son had become.

Thomas Lincoln was born in Rockingham County, Virginia, on January 6, 1778. The father of America's sixteenth president was the youngest of three sons and one of five children born to Abraham and Bathsheba Herring Lincoln. The first Abraham Lincoln had served in the Virginia militia during the American Revolution. In 1782 he settled in Kentucky where he staked a claim to 2,000 acres of farmland. That modest (for that time and place) estate cost him $800. At the age of six, Thomas was an eyewitness to his father's murder. Thomas had accompanied his father to a field they were clearing. While Abraham was working, an Indian furtively moved through the woods and killed Abraham with a single shot from a rifle. Thomas was about to be carried off by the Indian when a fatal shot fired by his brother, Mordecai, felled their father's killer.

Thomas then spent his childhood and teen years living with various relatives. Sometimes he was hired out as a farmhand. There is no record of him ever attending school. As an adult he could write his name. Some Lincoln biographers state that Thomas was illiterate, but Carl Sandburg claimed in his book, *Abraham Lincoln: The Prairie Years,* that Thomas "could read some."

While growing up Thomas learned the trades of cabinetmaking and carpentry. Exactly when he struck out on his own is not clear. According to Benjamin Thomas's biography, *Abraham Lincoln: A Biography,* it was "after his sixteenth year." Some of the jobs Thomas did while wandering through Kentucky and Tennessee were working as a laborer on a milldam, guarding prisoners, fighting Indians, cutting wood, and patrolling for slaves without permits. In 1803 Thomas purchased a 238-acre farm located on Mill Creek in Hardin County, Kentucky. He paid 118 pounds cash.

The fact that he was able to earn and save the money belies the common image of Thomas Lincoln as a lazy, shiftless, ne'er-do-well. In addition, as Benjamin Thomas points out, Thomas Lincoln always owned at least one horse, had a favorable credit rating, and apparently no unpaid debts.

In or around 1806 Thomas proposed to Sarah Bush, the daughter of his slave patrol captain. She turned him down. He then turned his amorous attentions to Nancy Hanks. She accepted. They were married on June 12, 1806, in the cabin of Richard Berry in Washington County, Kentucky. He was twenty-eight and she was twenty-three. Thomas and Nancy's first home was a crude, cramped (fourteen square feet) cabin in Elizabethtown, Kentucky. Sarah, the first of their three children, was born in February of 1807. Toward the end of 1808, the Lincolns left Elizabethtown to settle near what is now Hodgenville, Kentucky. Thomas made a down payment on three hundred acres, cleared the land, and built a log cabin.

On the morning of February 12, 1809, a son was born to Thomas and Nancy. They named the child after Thomas's deceased father, Abraham. It is believed that Thomas lived on the Hodgenville farm, which he called Sinking Spring, for about four years. He was able to provide the bare necessities for his family by hunting, farming, and doing carpentry.

Sandburg describes Thomas's lack of ambition and initiative: "He . . . would rather have people come and ask him to work on a job than to hunt the job himself. . . . He wasn't exactly lazy; he was sort of independent and liked to be where he wasn't interfered with." Richard N. Current fleshes out the character and personality of Thomas Lincoln in more detail in his book, *The Lincoln Nobody Knows*: "Both mentally and physically he was slow, dull, careless, inert. He liked his liquor though he drank no more than the average Kentuckian of his time. . . . Roving and shiftless, he moved from farm to farm in Kentucky and then migrated to Indiana and finally to Illinois, repeating in each place a tedious pattern of compulsive failure."

In 1813 Thomas abandoned the Sinking Spring farm after learning that a previous owner still had a lien upon the land. He moved his family to Knob Creek, Kentucky. After settling there, Thomas was once again plagued by legal troubles. His title to his Knob Creek farm was questioned, and a suit was filed to dispossess him. Thoroughly discouraged, Thomas decided to move to Indiana. Land there could be purchased directly from the federal government. Another factor in Thomas's decision to move may have been his unsolicited appointment as a road surveyor. In May of 1816 Thomas was ordered by the court to maintain the road from Muldraugh's Hill to Rolling Fork in the Knob Creek Valley. Unlike Abraham, Thomas never had any desire to be a public servant. Even though the duties were minimal, Thomas Lincoln was never one to take on work he did not want.

In the autumn of 1816 Thomas left Nancy, Sarah, and Abraham behind to explore land opportunities in Indiana. He traveled on a flatboat that Abraham had helped him build. Taking ten barrels of whiskey he had traded his farm for, tools, and household goods, Thomas traveled from Knob Creek to the Salt River to the

Ohio River. En route to Indiana, the boat capsized on the Ohio River. Thomas lost some of his tools but saved most of the whiskey. Arriving in Indiana, Thomas left his goods with a settler named Posey and went exploring the land armed with his hunting knife and axe. According to Albert J. Beveridge's biography, *Abraham Lincoln, 1809–1858,* he journeyed sixteen miles before choosing a place to settle his family. Thomas then turned around and began walking back to Knob Creek to get his family.

In November or December of 1816 the Lincolns loaded their few possessions on two borrowed horses and moved to Indiana. The Lincolns settled in what is now Spencer County, Indiana, near Little Pigeon Creek. Arriving in the middle of winter with no place to house his family, Thomas quickly threw up what was called a "half-faced camp"—a primitive shelter of logs and boughs enclosed on three sides. The fourth side of the structure was protected by a fire that had to blaze constantly to generate a minimal amount of heat. Benjamin Thomas calls the Lincolns' first winter in Indiana the low point of the Lincolns' fortunes. They lived in the crude shelter for about a year while Thomas cleared the land and built a cabin.

Lincoln biographers cite the year the Lincolns lived in the half-faced camp as additional evidence of Thomas's shiftlessness. However, they overlook that Thomas always had to hunt to feed his family. Eventually Thomas and Abraham cleared enough land for them to plant seventeen acres of corn, wheat, and oats. They also acquired sheep, hogs, and a few head of cattle. During their first year in Indiana, the Lincolns lived as "squatters," but by December of 1817 Thomas had paid $80—one/fourth of the purchase price for the 160 acres he claimed—at the government land office in Vincennes.

In the summer of 1818 an epidemic of a disease called milk sickness swept through southern Indiana. It is believed to have been caused by cattle eating poisonous plants and passing the poison on to people in their milk. The dreaded disease claimed the life of Nancy Hanks Lincoln on October 5, 1818. Thomas remained a widower for a little over one year. Then he traveled back to Kentucky to propose to a widow named Sarah Bush Johnston. According to Philip B. Kunhardt's book, *Lincoln: An Illustrated Biography,* Thomas said to her, "Miss Johnston, I have no wife and you no husband. I came a-purpose to marry you." She accepted, and they were married on December 2, 1819, in Elizabethtown, Kentucky.

Shortly thereafter, Thomas, Sarah, and her three children moved to Indiana with Thomas. Together with his cousin Dennis Hanks, there were now eight people living in the Lincolns' cabin. Sarah soon made her mark on the Lincoln cabin. She persuaded Thomas to finally put down a floor and hang some windows and doors in the structure.

Thomas appreciated Abraham more for his physical abilities than his mental ones and often hired him out as a farmhand or laborer. The money Abraham earned was turned over to his father. Until he turned twenty-one Abraham Lincoln apparently was not allowed to keep any of the money he earned.

Not all of Abraham's bosses were pleased with his attitude towards work. Abraham's fondness for reading, telling jokes and stories, and giving speeches at times caused him to shirk his work. Abraham Lincoln once said that his father taught him to work but never taught him to love it. Both the father and son shared a love of storytelling, but Thomas was utterly devoid of the love of books and reading that characterized Abraham. Physically, too, there was not much resemblance between father and son. Thomas was round-faced and of average height. Abraham was noted for his long face and lanky, six-foot-four-inch frame. They both had leathery skin, coarse black hair, and both were reputed to possess great physical strength.

The pronounced differences between the two gave credence to rumors that Thomas was not Abraham's biological father. Those rumors were buttressed by Thomas's harsh treatment of Abraham. Abraham Lincoln's cousin, Dennis Hanks, reported several instances of Thomas being physically abusive toward Abraham. "Sometimes a blow from the old man's fist would hurl the boy a rod," and "his father would sometimes knock him over," Hanks recalled. According to Beveridge, "Thomas Lincoln also thrashed the lad, who took his punishment in silence, tears the only outward sign of what he felt and thought."

Biographers of Lincoln cannot explain why Thomas singled out Abraham for such punishment. By all accounts, Abraham Lincoln was an extraordinarily good-natured boy and eager to please. The most common explanation is that Abraham Lincoln was often so absorbed in his books and reading, that he was slow to perform the manual labor Thomas required him to do. When he finally went off to perform a task, he usually took a book along.

Thomas became even more exasperated when his adolescent son interrupted his work and started orating. Abraham at times put down his tools, mounted a fence or a stump and began speaking to his fellow workers. They in turn put down their tools and stopped working so they could listen to Abraham. Abraham's stepmother, Sarah Bush Johnston Lincoln, recalled: "His father had to make him quit sometimes, as he would quit his own work to speak and made the other children as well as the men quit their work."

In February of 1830 Thomas Lincoln sold his farm to Charles Grigsby for $125. Thomas and Sarah Lincoln also sold some land she owned in Kentucky for $123. In addition, Thomas sold and bartered some of his household goods and bought some oxen. The meager returns of his farm and fears of another outbreak of milk sickness sent the Lincolns to Illinois, where they settled in Macon County. Abraham stayed with them for about a year before permanently leaving home. Once he left, he made little effort to stay in touch with his father. According to Beveridge, Abraham Lincoln from time to time gave his father small sums of cash or notes he received from his legal clients for services rendered.

In an 1848 letter to his father and his stepbrother, John D. Johnston, Lincoln agreed to send his father twenty dollars to keep Thomas from losing his land. In that letter he also advised his father to ascertain if the judgment had already been paid.

In the winter of 1850–51 Thomas Lincoln was seriously ill. John D. Johnston wrote Abraham a series of letters that went unanswered. In one he implores

Thomas Lincoln (1778–1851)

Thomas Lincoln. Courtesy of the Lincoln Museum, Fort Wayne, Indiana, a part of Lincoln National Corporation, #122.

Abraham, "I hast to inform you that father is yet a Live & that is all & he Craves to See you all the time & he wants you to Come if you ar able to git hure." It is not surprising that the letters remained unanswered. During his years in Springfield, Illinois, Abraham Lincoln never invited his father to visit him and his family. Benjamin Thomas explains this behavior: "Lincoln's inability to make even a pretense of affection for his father was in keeping with his fundamental honesty; for frankness, candor, and truthfulness were second nature with him."

In a letter to John D. Johnston dated January 12, 1851, Abraham finally communicated with his dying father. He explains that his letters have gone unanswered because

> It appeared to me that I could write nothing which would do any good. You already know I desire that neither Father nor Mother shall be in want of any comfort in health or sickness while they live; and I feel sure that you have not failed to use my name, if necessary, to procure a doctor, or any thing else for Father in his present sickness.

Abraham then writes that he cannot come to see his father and continues:

> I sincerely hope that Father may yet recover his health; but at all events tell him to remember to call upon and confide in, our great, and good, and merciful Maker; who will not turn away from him in any extremity. He notes the fall of sparrow, and numbers the hairs of our heads; and He will not forget the dying man, who puts his trust in Him. Say to him that if we could meet now, it is doubtful whether it would not be more painful than pleasant; but that if it be his lot to go now, he will soon have a joyous meeting with many loved ones gone before; and where the rest of us, through the help of God, hope erelong to join them.

Bibliography

Angle, Paul M., editor. *The Lincoln Reader.* New Brunswick, N.J.: Rutgers University Press, 1947.
Beveridge, Albert J. *Abraham Lincoln, 1809–1858.* Boston: Houghton Mifflin, 1928.
Current, Richard N. *The Lincoln Nobody Knows.* New York: McGraw-Hill, 1958.
Kunhardt, Philip B. *Lincoln: An Illustrated Biography.* New York: Random House.
Lincoln, Abraham. *Speeches and Writings, 1832–1858* and *1859–1865.* Library of America.
The Lincoln Kinsman. "Abraham Lincoln's Father: A Chronological Table of References to Him in Authentic Records." Fort Wayne, Indiana, March 1939.
Luthin, Reinard H. *The Real Abraham Lincoln.* Englewood Cliffs, N.J.: Prentice-Hall, 1960.
Rice, Allen Thorndike, editor. *Reminiscences of Abraham Lincoln.* New York: Harper, 1909.
Sandburg, Carl. *Abraham Lincoln: The Prairie Years.* New York: Scribner's, 1941.
Thomas, Benjamin P. *Abraham Lincoln: A Biography.* New York: Modern Library, 1952.

Jacob Johnson
(1778–1812)

*Sexton, soldier, porter, constable, caterer,
town bell ringer, factotum, and father of
President Andrew Johnson*

Like his famous son, Andrew, Jacob Johnson grew up impoverished and illiterate. Unlike his most famous son, the father of America's seventeenth president never bettered his lot in life. Jacob Johnson died when he was thirty-three and Andrew was three. Biographers of Andrew Johnson do not agree on where Jacob was born. According to Hans L. Trefousse's biography, *Andrew Johnson: A Biography,* Jacob was a descendant of a Virginia farmer named Silvanus Johnson, and Jacob's family moved to Johnston City, North Carolina, in 1754. According to Lately Thomas's book, *The First President Johnson,* on the other hand, Jacob was born in England and settled in America after sailing from Newcastle in 1795. A third source, Bill Severn's book, *In Lincoln's Footsteps,* gives Jacob's birthplace as either Virginia or somewhere in the north of England. There is agreement, however, that Jacob was born in 1778, and Joseph Nathan Kane's *Facts About the Presidents* gives April as the month of his birth. Johnson biographers agree on the character and personality of Jacob and generally describe him as genial, cheerful, easygoing, trustworthy, and devoid of ambition. In spite of a general lack of ambition, Jacob was hardworking. Severn records that at one time Jacob was holding a dozen odd jobs.

How and when Jacob came to settle in Raleigh, North Carolina, is not recorded. According to Severn he arrived there around 1800. That would be one year before Jacob Johnson met and married a petite, pretty, dark-haired girl named Mary McDonough. Mary was known around Raleigh as "Polly the weaver." She worked as a seamstress and laundress at a millinery shop and as a waitress at Peter Casso's inn in Raleigh. Like her husband, she was illiterate. After marrying Jacob, she augmented their meager family income by continuing to wash and mend clothes.

Jacob and Mary had three children. Their first child was a girl whose name is unrecorded and who died in infancy or early childhood. Their second child was a boy named William who became a carpenter in Texas. Andrew, their third and last child, was born in Raleigh on December 29, 1808. Just exactly where Andrew Johnson was born is another matter of disagreement among his biographers. The traditional story is that he was born in a log cottage located on the grounds of Casso's inn. Trefousse disputes this, claiming the actual birthplace was a log cabin that was eventually dismantled by souvenir hunters.

Some of the jobs Jacob held to support his family include milling, tending horses, ringing the town bell, serving as a church sexton (caretaker), being the town constable, and catering barbeques. Jacob also served in a unit of the state militia where his friends elected him captain.

According to Severn, local plantation owners offered Jacob opportunities to work in the country, but he preferred the urban environment of Raleigh. Because of his outgoing, gregarious nature, Jacob opted to stay where he could be with his friends.

Johnson biographers all agree that Jacob Johnson died as a result of performing an act of heroism in saving another's life. On a cold December day in 1811, Jacob Johnson accompanied several of Raleigh's well-to-do men on a fishing party at Walnut Creek. Jacob was most likely along to cater the affair and to clean the catch. During the party, Colonel Tom Henderson, editor of the *Raleigh Star,* and two other men boarded a canoe. Either accidentally, or as a prank, Henderson began rocking the canoe. It capsized, spilling the three men into the frigid waters.

A passenger named Callum could not swim, and he desperately clung to Henderson. As a result, both men sank to the bottom. While the other members of the party stood safely on shore, Jacob Johnson unhesitatingly dove into the icy waters. With much effort and exertion, Jacob rescued the two men while the third man swam to shore.

Since he was not able to change out of his freezing, wet clothes right away, Jacob caught a severe cold, which developed into a lingering illness. In January of 1812 Jacob collapsed while performing his duties as town bell ringer. He died on January 4, 1812.

Colonel Henderson paid homage to Jacob in his obituary in the January 12, 1812, issue of the *Star*:

> Died, in this city on Saturday last, Jacob Johnson, who for many years occupied a humble but useful station. He was the city constable, sexton and porter to the State Bank. In his last illness he was visited by the principal inhabitants of the city, by all of whom he was esteemed for his honesty, sobriety, industry, and his humane, friendly disposition. Among all whom he was known and esteemed, none lament him, except perhaps his own relatives, more than the publisher of this newspaper, for he owes his life on a particular occasion to the kindness and humanity of Johnson.

Over three decades after Jacob's death, a political attack compelled Andrew Johnson to defend the honor of his deceased father and elderly mother. In 1844 Andrew was seeking a second term as congressman for the first district of Tennessee. He was running as a Democrat, and his Whig opponent, the Reverend William

Brownlow, questioned Johnson's parentage. Brownlow claimed that Andrew could not possibly be the son of an illiterate, poor white man like Jacob Johnson, whom Brownlow also accused of being a chicken thief. Brownlow maintained that Andrew was the unacknowledged son of a Raleigh judge named John Haywood.

Andrew took time off from campaigning to travel to Raleigh and collect affidavits verifying that he was indeed the son of Jacob and "Polly the weaver." He published the affidavits in an open letter declaring, "The vandals and hyenas would dig up the grave of Jacob Johnson, my father, and charge my mother with bastardy."

On June 4, 1867, while serving as president, Andrew Johnson participated in a public tribute to his father. When Jacob had first been interred, his remains had been buried in Raleigh's equivalent of potter's field. Jacob's grave was marked by a small, gray stone slab with the inscription "JJ." His widow had not been able to afford anything more ornate. Now the small slab was replaced with a shaft of red limestone bearing the inscription: "In memory of Jacob Johnson; an honest man, beloved and respected by all who knew him. Born —. Died 1812, from a disease caused by an over-effort in saving the life of a friend."

Bibliography

Jones, James Sawyer. *Life of Andrew Johnson, Seventeenth President of the United States.* New York: AMS Press, 1975.
Kane, Joseph Nathan. *Facts About the Presidents.* Bronx, N.Y.: H. W. Wilson, 1989.
Severn, Bill. *In Lincoln's Footsteps: The Life of Andrew Johnson.* New York: Ives, 1966.
Stryker, Lloyd Paul. *Andrew Johnson: A Study in Courage.* New York: Macmillan, 1929.
Thomas, Lately. *The First President Johnson.* New York: Morrow, 1968.
Trefousse, Hans L. *Andrew Johnson: A Biography.* New York: Norton, 1989.
Winston, Robert W. *Andrew Johnson: Plebeian and Patriot.* New York: Holt, 1928.

Jesse Root Grant (1794–1873)

*Leather tanner, merchant, politician, postmaster, and father of
President Ulysses Simpson Grant*

The only obvious commonality between Jesse Root Grant and his son Ulysses was a fondness for whiskers. In his *Memoirs,* the famed soldier-president described his father as a voracious reader but said little else about Jesse's personality. However, Grant biographers have presented quite a bit of information about the father of America's eighteenth president. They generally describe him as proud, outspoken, verbose, boastful, opinionated, vigorously contentious, and blunt. The same biographers call Ulysses shy, sensitive, reticent, diffident, modest, and mild-mannered. One biographer characterized Jesse as a man who would stop a stranger in the rain to brag about his son Ulysses. Still, there are no letters or anecdotes to verify that Jesse ever gave Ulysses a single word of praise. In his book, *Ulysses S. Grant: His Life and Character,* Hamlin Garland sums up their differences succinctly: "'Ulysses got his reticence, his patience, his equable temper from his mother,' is the verdict of those who knew both father and mother. Others go further and say: 'He got his sense from his mother.'"

Jesse Root Grant was born in Westmoreland County, Pennsylvania, near the city of Greensburg on January 23, 1794. Jesse was the second of five children born to shoemaker Noah Grant and his second wife, Rachel Kelly Grant. Matthew Grant had been the first of the family to come to America. He had emigrated to Dorchester, Massachusetts, from Plymouth, England, in 1630.

Rachel died when Jesse was around eleven years old, and Noah could not afford to keep his family together. Some of the children went to live with relatives; others became apprentices. Jesse took the latter alternative and became apprenticed to George Tod of Youngstown, Ohio. According to William S. McFeely's *Grant: A Biography,* Tod was "a contentious, vigorous politician," and McFeely speculates that Jesse may have acquired his penchant for arguing politics from his association with Tod. Jesse left his apprenticeship with Tod to enter into another one with his half-brother, Peter Grant, in Maysville, Kentucky. The new apprenticeship became Jesse's introduction to the leather tanning business.

Jesse immersed himself in the business. Through hard work and enterprise, Jesse learned how to tan leather and buy hides cheaply while selling the finished product for a handsome profit. With his newly acquired knowledge of manufacturing and merchandising, Jesse was able to go into business for himself. He set up shop in Point Pleasant, Ohio.

According to some biographers of Grant, Jesse's abhorrence of slavery caused him to leave Kentucky. *The American Heritage Book of Presidents and Famous Americans* quotes Jesse on this subject: "I would not own slaves and I will not live where there are slaves." However, McFeely points out that the only contemporary evidence of Jesse's antislavery sympathies is the fact that he wrote for an antislavery paper called the *Castigator.* McFeely also indicates that after Ulysses had left home, Jesse moved back to the slave state of Kentucky.

While living in Point Pleasant, Jesse met and married Hannah Simpson. They were wed on June 24, 1821, when he was twenty-seven and she was twenty-two. According to Doris Faber's book, *The Mothers of American Presidents,* their courtship was devoid of romance. Jesse needed a wife and he heard that Hannah was available. McFeely adds: "Because of his early experiences, the comfortable idea that a family is a secure joining of people in a relationship of mutual affection was foreign to him." Jesse regarded marriage and family as a business deal, a merger, an acquisition, and an investment with an anticipated return. Marriage would provide heirs to help with the business and someday take it over. The first of Jesse and Hannah's six children was born on April 27, 1822. One month later, the parents named the child Hiram Ulysses Grant. When Hiram entered West Point, he adopted the name Ulysses Simpson Grant. When Ulysses was one year old, Jesse moved his family to Georgetown, Ohio. In Georgetown Jesse built a house and became the proprietor of the tannery he established.

William DeGregorio's book, *The Complete Book of U.S. Presidents,* mentions that Ulysses S. Grant was quite squeamish and could not bear the sight of animal blood. The aversion is easy to understand. Ulysses lived across the street from a tanyard where animals were caged, slaughtered, and skinned. The stench of death and the shrill screams of dying animals were constantly around him. Ulysses often said that he loathed his father's tannery. Apparently Jesse had no trouble accepting the fact that his oldest child had neither interest in nor aptitude for the tannery. When Jesse added a livery stable to his business, he found that Ulysses had an affinity for working with horses. By the age of ten Ulysses was driving a pair of horses to Cincinnati, forty miles away, to pick up and deliver passengers and freight. Before he was in his teens, Ulysses was virtually running the stable by himself.

Ulysses Grant's love of horses is responsible for one of the most commonly told anecdotes about his relationship with his father. When Ulysses was eight, he begged his father to purchase a colt he had become attached to. Jesse agreed only after giving his son detailed and precise instructions on how to bargain. Ulysses rode out to the owner's farm and told him: "Papa says I may offer you twenty dollars for the colt, but if you won't take that, I am to offer twenty-two and a half, and if you won't take that I am to give you twenty-five." The owner gladly accepted the highest of-

Hannah and Jesse Root Grant. Courtesy of the Library of Congress.

fer, and for weeks the chagrined father listened to the townspeople ridicule his son whenever the story was repeated.

Garland relates an anecdote about how Jesse's hubris brought scorn and ridicule upon his shy and sensitive son. When Ulysses was twelve, a traveling phrenologist came to their town. During one of his public lectures, a local doctor challenged the phrenologist to examine someone's head while blindfolded. The phrenologist agreed and Ulysses became the reluctant guinea pig. The phrenologist proclaimed that this was no ordinary head, and it would not be strange if the subject someday became president of the United States. This confirmed proud Jesse's firm belief that Ulysses was destined for greatness.

As Hamlin explains, in all likelihood the pronouncement was made with a nod and a wink and Jesse and Ulysses had been played for fools. The village version of the incident was that the Grants were the gullible victims of a mean-spirited practical joke.

There was, however, a positive side to Jesse's overweening pride in his oldest child. That pride made Jesse determined that Ulysses should get the best education his father could afford. Jesse only had a few months of formal schooling, and he was always acutely aware of his lack of education. In spite of that, he was a voracious reader. In his *Memoirs*, Ulysses Grant recollected that his father "read every book he could borrow," and that Jesse's "thirst for education was intense." He also recalled that "when he got through with a book, he knew everything in it."

Ulysses started school when he was five and attended various subscription schools into his teens. When he reached high school age, he attended the Maysville (Kentucky) Seminary and then the Presbyterian Academy in Ripley, Ohio. In 1838, without consulting his son, Jesse secured a West Point appointment for Ulysses. Ulysses balked at going there. He felt that he lacked the academic preparation, and in his *Memoirs* he explained that he "could not bear the idea of failing." According to Ulysses's *Memoirs*, Jesse's reaction was simply to say "he thought I would [go to West Point], and I thought so too, if he did." In other words, Jesse did the thinking and deciding for both of them.

By getting Ulysses into West Point, Jesse accomplished two objectives: he provided his son with an inexpensive college education and a career outside of the tannery. Jesse's seemingly perfect solution went awry when Ulysses resigned his commission.

After graduating from West Point in 1843, Ulysses served with distinction in the Mexican War (1846–48). Following his war service, Ulysses married Julia Dent on August 22, 1848. He then served at army posts in Sackett's Harbor, New York; Detroit; San Francisco; and the Oregon Territory, but the cumulative effects of being separated from wife and children, being too poor to send for them, boring, routine duties, and serving under a fastidious superior officer were more than Ulysses could endure. Reportedly, he began drinking heavily to ease his depression. When he was assigned to a post in Humboldt Bay, California, his situation was at its worst. On April 11, 1854, Ulysses resigned his commission.

Jesse, in his typically well-meaning but meddlesome manner, attempted to get the resignation rescinded. Ulysses had requested for his resignation to become effective on July 31, 1854. Jesse learned of the resignation in June and wrote to Ohio Congressman Andrew Ellison asking him to use his influence with Secretary of War Jefferson Davis. When that did not work, Jesse directly contacted Secretary Davis. In a prophetic letter to the future president of the Confederacy, Jesse wrote: "I never wished him to leave the servis. I think that after spending so much time to qualify himself for the army and spending so many years in the servis, he will be poorly qualified for the pursuits of private life." However, all his efforts were to no avail. Secretary Davis wrote Jesse and informed him that the resignation stood.

Discouraged, disgraced, and despondent, Ulysses reluctantly returned to Ohio to face his father. After what is believed to have been a tense reunion, Ulysses took his wife and children to live with Julia's parents in Missouri. Ulysses began farming an eighty-acre tract his father-in-law had given him as a wedding gift.

Father and son became even more estranged when Ulysses turned down a job offer from Jesse. According to McFeely, in 1854 Jesse offered Ulysses a job in his leather goods store in Galena, Illinois. The offer came with the proviso that Ulysses's wife and children would live either with Jesse and Hannah or with Julia's parents. Ulysses found those terms unacceptable and unequivocally refused the offer.

Grant biographers concur that the period from 1854 to the outbreak of the Civil War in 1861 was the bleakest and most miserable time of Ulysses Grant's life. Letters from his father show Ulysses going from sanguine expectations to the humiliation of asking for his father's help. In a letter written in December of 1856, Ulysses tells his father: "Evry day I like farming better and I do not doubt but that money is to be made at it." Two months later, Ulysses was writing Jesse and asking him for a $500 loan. According to McFeely, the request was denied. After failing at farming and real estate, Ulysses swallowed what pride he had left. He took the job in Galena he had turned down six years earlier. However, this time Jesse allowed him to bring his family along.

When the Civil War erupted and Ulysses returned to the army, Jesse was unimpressed by his son's show of patriotism. According to McFeely, when Ulysses assumed command of the volunteer Twenty-First Illinois Infantry, Jesse chided his son for leading volunteers instead of a regular army. Ulysses explained to his father in a letter that he was in the army to fight a war, not to advance his military career.

As Ulysses ascended from colonel to commander of the Union Army, a transformation occurred in his relationship with his father. Ulysses finally began standing up to the man who had largely controlled his life. In a letter written in September of 1862 Ulysses rebuked his father's attempts to defend him from his critics: "I have not an enemy in the world who has done me so much injury as you in your efforts in my defense. I require no defenders and for my sake let me alone." Two months later, in another letter to his father, Ulysses expressed his strong displeasure over how Jesse speaks of Julia: "I am only sorry your letter, and all that comes from you speaks so condescendingly of everything Julia says, writes or thinks.

You without probably being aware of it are so prejudiced against her that she could not please you. This is not pleasing to me."

When writing his father during the war, Ulysses omitted any news of troop movements because he knew that Jesse would leak the news to the press. After the peace at Appomattox, Jesse began actively promoting his son for president. This prompted Ulysses to write his father and ask: "From your letter you seem to have taken an active feeling, to say the least, in this matter, that I would like to talk to you about. I could write, but do not want to do so. Why not come down here and see me?" If they did meet, Jesse was undeterred. In 1868 Jesse addressed a Chicago convention of Civil War veterans, which "nominated" Ulysses S. Grant for president. Jesse also attended the 1868 Republican National Convention despite requests from Ulysses's campaign managers to stay at home. They were worried that the garrulous old man might say something to damage his son's candidacy. According to one report, journalists hovered around Jesse as though he were on the "verge of the grave."

Once Ulysses became president, Jesse went from being a private embarrassment to becoming a public one. After being appointed postmaster of Covington, Kentucky, Jesse neglected the office to spend time in Washington with his son. Another postmaster's appointment went to a woman whose mother was an acquaintance of Jesse's. That post office was in the district of congressman and future president, James A. Garfield. Garfield vigorously opposed the appointment, but later backed down rather than force the president to say no to Jesse.

On March 4, 1873, Jesse attended his son's inauguration for a second term. After the ceremony, Jesse slipped and fell on some icy steps. He returned to Covington insisting all was well and that he would soon be back in Washington giving his sage advice to the president. On June 29, 1873, he died in Covington at the age of seventy-nine.

Jesse Grant's obituary in the July 4, 1873, issue of the *Covington Journal* read:

> Last December paralysis, which lingers on the verge of advanced years, prostrated Mr. Grant. From this he partially recovered, but there was evidenced from this time forth in the trembling frame and feeble step the near approach of death.... He lingered in his unconscious state until eighteen minutes past 7 o'clock Sunday night, when, in the presence of his wife, his daughter, Mrs. Cramer, and her children, together with several friends of the family, he quietly breathed his last.

Following Jesse's funeral, the *Journal* reported: "The ceremonies were conducted without parade or ostentation.... The procession, numbering twenty-five carriages, moved to Spring Grove Cemetery, back of Cincinnati, where the remains were interred." The newspaper also listed President Grant as among the mourners and reported that "the President, in consequence of some delay in receiving dispatches, did not reach Covington in time to see his father alive."

McFeely concisely sums up the relationship between Jesse and Ulysses: "Ulysses spent his life alternately repudiating Jesse Grant's bleak world and trying to prove himself worthy of it."

Bibliography

Coolidge, Louis A. *Ulysses S. Grant.* Boston: Houghton Mifflin, 1922.
Covington (Ky.) Journal. July 4, 1873.
DeGregorio, William A. *The Complete Book of U.S. Presidents.* New York: Barricade Books, 1993.
Faber, Doris. *The Mothers of American Presidents.* New York: New American Library, 1968.
Falkof, Lucille. *Ulysses S. Grant: Eighteenth President of the United States.* Ada, Okla.: Garrett Educational Corporation, 1988.
Garland, Hamlin. *Ulysses S. Grant: His Life and Character.* New York: Macmillan, 1920.
Grant, Ulysses S. *Memoirs and Selected Letters.* The Library of America, 1990.
Hesseltine, William B. *Ulysses S. Grant: Politician.* New York: Ungar, 1957.
McFeely, William S. *Grant: A Biography.* New York: Norton, 1981.
Simon, John Y., editor. *The Personal Memoirs of Julia Dent Grant.* New York: Putnam's, 1975.
Sullivan, Wilson. "Ulysses Simpson Grant." In *The American Heritage Book of the Presidents and Famous Americans,* pp. 481–515. New York: Dell, 1967.
Todd, Helen. *A Man Named Grant.* Boston: Houghton Mifflin, 1940.
Woodward, W. E. *Meet General Grant.* New York: Liveright, 1928.

Rutherford Hayes Jr.
(1787–1822)

Merchant, framer, distiller, and father of
President Rutherford B. Hayes

Rutherford Birchard Hayes was born seventy-six days after his father had died. Although he never knew his father, America's nineteenth president certainly knew of him. The most complete biography of Rutherford Hayes Jr. (the father) comes from the diary of Rutherford B. Hayes (the son).

Rutherford Hayes Jr. (hereinafter referred to as Ruddy to avoid confusion with the son) was born in Brattleboro, Vermont, on January 4, 1787. Ruddy was the fourth child and second son of Rutherford Hayes Sr. and Chloe Smith. The first members of the Hayes family to come to America had emigrated from Scotland in 1680. Hayes Sr. worked at various times as a blacksmith, a farmer, and an innkeeper. Ruddy attended school when he could and received what his son termed a "common-school education." At about the age of fifteen Ruddy became a clerk in the mercantile firm of Noyes and Mann in their Wilmington, Vermont, store. Ruddy's parents felt that he should pursue a business career because they felt that he was not sufficiently robust for performing much manual labor. Apparently, family connections helped Ruddy to get his first clerical job. John Noyes, the firm's senior partner, was Ruddy's brother-in-law.

While working as the "managing clerk" of the Wilmington store, Ruddy met Sophia Birchard. Sophia had ridden the family workhorse into town and came to the store to sell Ruddy a bag of rags. The sight of a slim, bright-eyed, energetic young lady lugging a heavy sack of rags into the store made an immediate and lasting impression on Ruddy. He was soon wooing Sophia.

In 1810 Ruddy was transferred to the firm's main store in Brattleboro. Ruddy and Sophia could see each other only on weekends, but he kept the flame of romance burning with frequent letters. One of them read:

> My dear — I am not fond of far-fetched sentiment. But do not think that I mean to throw out all Ceremony out of the Question and by a careless indif-

ference alienate your affections and weaken the bonds of friendship. No, rather than be accused of that, I would search the tales of romance . . . and the Dictionary for all the long words I can find. . . . I suppose you can guess by this time who this is from. But that you may be certain that it is from a real friend, I subscribe in full truth the name of RUTHERFORD HAYES JR. P.S. Pardon me, I love you, Sophia.

Once Sophia decided to test Ruddy's love by attending a dance or two in Wilmington with other male escorts. Ruddy reassured her of his feelings: "No, Sophia, the lass with the roseate cheeks shall not be long forgotten by the lad with the rubicund hair." In his diary, Rutherford B. Hayes described his father as of "medium height — about five feet, nine inches, straight, slender, healthy and active; full of energy and life — a witty, social, popular man, who made warm friends and few enemies. . . . He was red-headed — fiery red — and rather handsome." Sophia had once exclaimed: "I will never marry a redhead!" However, that proved to be a false prophecy. On September 13, 1813, Miss Birchard became Mrs. Hayes. The ceremony was held in the home of Sophia's late father.

Ruddy may have broken a few hearts in Wilmington when he wed Sophia. It was said of him that "Mr. Hayes, being a young man of good character and position, was a very desirable escort for the ladies." The newlyweds moved to Dummerston, Vermont, where Ruddy was a junior partner in the Noyes & Mann store. Unfortunately, business was not very good. Since June 18, 1812, the United States had been officially at war with England. Federal law prohibited the store from dealing in English products even though there was a great demand for them.

In New England, there was strong and bitter opposition to the war. John Noyes had been an outspoken opponent of the war and ran for Congress in 1814 as a Federalist candidate on the "peace" ticket. Noyes was elected and Ruddy profited by being promoted to a full partner in the firm now known as Noyes and Hayes. When the war ended in May of 1815, Ruddy anticipated an upswing in business, but the opposite occurred. Land that Vermont farmers had used to provide the army and navy with farm produce seemed to suddenly "give out." The store's base of customers was dwindling because of a steady migration from Vermont to western New York and Ohio. Fewer people were raising fewer crops and spending less money.

In the midst of this economic uncertainty came the sudden birth and death of the first Rutherford Birchard Hayes. On August 14, 1814, the first child of Ruddy and Sophia was born. A red-haired boy who had the same name as the future president. Tragically, the baby was born dead. Ruddy went into a deep depression. He often cried out loud and seemed to have no control over his emotions. It took the tenderness and tenacity of Sophia to bring him out of his profound depression. Sophia could comfort Ruddy in his grief because she had already experienced so much of it herself. Her father had died when she was thirteen. Her mother had died six months before she married Ruddy. She would ultimately outlive her husband and four of her five children. Of her five children, only the future president and one daughter reached maturity.

After serving one term in Congress, John Noyes decided to retire from both politics and business. He offered to sell Ruddy his share of the business, but Ruddy had other plans. Ruddy had wanted to join the westward migration, but he was never able to talk Sophia into uprooting their family. However, after two years of resisting, she finally acquiesced. On March 20, 1817, an ad was placed in the *Brattleboro Reporter* giving notice that the firm of Noyes and Hayes was to be dissolved on April 15. In June of 1817 Ruddy rode west to investigate business opportunities in Ohio. Three months later, the Hayes family, consisting of Ruddy, Sophia, a son and a daughter, an orphan girl relative, and Sophia's fifteen-year-old brother, Sardis Birchard, began their move west.

Ruddy had decided that the town of Delaware was just right for his family. It was small (around four hundred people) and had a large population of transplanted Vermonters. More importantly, there were churches and choice farm land. Ruddy had chosen a tract of land "by estimation 124 acres and 64 perches," that was located 1.5 miles north of town. Ruddy paid $2,888 for the property. In his diary, Rutherford B. Hayes wrote that his father "brought a considerable sum of money to Ohio, perhaps $8,000."

It took forty days for the Hayes caravan to travel from Vermont to Delaware, Ohio. They loaded their possessions onto two covered wagons and a spring wagon and traveled on the Cumberland Road. Once the family was settled, the energetic and enterprising Ruddy quickly went to work. Ruddy invested some of his capital by buying land in and around Delaware. He also began dealing in imported merchandise and entered into a partnership to distill whiskey. The latter venture appears to have been the most lucrative. It was reported that the distillery had a large number of kettles and other equipment.

Interestingly enough, the son of a distiller later became a member of the Sons of Temperance. Rutherford B. Hayes was a light drinker, and he stopped drinking altogether when he became president. His wife became known as "Lemonade Lucy" because she banned alcoholic beverages from the White House during the Hayes administration.

During the time he lived in Delaware, Ruddy Hayes earned the respect and admiration of his neighbors. He had a reputation for being hard-working and unfailingly honest. According to the praise of one of his associates, he was "as good a man as ever lived in the town of Delaware."

Ruddy apparently was successful in his business enterprises. He owned the first brick house in Delaware, and it was said to be "more genteelly furnished" than the other homes in the neighborhood. Biographies of Rutherford B. Hayes record that Ruddy was able to leave a large estate, which gave his widow and orphans financial security. Ruddy left a farm, a house, landholdings, and presumably an interest in a distillery. When Ruddy died, both the farm and the house were generating income. The farm was rented out and the house had two boarders.

However, in *Rutherford B. Hayes and His America,* Harry Barnard paints a different picture: "But despite all his energy and daring, the fortune he [Ruddy] had so confidently expected eluded him. For all his natural optimism, he found himself feeling defeated. . . . For no sooner had he got started than the western boom suffered an excruciating collapse." The truth is probably that Ruddy made money, but not nearly as much as he had hoped to. Barnard speculates that business failures motivated Ruddy to join the Presbyterian church shortly before his death. While working in his fields on July 17, 1822, Ruddy was stricken with typhus fever. He died three days later. He was thirty-five years old.

The July 22, 1822, edition of the *Delaware Patron and Franklin Chronicle* noted his death as follows:

> Died. In this town on Saturday last of the typhus fever, Mr. Rutherford Hayes, aged 35 years, formerly of Vermont; leaving an amiable wife and two children, to mourn the irreparable loss. Mr. Hayes had resided in this place about four years, in which time he had secured the respect and confidence of all who knew him. In his death, society sustains a loss of one of its most valuable members; and every good citizen may truly lament the loss of a friend and brother. His funeral was attended on Sunday, by the largest collection of citizens, which we recollect to have seen on a similar occasion, who thus testified their respect for the deceased and mingled their sympathies, for the bereavement to the widow and orphans.

Rutherford's uncle, Sardis Birchard, became his surrogate father throughout Rutherford's life. Sardis stayed in Delaware for about the first three years of Rutherford's life, but he moved away permanently in 1826, telling Rutherford, "I find living with so many womenfolk tiring."

Sardis had both the means and time to look after Rutherford's welfare. A successful career as a merchandiser and land speculator made Sardis independently wealthy. He never married and was able to pay for Rutherford's education at Kenyon College and Harvard Law School. Sardis also helped Rutherford to establish himself in his law practice, and he even paid for Rutherford's wedding. In *Rutherford B. Hayes: Statesman of Reunion,* H. J. Eckenrode summed up the influence of Uncle Sardis upon the life of Rutherford B. Hayes in these words: "Because of Sardis Birchard, Rutherford Hayes had been reared in modest, easy circumstances, educated, comfortable, settled in business, married, started in politics, and had enjoyed leisure for study, society and personal publicity. It was to Birchard that he was to owe the presidency, though Uncle Sardis did not live to see this."

Perhaps the most important thing Ruddy was able to pass on to Rutherford B. Hayes was his name. Rutherford grew up knowing that he shared the name of a deceased grandfather, father, and older brother. Sophia and Uncle Sardis no doubt reminded him that he could not spend his life being a wastrel or the prodigal son of Rutherford Hayes Jr.

Bibliography

Barnard, Harry. *Rutherford B. Hayes and His America*. Indianapolis and New York: Bobbs-Merrill, 1954.
Delaware (Ohio) Patron and Family Chronicle. July 24, 1822.
Eckenrode, H. J. *Rutherford B. Hayes: Statesman of Reunion*. New York: Dodd, Mead, 1930.
Faber, Doris. "Sophia Birchard Hayes." In *The Mothers of American Presidents*. New York: New American Library, 1968.
Hayes, Rutherford. *Diaries of Rutherford B. Hayes*.
Hayes Scrapbook. Vol. 91, p. 74.
Hogenboom, Ari. *The Presidency of Rutherford B. Hayes*. Lawrence, Kansas: University Press of Kansas, 1988.
Myers, Elisabeth P. *Rutherford B. Hayes*. Chicago: Reilly & Lee, 1969.
Pessen, Edward. *The Log Cabin Myth: The Social Background of the Presidents*. New Haven and London: Yale University Press, 1984.
Williams, Charles Richard. *The Life of Rutherford Birchard Hayes: Nineteenth President of the United States*. Columbus, Ohio: Ohio State Archaeological and Historical Society, 1928.

Abram Garfield
(1799–1833)

*Farmer, canal constructor, and father of
President James A. Garfield*

Abram Garfield is a presidential father who had little influence upon the life of his famous son. The father of America's twentieth president died when James Garfield was only eighteen months old. In his published *Diary,* James mentions his father only when describing a a visit to an orchard with trees that were planted by his father.

Abram Garfield was born on December 28, 1799, in Worcester, New York. He was christened Abraham, but he went by the name of Abram. The first known member of the family to settle in America was Edward Garfield. He had come to Massachusetts in 1630. As recorded in the biography, *Garfield,* by Allan Peskin, Abram's grandfather, Solomon, settled in Worcester shortly after the Revolutionary War. Biographers of Garfield do not provide any information about Abram's childhood. Abram's father, Thomas, died when Abram was still a child. His mother remarried; her second husband was Thomas Boynton. It is unknown if Abram ever attended school. In Margaret Leech and Harry J. Brown's book, *The Garfield Orbit,* Abram is described as having "little interest in book learning." However, written bids submitted by Abram when he was a canal constructor verify that he was literate.

When he was fourteen, Abram met his future wife, Eliza Ballou. She was twelve and had moved with her family from New Hampshire to Worcester. It was not a case of love at first sight; when they met, Abram had his eye upon Eliza's older sister, Mehitabel. While Abram was still a teen, the Ballous moved to Muskinghum County, Ohio. Before the family left, Abram and Mehitabel agreed that they would get married when they were older. Abram promised Mehitabel that someday he would come to Ohio and make her his bride. When Abram was seventeen, he set off for Ohio. He turned back after reaching Buffalo and learning that the love of his life had married another man.

In 1819 Abram once again headed west with Muskinghum County as his destination. Leech and Brown write that Abram came to Ohio because his mother, stepfather, and their children had all settled there. When he arrived in Ohio, Abram learned that an uncle of Mehitabel's was living in the area. When Abram visited the uncle, he found that Eliza was living with him. They quickly became reacquainted and were married on February 3, 1820.

When she was in her seventies, Eliza wrote James Garfield a letter with a detailed description of his father. Despite having been a widow for four decades, Eliza still sounded like she was very much in love with Abram:

> Your father was five feet and eleven inches high, large head, broad shoulders and chest, high forehead, brown hair, blue eyes, light complexion, as beautiful a set of teeth as any man ever had. They were just as even as they could be and very white. Cheeks very red, lips tolerably full, but to me very handsome. His hands and feet small for a man of his size. His boots I think were eights, his bearing noble and brave, his bump of benevolence was fully developed, fond of his friends, everybody liked him, his judgement very good, more than common.

For the first eight years of their marriage, Eliza and Abram did not have a home of their own. They stayed with relatives while Abram hired himself out as a farm worker. Eventually Abram left farming for canal construction. After going into the business with two of his friends, Abram enjoyed a brief taste of success. After building a section of canal along the Cuyahoga River, Abram was able to purchase a parcel of land in Orange Township, Ohio. There he built the log cabin in which James was born. Unfortunately, Abram's prosperity was short-lived. A second canal building job in Tuscarawas County, Ohio, was a losing venture. Virtually all the profits from the first job were eaten up by losses on the second, and Abram returned to farming.

Whether in farming or canal building, Abram was well suited for manual labor. Garfield biographers make mention of Abram's enormous strength. He was known throughout frontier Ohio as a champion wrestler, and it is recorded that people came from miles around to witness Abram's prowess as a wood-chopper. Eliza once boasted that Abram "could outlift any man he came in contact with" and could "do as much work in a day as any man would do in two." There are also reports that Abram sometimes used his muscles for imbibing. According to John M. Taylor's book, *Garfield of Ohio: The Available Man*, Abram "could take a barrel of whiskey by the chime, and drink out of the bung hole."

Abram Garfield was also a virile man. He fathered five children during his thirteen years of marriage. James Abram Garfield was the last of the five Garfield children. He was born on November 19, 1831, in the family's log cabin in Orange Township. He was named for his father and an older brother, James Ballou Garfield, who had died in infancy.

Garfield biographers explain that the death of James Ballou Garfield caused Abram and Eliza to turn to religion for solace. They found comfort in the prayers and preachings of the Disciples of Christ and became ardent practitioners of that faith. That was the same faith James A. Garfield embraced. The twentieth president was baptized when he was a teen, and he later became a lay preacher for a time.

In May of 1833 Abram caught a severe cold after exerting himself in fighting a forest fire. He died on May 8, 1833. One biographer lists pneumonia as the cause of death, but another claims Abram developed complications after being attended to by a local quack. According to Doris Faber's book, *The Mothers of American Presidents*, Abram leaped from his bed shortly before dying, gazed into his wife's eyes, and said: "Eliza, I have brought four young saplings into these woods. Take care of them."

There is agreement that growing up without a father had a profound influence on James Garfield's personality. As Leech and Brown put it, "The want of a father was an obvious factor in the emotional disturbances that James began to manifest in boyhood." As a youth, James A. Garfield was pugnacious and highly sensitive to slights and insults, both real and imagined. As William DeGregorio describes him in *The Complete Book of U.S. Presidents*, "Throughout his life, his [James's] self-confidence was fragile."

When he was thirty-nine years old, James was finally able to make some tangible connection to his deceased father. While campaigning for reelection to Congress, James persuaded someone at the Board of Public Works in Columbus, Ohio, to dig through their files for a canal construction bid that Abram had submitted. Holding the yellowing paper, James read a faded script that said: "If eny of them is struck to us, we will commence them soon." James liked what he read. It showed him that the father he could not remember had been an honorable and forthright man in his business dealings.

Bibliography

Brown, Fern G. *James A. Garfield: Twentieth President of the United States*. Ada, Okla.: Garrett Educational Corporation, 1990.
DeGregorio, William A. *The Complete Book of U.S. Presidents*. New York: Barricade Books, 1993.
Faber, Doris. *The Mothers of American Presidents*. New York: New American Library, 1968.
Leech, Margaret, and Harry J. Brown. *The Garfield Orbit*. New York: Harper & Row, 1978.
Peskin, Allan. *Garfield*. Kent, Ohio: Kent State University Press, 1978.
Taylor, John M. *Garfield of Ohio: The Available Man*. New York: Norton, 1970.

William Arthur
(1796–1875)

*Clergyman, teacher, author, editor, and father of
President Chester A. Arthur*

The Reverend William Arthur and his son, Chester Alan, apparently did not have much in common. William led an austere, almost hardscrabble existence as an itinerant Baptist preacher. It has been estimated that he never made more than $500 a year. Chester made $50,000 a year while serving as America's twenty-first president, and he certainly enjoyed the finer things in life during his administration. Chester Arthur was the first American president to have a valet, and he hired a French chef to cook gourmet meals at the White House. White gloves and silk handkerchiefs were common fashion accessories for the chief executive who was nicknamed "Elegant Arthur."

The Reverend William Arthur, on the other hand, was blunt, tactless, and never neutral. Reverend Arthur had no qualms about alienating parishioners who disagreed with him. That personality trait kept him moving from church to church. From 1828 to 1863 William Arthur had eleven different pastorates. Chester is described by his biographers as amiable, genial, and easygoing, a suave politician who was always careful not to offend. In contrast, William Arthur was a man of deep religious convictions. Chester disappointed his parents because he never joined a church. According to contemporary physical descriptions father and son did not look much alike. William Arthur is described as a man of medium height with dark hair; Chester was above average height (6'2") with wavy brown hair.

William Arthur was born in 1796 in the townland of Dreen in County Antrim, Ireland. Little is recorded about his childhood beside the fact that when he was a child, a brick wall collapsed on his feet and left him with a permanent limp. Acceding to his parents' wishes, William directed his attention and energies to scholarly pursuits. Around the age of eighteen, William graduated from the University of Belfast. About three or four years later, he emigrated to Canada from Ireland.

Shortly after settling in Quebec, William found employment as a teacher, first at Stanstead, Quebec, and then at the Free School of Royal Foundation in Dunham, fifteen miles north of the Vermont border. While teaching at Dunham, William Arthur met and married eighteen-year-old Malvina Stone. They were married in 1821.

After teaching for about three years, William Arthur decided to make a career change to the more lucrative profession of law. In or around 1824 William moved his wife and infant daughter, Regina, across the border to Burlington, Vermont. William chose Burlington because it was a county seat and afforded him the opportunity to read and learn law in a lawyer's office. Three years, two children, and two address changes later, William Arthur experienced a religious conversion, which permanently changed his life and career plans.

While taking a break from his law studies in Waterville, Vermont, Arthur attended a Baptist revival and had a religious experience that convinced him that he had been called to preach the gospel. William's family had been Presbyterians, and he had taken his wedding vows in an Episcopal church. However, the effect of his conversion was of such magnitude, that he promptly decided to become a Baptist minister. In 1827 William was licensed to preach. One year later, he joined the "closed communion" sect of the faith and passed a formal examination to become an ordained Baptist minister.

There can be no doubt about the strength and sincerity of William Arthur's religious convictions. When he was ordained, Arthur was thirty-two years old with a wife and four daughters to support. Forsaking a potentially remunerative career as a lawyer to serve as an itinerant Baptist preacher is ample evidence that William Arthur truly believed the Lord would provide.

On October 5, 1829, something happened to make the Reverend William Arthur momentarily abandon the strict conduct of a Baptist clergyman. He gleefully broke into a spontaneous dance of joy when he was told that his fifth child was a boy. The nine-pound baby was named Chester for Dr. Chester Abell, the physician who delivered him, and Alan for William's father. According to entries in the Arthur family Bible, Chester Alan Arthur was born in the parsonage of the North Fairfield, Vermont, church where William was the minister. Years later, Chester Arthur's political opponents would unsuccessfully claim that Arthur was born in Canada and was therefore prohibited by the Constitution from serving as president. After Chester's birth, William and Malvina had three more children who lived to maturity. A fourth child died a few weeks before his second birthday.

In the two major biographies of Chester A. Arthur — George Howe's *Chester A. Arthur: A Quarter-Century of Machine Politics* and Thomas Reeves's *Gentleman Boss: The Life of Chester A. Arthur*— there is scant information or speculation on what influences William may have had on Chester. Chester A. Arthur never wrote an autobiography, and he had many of his public and private papers destroyed shortly before his death.

Chester likely experienced some childhood feelings of rootlessness and insecurity because his family led an economically marginal existence and moved at least seven times before he left home. Perhaps because of all that moving, Chester stayed put. Chester spent practically all of his adult life in New York City or Washington,

William Arthur. Courtesy of the Library of Congress.

D.C.; a pair of cities a world apart from the rural Vermont and upstate New York hamlets and villages of his childhood.

The greatest influence the Reverend William Arthur had on Chester appears to be in the area of race relations. William Arthur was an implacable abolitionist and is credited with being a cofounder of the New York Antislavery Society. William Arthur's unmitigated abhorrence of slavery undoubtedly made him unpopular with some members of his congregations. Although he was never an outspoken advocate of racial equality and civil rights, Chester Arthur's most famous court cases were ones in which he defended the civil rights of blacks. In the Lemmon Slave Case, Chester A. Arthur was the attorney for the people under the counsel of William M. Everts. They successfully argued that eight slaves belonging to Jonathan Lemmon of Virginia became free when they entered the free state of New York and could not be returned to bondage under the Fugitive Slave Law. The decision was later sustained by the Supreme Court of New York and the Court of Appeals.

Almost a century before Rosa Parks triggered the Civil Rights Movement by refusing to surrender her bus seat to a white passenger, Chester A. Arthur successfully represented a black New York City teacher in a strikingly similar situation. in 1856 Elizabeth Jennings had been forcibly ejected from a whites only streetcar in New York City after she had already paid her fare. Arthur obtained a verdict against the streetcar company that forced the desegregation of public transportation in New York City.

William also influenced his son significantly through his insistence that Chester get a good education. In the early 1840s William had Chester attend various academies in preparation for college. In 1843 Chester was able to enter Union College in Schenectady, New York, as a sophomore. William was a classical scholar who spoke Latin, Greek, and Hebrew. Not surprisingly, Chester chose to pursue the school's classical curriculum. Chester graduated from Union College in 1848, and, like his father, he combined teaching with part-time law studies. Unlike his father, Chester never got the call to preach, so he became an attorney. With six other children living in a crowded parsonage, William was not able to provide much financial assistance for Chester's law studies. However, he was able to help him with employment. In 1851 William got Chester a job as the principal of an academy that met in the basement of the church where Reverend Arthur preached. Three years later, Chester was admitted to the bar of the state of New York.

For the rest of his father's life, Chester was able to provide financial aid for his parents. Sometimes, this charity had to be coaxed. In a letter to William Arthur Jr., Chester's sister, Regina, described how their father's income had seriously declined and added, "Chester knows this, for Mary told him and perhaps he will volunteer to do something without being called upon."

After retiring from the clergy in 1863, William Arthur returned to teaching. He took in male boarding students and prepared them for college. He also resumed his literary pursuits. In the 1840s William Arthur had edited a periodical entitled *The Antiquarian and General Review*. Arthur had proclaimed the purpose of the publication as "comprising whatever is useful or instructive in ecclesiastical or historical antiquities; serving as a book of useful reference on subjects of research and curiosity." The publication had appeared for four years before ceasing publication in 1849. William Arthur had also authored a book, *Derivation of Family Names*, published in 1857 with the esoteric subtitle "an Etymological Dictionary of Family and Christian Names with an Essay on their derivation and import."

Malvina Arthur died in 1869 in Newtonville, New York. William spent the rest of his life in that community. He remarried at some unspecified date. The remarriage was not well received by his children, and William was not well received by the second Mrs. Arthur. Reportedly, she locked her newlywed husband in a barn and refused to live with him. Other members of the Arthur family shunned her, and she is not even mentioned in the biographical accounts of William Arthur that appeared at the time of his death.

By the fall of 1875 William Arthur was seriously ill. Chester was summoned to his father's bedside. Regina Caw wrote:

> Chester came of Wednesday about twelve. I said to Pa, "Chester is here." "Who?" said he. "Chester." Oh, how his face brightened up as he tried to take his hand from under the bedclothes that he might try to shake hands with him, and when Chester said, "You know me, don't you Pa?" He answered, "Oh yes," and raised both arms and put them about Chester's neck. . . . From the time that Chester came, he seemed to rest on him, asking me how long he was going to stay and giving such a satisfied look when I said "All night and all tomorrow and a long time."

Actually, Chester quickly returned to New York City and his duties as the collector of the port of New York.

William Arthur died quietly, probably from stomach cancer, on October 27, 1875. He left Chester little in the way of material goods, but he did leave him with an abundance of memories of fiery Sunday sermons and impassioned exhortations against sin and slavery. When he died, William was most likely unaware that Chester had left.

Bibliography

Doenecke, Justus D. "Chester A. Arthur." *Research Guide to American Historical Biography.* Vol. 1. Washington: Beachem, 1988.

Garrett, Romeo B. *The Presidents and the Negro*, pp. 178–179. Peoria, Ill.: Associated Publishers, 1982.

Howe, George F. *Chester A. Arthur: A Quarter-Century of Machine Politics.* New York: Ungar, 1935.

Reeves, Thomas. *Gentleman Boss: The Life of Chester A. Arthur.* New York: Knopf, 1975.

Seuling, Barbara. *The Last Cow on the White House Lawn and Other Little-Known Facts About the Presidency.* Garden City, N.Y.: Doubleday, 1978.

Richard Falley Cleveland (1804–1853)

*Clerk, teacher, clergyman, and father of
President Grover Cleveland*

When Richard Falley Cleveland was born, his parents decreed that he would become a minister. Being a dutiful son, that is how Richard spent most of his adult life. From his ordination in 1829 to his death in 1853, the Reverend Richard Falley Cleveland spread the word of God to anyone who would listen. The father of America's twenty-second and twenty-fourth president (Grover Cleveland served two nonconsecutive four-year terms) was born in Norwich, Connecticut, on June 19, 1804. Richard was the fifth of six children of watchmaker William Cleveland and Margaret Falley Cleveland. The first of Richard's ancestors to come to America was Moses Cleveland, an indentured carpenter's apprentice who had emigrated from Ipswich, England, to Plymouth, Massachusetts, in 1635.

Biographers of President Cleveland do not offer much information about Richard's childhood. They report that he worked in an uncle's cotton mill and as a clerk in a dry goods store in Norwich. In his book, *Grover Cleveland: A Study in Courage*, Allan Nevins describes Richard as "a thin, pale and intelligent boy." Richard attended Yale University and graduated with high honors in 1824. Almost immediately after graduation, Richard moved to Baltimore. In that city he found employment as a teacher in a private school. While teaching, Richard also began his theological studies under the tutelage of the Reverend William Nevins.

While in Baltimore, Richard met his future wife, Ann Neal, the daughter of William Neal, a well-to-do bookseller and publisher of law books. Before leaving for advanced studies at the Princeton Theological Seminary, Richard promised Ann that he would come back for her. Richard and Ann were married in Baltimore on September 10, 1829. On October 15 of the same year, Richard was ordained as a minister in the Congregational Church. He quickly assumed his first pastorate at the First Congregational Church in Windham, Connecticut. Ann soon learned that being a minister's wife would compel her to make some lifestyle changes.

When Ann moved to Connecticut, she took along a Negro woman who had

Rev. Richard Falley Cleveland. Courtesy of the New Jersey State Park Service. (Sharon Farrell, photographer).

been her maid. The populace of Windham abruptly let her know that they did not approve of someone from a slave state bringing a Negro servant into the free state of Connecticut. Ann had also taken along a considerable wardrobe and her jewelry collection. Richard's congregation informed the Clevelands that bright, colorful clothes and jewelry were entirely inappropriate for a minister's wife. In 1833 Richard left Windham to become the "stated supply" or acting minister of a Presbyterian church in Portsmouth, Virginia. He stayed there for approximately two years before moving on to the Presbyterian church in Caldwell, New Jersey, in November of 1834.

By the time the Clevelands had settled in Caldwell, four of their nine children had been born. Their fifth child, Stephen Grover Cleveland, was born in the Presbyterian manse in Caldwell on March 18, 1837. Richard and Ann named their newborn son after the Reverend Stephen Grover who had preceded Richard as the minister of the Presbyterian church in Caldwell. By the time he was twenty-one, the future president had stopped using his first name.

Richard's tenure at the church in Caldwell was a highly productive time for him. Nevins writes that during his ministry, 109 members were added to the church rolls. The church was also remodeled and repaired at a cost of $22,000. While there may have been ample money for fixing up the church, there were scant funds for Reverend Cleveland's salary. Cleveland biographers repeatedly mention that Reverend Cleveland never made more than $1,000 a year. When Grover was four, Richard took a position as the pastor of a church in Fayetteville, New York, and he stayed there for nine years.

In the home of the Reverend Richard Cleveland, frugality was a way of life and extravagance of any kind was a sin. The parents' word was law. As Robert McElroy describes the Cleveland household in *Grover Cleveland: The Man and the Statesman*, "Filial reverence, strict obedience, unquestioning belief in parental wisdom, and ready compliance with parental commands were the presuppositions of life, according to the Puritan code which dominated the family." As long as the Reverend Richard Cleveland was alive, his family never knew what it was like to disobey the fourth commandment (Remember the sabbath day, to keep it holy . . .). Every Sunday, the Cleveland children attended Sunday school and two worship services to hear their father preach. Outside of the worship services, their time was spent reading and learning scripture and the Westminster Confession. Time on the sabbath was also set aside for silent prayer and reflection on how one could serve God. A week in the Cleveland home consisted of six days of labor and one day of worship.

According to Nevins, Richard Cleveland's life was "laborious and impoverished." With the birth of his last child, Rose, in 1846, Richard Cleveland had to house, clothe, and feed a family of eleven. He started looking for more lucrative employment, and late in 1850, he found it. The American Home Missionary Society offered Richard the position of district secretary of their central New York agency at the salary of $1,000 a year. That stipend must have seemed like a small fortune to Richard since his ministerial positions usually paid only between $500 and $600 a year. The new position moved the Clevelands to Clinton, New York. Unfortunately, the comparatively well-paying new position took a serious toll on Richard's health. Richard developed a severe gastric ulcer. The job of district secretary required constant travel. Nevins speculates that the incessant travel over rough, unpaved roads in all kinds of weather seriously aggravated Richard's condition. Richard had to find a job that was not as demanding physically.

The September 22, 1853, issue of the *New York Evangelist* announced that the Reverend Cleveland's work for the Home Missionary Society "has been successful, and much approved by the friends of the said Society." The publication also said that Cleveland's resignation was "greatly regretted" by the Society.

The best available position was at a Presbyterian church in Holland Patent, New York, a small town about twelve miles north of Utica. On September 14, 1853,

Richard was installed as the minister there. The following Sunday, he delivered his first, last, and only sermon from the pulpit of the Holland Patent Presbyterian Church. On October 1, 1853, Grover and his sister, Mary, hitched up the family wagon and drove to Utica to go shopping. While Grover sat in the carriage waiting for his sister, he learned of their father's death. According to Dennis Tilden Lynch's book, *Grover Cleveland: A Man Four-Square,* Grover heard the news from the cries of a newsboy hawking the evening paper.

Richard's unexpected death at the age of forty-nine made Ann an impoverished widow with seven children still living at home. The congregation came to her aid by buying the home she lived in. Fatherless at sixteen, Grover Cleveland spent the rest of his life helping his mother and siblings. On the fourth of October, 1853, the Reverend Richard Cleveland was buried beneath a small tombstone with the inscription: "Blessed in the sight of the Lord is the death of his saints."

In George F. Parker's book, *Recollections of Grover Cleveland,* the former president recalled his father in these words:

> Looking back over my life nothing seems to me to have in it more both of pathos and interest than the spectacle of my father, a hard-working country clergyman, bringing up acceptably a family of nine children, educating each member so that, in after life, none suffered any deprivation in this respect, and that, too, upon a salary which at no time exceeded a thousand dollars a year. It would be impossible to exaggerate the strength of character thus revealed.

If he did not leave his famous son anything else, the Reverend Richard Cleveland left Grover with the firm conviction that one should always tell the truth. Even Grover Cleveland's opponents and detractors concede that he was a man of remarkable honesty. In 1884 Grover Cleveland was running for president and his supporters were gravely concerned about charges that he had fathered a child out of wedlock. When asked how to respond, Grover bluntly told them: "Tell the truth." The truth was that the father could have been any number of men, but since Grover was the only bachelor among them, he accepted responsibility for the child's welfare.

When Grover Cleveland died in 1908, he could have been thinking that he was speaking to his deeply pious and moral father when he uttered his last words: "I've tried so hard to do right."

Bibliography

Collins, David R. *Grover Cleveland: Twenty-Second and Twenty-Fourth President of the United States.* Ada, Okla.: Garrett Educational Corporation, 1988.

Lynch, Dennis Tilden. *Grover Cleveland: A Man Four-Square.* New York: Horace Liveright, 1932.

McElroy, Robert. *Grover Cleveland: The Man and the Statesman: An Authorized Biography.* New York: Harper, 1923.

Nevins, Allan. *Grover Cleveland: A Study in Courage.* New York: Dodd, Mead, 1966.
Parker, George F. *Recollections of Grover Cleveland.* Freeport, N.Y.: Books for Libraries Press, 1971.
Welch, Richard E., Jr. *The Presidencies of Grover Cleveland.* Lawrence, Ks.: University Press of Kansas, 1988.

John Scott Harrison (1804–1878)

*Farmer, politician, U.S. congressman, and father of
President Benjamin Harrison*

John Scott Harrison was a farmer who loved farming and a politician who detested politics. Since he had the singular distinction of being both the son and father of an American president, running for public office was thrust upon him. John Scott Harrison was born on October 4, 1804, in Vincennes, Indiana, while his father, William Henry Harrison, was serving as governor of the Indiana Territory. John Scott was the fifth of ten children (six boys and four girls) sired by the ninth president of the United States. John Scott was the only one of the six Harrison sons to live to see William Henry Harrison serve as president.

According to Harry J. Sievers's book, *Benjamin Harrison: Hoosier Warrior*, John Scott Harrison was the valedictorian of his class when he graduated from Cincinnati College. Sievers also reports that John Scott Harrison "entered the law firm of Longworth and Harrison" but left the profession when his father was appointed minister to Colombia by President John Quincy Adams. When his father left for Colombia, John Scott Harrison took on the job of overseeing William Henry Harrison's farm and estate in North Bend, Ohio. The arrangement was mutually beneficial to father and son. It gave John Scott a new livelihood, and it gave William Henry the time and freedom to pursue a career in politics.

In 1824 John Scott Harrison married Lucretia Knapp Johnson. Their marriage produced three children. Lucretia died in 1830 at the age of twenty-five. John Scott Harrison had been a widower for just over eighteen months when he married Elizabeth Ramsey Irwin on August 12, 1831. No father of an American president fathered more children than John Scott Harrison. This very virile man had ten more children by his second wife, for a total of thirteen. Benjamin was the second of the ten produced by John Scott's second marriage. He was born at his grandfather's home in North Bend on August 20, 1833.

When Benjamin was three, William Henry deeded John Scott some six hundred acres of farmland located five miles below North Bend at the intersection of

John Scott Harrison. Courtesy of the Cincinnati Historical Society.

the Ohio and Big Miami Rivers. That farm was called The Point and it became the boyhood home of Benjamin Harrison.

In spite of his children's isolation from any nearby schools, John Scott Harrison saw to it that they received an education. He built a one-room log schoolhouse on his property and hired tutors to educate his children. As soon as Benjamin was deemed old enough, he was assigned regular chores on the family farm. Planting and harvesting crops, milking cows, watering the garden, and feeding livestock were a few of the tasks Benjamin performed during a typical working day.

While not impoverished, the large Harrison clan certainly was not wealthy. Despite his fame, William Henry Harrison was not a wealthy man. John Scott Harrison was but one of ten children that William Henry had to feed, clothe, educate, and sometimes help support.

Along with an education and an "everyone pitches in" work ethic, John Scott Harrison provided Benjamin and his other children with a strong religious upbringing. The Harrison family attended services at nearby Presbyterian churches, and they observed Sunday as a religious day. When they could not attend Sunday services, they set Sundays aside for prayers and hymns. Sunday evenings were reserved for scripture readings.

Recurring financial problems were a lifelong problem for John Scott Harrison. Sievers reports that floods, low prices for hay, and financial difficulties nearly caused John Scott Harrison to lose his farm when Benjamin was a child. Another constant drain on John Scott Harrison's cash reserves was the ill health of family members. Such common afflictions as cholera, smallpox, dysentery, and respiratory ailments constantly plagued the Harrisons. Six of the thirteen children fathered by John Scott Harrison died before their third birthday.

By 1847 John Scott Harrison had decided that his two oldest sons, Irwin, sixteen, and Benjamin, fourteen, would attend college. In preparation for that goal, John Scott Harrison chose to send them to a preparatory school called Farmer's College in Walnut Hills, Ohio. In a letter to his brother-in-law, Harrison explained: "Sending the boys to Cary's last week consumed all my ready capital. But I have corn and hay . . . both which are cash articles in Lawrenceburg." Somehow, John Scott Harrison managed to keep Benjamin in school. Benjamin Harrison graduated from Farmer's College in 1850, and in the fall of that year, he entered Miami University in Oxford, Ohio, as a junior.

When Benjamin left for college, he had a letter from his father to the college president, Reverend William C. Anderson. As reprinted in Sievers's book, the letter read:

> My son Benjamin, the bearer thereof, leaves home tomorrow for Oxford, with a view of attaching himself to one of the classes in your institution. Benjamin had been for several years a student of Farmer's College in this county . . . and will hand you a statement of standing in that school.

John Scott Harrison had hoped to send Benjamin to a well-respected "Yankee College," but his financial difficulties did not permit it. Still, in his letters to his son, he urged Benjamin to diligently pursue his studies. In one letter he told Benjamin "to try hard to stand high in the estimation of both professors and fellow students." In another letter, he told Benjamin, "we should never seek to make a witty remark at the expense of the feelings of a less gifted friend or acquaintance."

Benjamin Harrison graduated from Miami University in 1852. After leaving college, he returned to The Point to seek his father's counsel about pursuing a career in law. For the first time, John Scott had a frank and open discussion about family finances. Benjamin was appalled to learn that his father had loaned money and signed notes without proper collateral. When the notes came due and his friends could not pay, John Scott Harrison mortgaged parcels of his farmland to make the payments. An estate that had once been several hundred acres was now just a few.

Paying for any further education for Benjamin was out of the question, and Benjamin was determined that he would not add to his father's financial burdens. However, his father was still able to help him out. John Scott was able to help Benjamin obtain a position as a law clerk in the Cincinnati firm of Storer and Gwynne.

The year of 1853 was a landmark date in the lives of both father and son. John Scott Harrison was elected to the first of two terms as a Whig congressman from Ohio, and Benjamin Harrison married Caroline Lavina Scott at Oxford, Ohio, on October 20.

During his four-year tenure (1853–1857) in the U.S. House of Representatives, John Scott Harrison made only two speeches. In his first, he denounced the Kansas-Nebraska Act, which would have permitted the territories of Kansas and Nebraska to be admitted to the union as either free or slave states, depending on the decision of the voters in those territories. The act would virtually repeal the 1820 Missouri Compromise, which prohibited slavery north of the 36°30′ line. Harrison spoke out against the further expansion of slavery and urged that the union be preserved:

> But, sir, when you ask us to aid you in breaking down a wall which our fathers erected between the land and the free, that slavery may cover the land with its raven-wing, we say to you, no. . . . Let the conservatives of the South stand by the conservatives of the North in support of the Constitution and the compromises, and the country is safe — our union preserved.

In spite of Harrison's opposition, the act was passed by Congress.

Harrison's second speech was made after South Carolina Congressman Preston Brooks brutally assaulted Massachusetts Senator Charles Sumner while the Senator was seated at his desk on the senate floor. On May 19 and 20, 1856, Sumner delivered a speech he had entitled "The Crime Against Kansas." In that speech Sumner had called Senator Andrew Perkins Butler of South Carolina the "Don Quixote of slavery" and said Butler "has chosen a mistress to whom he has made his vows, and who, though ugly to others, is always lovely to him; though polluted in the sight of the world, is chaste in his sight . . . the harlot slavery." Representative Brooks was a nephew of Butler. After reading the published account of Sumner's speech, Brooks was convinced that his uncle had been slandered. Brooks decided that Sumner deserved a beating.

On May 22, 1856, Brooks thrashed Sumner about the head and shoulders with an eleven-and-a-half ounce gutta-percha cane. The beating lasted less than one minute, but it kept Sumner incapacitated for over two years. Sumner was not able to resume his Senate duties full-time until 1859.

A congressional committee investigating the assault recommended that Brooks be expelled from the House of Representatives. On July 14, 1856, John Scott Harrison explained to his colleagues why he was opposed to the expulsion:

> I cannot understand why the gentleman from South Carolina should bring down upon himself the indignation of this House for an offense less aggravated, in my opinion, than many I have witnessed on this floor. . . . The Senator from Massachusetts certainly descended from his high position when he attacked the character and institutions of one of the states. It is also true that the Representative from South Carolina forgot, for a time, the respect and consideration which are due from every American to the highest forum of his country.

John Scott Harrison's decision to vote against the expulsion of Brooks was quite unpopular with his constituents. He was defeated for reelection in 1856 and never again sought political office. John Scott Harrison never grieved his retirement from politics. In an 1854 letter to his brother-in-law he had written: "and still my thoughts are continually wandering from the hall of legislation to my children and to my home."

In August of 1861 the Ohio Democratic State Convention was held at Columbus and John Scott Harrison was nominated for lieutenant governor. When notified of the nomination, John Scott Harrison declined it in a letter to the secretary of the central committee: "I have no inclination to be a candidate for any office. If I ever cherished ambition for such distinction I have been cured of it."

During the first years of John Scott Harrison's retirement from politics, he and Benjamin had a brief falling out because of their differing political beliefs. Aware of the impending demise of the Whig Party, John Scott Harrison looked for a new party to join. Since he did not feel completely comfortable with either the Republicans or the Democrats, John Scott Harrison opted to join the American or Know-Nothing Party and supported their presidential candidate, ex-President Millard Fillmore, in the election of 1856. The party's rank and file consisted of Americans who were opposed to immigrants, particularly Roman Catholic immigrants from Italy and Ireland. The party members believed that immigrants were taking jobs away from native-born Americans and that Catholic immigrants would be more loyal to their church than to their adopted country.

Benjamin Harrison had aligned himself with the Republican Party because he was a staunch opponent of slavery and because he supported the abolitionists. John Scott Harrison was also opposed to slavery, but he believed that the abolitionists were dangerous extremists whose uncompromising beliefs would cause a permanent rift between the slave and free states. The American Party did not take a firm antislavery stand.

In May of 1856, John Scott wrote Benjamin and chided him about his political affiliation: "I see by the papers that your Republican ticket was badly beaten [in

Indiana]. If you want to be successful you must run up the true blue American flag." The break between the father and son reached its zenith when Benjamin Harrison was nominated by the Indianapolis Republicans to run for city attorney in 1857. Benjamin was elected in May, and his father rejected an invitation to visit with Benjamin and his family in Indianapolis.

However, by January of 1858 father and son had reconciled. John Scott told Benjamin in a letter, "I look forward to a period in the future when you may occupy a high position among the political men of Indiana." Benjamin then began to visit his father regularly on weekends. They still disagreed and argued about politics, but now they were able to do so in a restrained and gentlemanly fashion.

In 1860, while running for reporter of the Indiana Supreme Court, Benjamin Harrison made a speech in Lawrenceburg, Indiana, denouncing "the slave oligarchy and slave aristocracy of the South." News of those remarks prompted a strong rebuke from his father. John Scott Harrison had made several Southern friends during his four years in Congress. He wrote to Benjamin: "You will allow me to correct you . . . I have resided in Washington and you have not."

Four years later, Indiana Democrats attempted to capitalize on the political differences between father and son. Benjamin had resigned as reporter of the Indiana Supreme Court in 1862 to enlist in the Union Army. An editorial in the October 11, 1864, issue of the *Indianapolis Daily State Sentinel* entitled "Hon. J. Scott Harrison" stated:

> This distinguished citizen and patriot, the father of a gentleman who is running in this state on the Abolition ticket For Supreme Court Reporter, assures the Democratic Executive Committee, of Hamilton County, Ohio, that he is with "the Democracy in this contest, and will support the October and November Democratic tickets." The honorable gentleman, if he lived in Indiana, would not therefore, vote for his own son.

As it turned out, Benjamin did not need his father's support. He was elected by a margin of over 20,000 votes.

In 1872 Benjamin was being touted by Indiana Republicans as a gubernatorial candidate. He sought his father's advice. Recalling his own experiences, John Scott suggested that Benjamin acquire more money before taking a leave of absence from his increasingly lucrative law practice. Benjamin took his father's advice and waited until 1876 to seek the governorship.

John Scott Harrison died at his farm in North Bend, Ohio, on May 25, 1878. He was seventy-three years old. He left no estate, and when he died, he did not own the house he lived in or the land he lived on. The distinguished son and father of an American president died virtually penniless and dependent on the kindness and generosity of friends and relatives. However, what happened to John Scott Harrison after his death was even worse.

During John Scott Harrison's burial, some mourners noticed that the grave of Harrison's recently deceased grandnephew, Devin, had been disturbed. A subsequent search revealed an empty coffin. Ostensibly, body snatchers had stolen the corpse and sold it to a medical school. Watchmen were hired to guard John Scott Harrison's grave and John Scott's son, John, went to Cincinnati to search for Devin's body. After acquiring a search warrant, John, a nephew named George Eaton, and three police officers began a search of the Ohio Medical College. The search party discovered a cloth-covered corpse with a noose about its neck hanging in an air shaft. The corpse was then removed from the air shaft and placed on the floor. When the shroud was removed from its face, John Harrison recoiled in shock and horror, for the corpse was not Devin, but his father, John Scott Harrison. Despite two guards, mounds of earth, and nearly a ton of cemented stone slabs, the tomb of John Scott Harrison had been defiled by graverobbers.

John Scott Harrison was reburied in the vault of a family friend. In June of 1878 Devin's body was found at a morgue in Ann Arbor, Michigan. A Hamilton County grand jury indicted two men for the thefts, but there were no convictions. Since he was the lawyer in the family, Benjamin filed suits for $10,000 in exemplary damages for the widow and for his father's estate. There is no record on the outcome of those suits. The matter may have been settled out of court.

In 1880 Ohio passed new laws increasing the penalties for "body-snatching." According to Sievers, Benjamin Harrison was so traumatized by the crime he could rarely say the word "father" for the rest of his life. This is a strange and sad legacy for a man who had simply wanted to be a farmer.

Bibliography

Harney, Gilbert L. *The Lives of Benjamin Harrison and Levi P. Morton*. Providence, R.I.: Reid Publishers, 1888.
Indianapolis Daily State Sentinel. October 11, 1864.
Letter from the Benjamin Harrison Memorial Commission, Indianapolis, Indiana. Washington, D.C.: U.S. Government Printing Office, 1941.
Myers, Elisabeth P. *Benjamin Harrison*. Chicago: Reilly & Lee, 1969.
Sievers, Harry J. *Benjamin Harrison: Hoosier Statesman*. New York: University Publishers, 1959.
Sievers, Harry J. *Benjamin Harrison: Hoosier Warrior*. New York: University Publishers, 1952.
Stevens, Rita. *Benjamin Harrison: Twenty-Third President of the United States*. Ada, Okla.: Garrett Educational Corporation, 1989.
Wallace, Lew. *Life of General Benjamin Harrison*. Indianapolis: Union Publishing, 1888.

William McKinley Sr. (1807–1892)

*Iron manufacturer and father of
President William McKinley*

William McKinley Sr. was hardworking and industrious but not prosperous. He was ambitious for his nine children, if not for himself. William Sr. passed on his name and displaced ambition to his third son and seventh child, William Jr., who served as America's twenty-fifth president. Along with his name, ambition, and work ethic, William Sr. also passed on his looks to William Jr. A photo of the elder McKinley suggests what William Jr. would have looked like if he had lived long enough to put a few more lines and wrinkles in his face. Father and son had the same receding hairline, broad forehead, bushy eyebrows, and firm jaw.

William McKinley Sr. was born in Mercer County, Pennsylvania, on November 15, 1807. His forebears were Scotch-Irish and English Puritans who settled in Pennsylvania. Both of William Sr.'s grandfathers fought in the Revolutionary War. William Sr.'s grandfather McKinley and his father, James McKinley, were both "founders" or managers of blast furnaces used in the manufacture of pig iron. William Sr. became the third generation of McKinley men to ply that trade. It is not known if he ever had other aspirations. In all likelihood, William Sr. did not have many career choices or options.

At best, William Sr. had perhaps the equivalent of a grade school education. He was the second of ten children, so there were no funds available for him to pursue educational opportunities. Whatever formal education William Sr. received ended at around age sixteen when he began working full-time as a founder. In 1829, while working and living in New Lisbon (now called Lisbon), Ohio, William Sr. married Nancy Allison. They were wed on January 6. He was twenty-one and she was nineteen. Biographers of William McKinley describe Nancy as thrifty, pious, and strong-minded. The same biographers characterize William Sr. as stubborn, industrious, and a good but never prosperous businessman. Both William Sr. and Nancy McKinley were deeply religious Methodists who told their children: "Whatever you be, you will be a credit to your family and to your God."

William McKinley Sr. Courtesy of the Stark County Historical Society, Canton, Ohio.

In 1830 William Sr. became a partner in the iron manufacturing firm of Campbell, McKinley, and Dempsey. He rented a furnace in Niles, Ohio, that was owned by a James Heaton. How long that three-way partnership lasted is unclear. However, it is known that at an unspecified later date McKinley Sr. formed another partnership with a brother-in-law named Jacob Reep. While in partnership with Reep, McKinley Sr. rented furnaces in the Ohio towns of Fairfield, New Lisbon, and Niles.

In the course of a typical twelve-hour day tending a blast furnace, McKinley Sr. would chop down trees, split the logs until they would fit into the furnace, burn the wood to produce charcoal, and also look for iron ore. In spite of the long hours and the constant physical exertion, McKinley Sr. was never known to complain about his work. He often cheerfully called it "useful labor, suitable for a strong man and a hearty Christian soul."

On January 29, 1843, the seventh child of William Sr. and Nancy was born in the McKinley's cottage in Niles, Ohio. William McKinley Jr. was preceded by four sisters and two brothers. Two more children followed, Abbie Celia who died in infancy and Abner who later became a partner in William Jr.'s Canton, Ohio, law firm. In 1852, when William Jr. was nine, the McKinleys moved to Poland, Ohio. The move was prompted by parental concern about the children's education. In Poland there was a school called the Poland Seminary, which was operated by the Methodist Episcopal church and enjoyed a superior academic reputation. It was there that William Jr. received his college prepatory education.

William Sr. gave William Jr. what attention he could, which was probably not much. Supervision and discipline were mostly left to Nancy and William Jr.'s older siblings. Working twelve-hour days left precious little time for William Sr. to bond with his son or spend quality time with him. Besides sending him to school, William Sr. and Nancy did their best to give William Jr. a home life fostering intellectual stimulation. According to McKinley biographers, the family library included David Hume's *History of England*, Gibbon's *Decline and Fall of the Roman Empire*, and various works of Dickens and Shakespeare. The McKinleys also subscribed to several magazines and Horace Greeley's *Weekly New York Tribune*. According to Charles S. Olcott's *The Life of William McKinley*, William Sr. kept three books constantly on hand and read from them a few minutes at a time whenever he had the opportunity. They were the *Bible* and works of Shakespeare and Dante.

Reading was not only encouraged in the McKinley household, it was a mandatory daily activity. After the evening meal, each member of the family took turns reading aloud while the others sat and listened. William Sr. and Nancy also strongly encouraged the development of religious convictions. They were devout Methodists and were supportive of their church, and they made sure that all their children regularly attended worship services.

In his biography of McKinley, *William McKinley: Stalwart Republican*, William Carl Spielman states that William McKinley Jr. "probably acquired a taste for politics and political discussion from his father." However, biographies of William McKinley make no mention of William Sr. ever running for office or being actively engaged in a political campaign. It appears that he was never involved in any of William Jr.'s campaigns even though he lived long enough to see his famous son get elected to the U.S. House of Representatives six times and to governor of Ohio once.

William McKinley was the third of four American presidents to fall prey to an assassin. For that reason, no memoirs or autobiography written by him exist. His most intimate feelings about his father remain unknown.

William McKinley Sr. died on November 24, 1892, at his home in Canton, Ohio. He was eighty-five years old. William Jr. was governor of Ohio at the time. According to the obituary in the *Canton Repository*, William Jr. was by his father's side when William Sr. died: "As his death has been anticipated for a few days all of the family were in attendance."

The obituary summarized William Sr.'s life: "Mr. McKinley was one of Canton's most respected citizens. Mr. McKinley was one of the pioneer manufacturers in the state in Trumbull and Columbiana counties. He was a staunch advocate of the principles that have made his son famous."

Myron Herrick, a member of Governor McKinley's staff, offered William Jr. his condolences by sending him a poem entitled "Recompense." The poem's last lines were:

> When we shall wake,
> I am quite sure that we will be very glad
> That for a little while we were so sad.

William Jr. had the poem read at his father's funeral. He wrote Herrick a letter of thanks and told him that the poem was one of the most beautiful things he had ever read.

After his father's death, William McKinley dropped the junior from his name, which he had not been able to do during his father's lifetime. He still was and would always be William Sr.'s son, but he was no longer William Junior.

Bibliography

Canton (Ohio) Repository. November 25, 1892.
Collins, David R. *William McKinley: Twenty-fifth President of the United States.* Ada, Okla.: Garrett Educational Corporation, 1990.
Everett, Marshall. *Complete Life of William McKinley.* 1901.
Hoyt, Edwin P. *William McKinley.* Chicago: Reilly & Lee, 1967.
Leech, Margaret. *In the Days of McKinley.* New York: Harper, 1959.
Morgan, H. Wayne. *William McKinley and His America.* Syracuse, N.Y.: Syracuse University Press, 1963.
Olcott, Charles S. *The Life of William McKinley.* Boston: Houghton Mifflin, 1916.
Spielman, William Carl. *William McKinley: Stalwart Republican.* New York: Exposition Press, 1954.

Theodore Roosevelt Sr. (1831–1878)

*Glass importer, merchant, and father of
President Theodore Roosevelt*

In his *Autobiography*, Theodore Roosevelt unequivocally stated his feelings about his father:

> My father, Theodore Roosevelt, was the best man I ever knew. He combined strength and courage with gentleness, tenderness and great unselfishness. He would not tolerate in us children selfishness or cruelty, idleness, cowardice, or untruthfulness. As we grew older he made us understand that the same standard of clean living was demanded for the boys as for the girls; that what was wrong in a woman could not be right in a man.

He also added, "he was the only man of whom I was ever really afraid."

Theodore Roosevelt Sr., the father of America's twenty-sixth president, was born in New York City on September 22, 1831. Theodore Sr. was one of six children (five boys and one girl) born to Cornelius Van Schaak Roosevelt and Margaret Barnhill Roosevelt. Theodore Sr. was the youngest of the five boys. According to one Roosevelt biographer, the most unpleasant experience of Theodore Sr.'s childhood was having to wear his brothers' hand-me-down clothes. As Allen Churchill records in his book, *The Roosevelts: American Aristocrats,* Theodore Sr. once burst into tears when he heard his parents discussing which hand-me-downs could be altered to fit him.

Theodore Sr. did not attend college. When he was twenty, he joined his father and an older brother in the family business. The business was originally named Roosevelt and Kobbe. The business, founded after the American Revolution, originally dealt in hardware. When Theodore Sr. joined the enterprise, the business was called Roosevelt and Son and was involved in the importation and sale of plate glass.

In the summer of 1850 Theodore Sr. traveled to Georgia with an in-law, Dr. Hilborne West. There he met fifteen-year-old Martha Bullouch for the first time. Churchill describes Martha as "beautiful, fragile and willowy." She quickly became the object of Theodore Sr.'s intense attention and affection. Roosevelt biographers unaminously depict Martha as a woman of striking beauty. Her hair was fine and silky black and her skin was colorfully described as "more moonlight white than cream white." Some sources claim that Theodore Sr. and Martha became secretly engaged before he returned to New York. According to other sources, Theodore Sr. courted Martha for three years via frequent letters. At any rate, they were married on December 22, 1853, at Roswell, Georgia, when he was twenty-two and and she was nineteen. Churchill reports that their wedding was preceded by "a full week of gay receptions, parties and sundown-to-sunup dances." After their honeymoon, the newlyweds moved into a four-story brownstone at 28 East Twentieth Street in New York City. Their home was next door to Theodore Sr.'s brother, Robert, and just six blocks away from Cornelius's home.

Theodore Sr. and Martha had been married slightly over a year when their first child, Anna, was born on January 7, 1855. Theodore, their first son and second of four children (two boys and two girls), was born in New York City on October 27, 1858.

In addition to working long hours at Roosevelt and Son, Theodore Sr. actively and enthusiastically engaged in a host of civic and philanthropic activities. In his *Autobiography,* Theodore Roosevelt lauded his father: "I never knew anyone who got greater joy out of living than did my father, or anyone who more wholeheartedly performed every duty: and no one whom I have ever met approached his combination of enjoyment of life and performance of duty."

A partial list of charitable, civic, and humanitarian activities and organizations that Theodore Sr. generously supported with his time and money includes: teaching Sunday School at the Madison Square Presbyterian Church, helping to found the Children's Aid Society for homeless children, serving on the boards of United Charities and State Board of Charities, helping to found the New York Orthopedic Dispensary and Hospital, working to aid the blind, and helping to found the Society for the Prevention of Cruelty to Animals. Theodore Sr. was also a driving force behind the establishment of the Metropolitan Museum of Art and the Museum of Natural History.

Theodore Sr. had what one associate called "a troublesome conscience." He also had a penchant for soliciting charitable donations from his well-to-do friends. They instinctively reached for their checkbooks when they saw Theodore Sr. approaching. Reputedly, they usually asked him, "How much this time, Theodore?"

Despite his very busy schedule, the indefatigable Theodore Sr. also managed to have an extremely active social life. He and Martha were well known for their lavish hospitality. When not acting as host and hostess, the Roosevelts regularly attended dinner parties and balls where Theodore Sr. would dance all night.

Because of his unmitigated zest for living, gregarious personality, and high energy level, women found themselves attracted to Theodore Sr. According to David McCullough's book, *Mornings on Horseback,* Theodore Sr. "seems to have genuinely preferred the company of women," and the attention he showed to Martha was "exceptional even for that day and those circles." Women also found Theodore Sr. attractive because he was a genuinely handsome man. Usually described as square-jawed, with leonine features, physically imposing with big, sloping shoulders, a chestnut beard and china-blue eyes, Theodore Sr. was a man who left a lingering impression on practically everyone he met.

In his *Autobiography*, Theodore Roosevelt recalled that his father physically punished him only once, when he was four years old and had bitten his older sister. After a short chase, Theodore Sr. had caught up with his misbehaving son and administered the appropriate punishment. As Theodore put it, "the punishment that ensued fitted the crime."

When Theodore Roosevelt writes that his father was the only man he ever really feared, it was not a fear born of abusive behavior. Most of Theodore's early memories of his father are of Theodore Sr. being a caring, compassionate man tenderly attending to his sickly, asthmatic son. In his *Autobiography*, Theodore Roosevelt remembered his "father walking up and down the room with me in his arms at night," while Theodore struggled to breathe. Theodore's delicate constitution forced Theodore Sr. to be an overprotective parent who had to plan his activities around the ever-changing condition of Theodore's health.

The outbreak of the Civil War divided the Roosevelts. The war also marked the only time that Theodore may have felt that his father was letting him down. As a Lincoln Republican, Theodore Sr. had joined with other New York businessmen to petition Congress to avoid war at any cost. Theodore Sr. had also assisted in the promotion of a large antiwar rally. However, Martha, her mother, and her sister, Annie, were all Georgia-born sympathizers with the Confederate cause. When the Civil War began, all three women were living in the same house as Theodore Sr.

During the war Theodore Sr. continued to support the Union. However, he avoided military service by hiring a substitute to serve in his place. In his *Autobiography*, Theodore Roosevelt did not relate what his father did during the Civil War. He had a habit of glossing over painful memories. Roosevelt biographers and Theodore's sister, Corinne, have contended that Theodore Roosevelt's near hysterical yearning to wage war was a result of the guilt and shame he felt because his father had hired a substitute soldier. However, Theodore Sr.'s "troublesome conscience" would not permit him to be completely passive and idle during the war. He told his wife, "I would never feel satisfied with myself after this war is over if I do nothing."

In his work with charities, Theodore Sr. had seen that the families of soldiers were destitute because there was no plan or program for military dependents to receive any portion of a soldier's pay. After consulting with two associates, Theodore Sr. conceived the idea of allotments — a small voluntary deduction that would be sent home to dependents. Theodore Sr. traveled to Washington and energetically lobbied a reluctant and skeptical Congress. The major obstacle was convincing cynical lawmakers that he neither sought nor desired any personal gain from the proposed legislation. After about three months of intensive lobbying, the legislation became law. Theodore Roosevelt Sr. was named one of the three allot-

Theodore Roosevelt Sr. Courtesy of the Theodore Roosevelt Collection, Harvard College Library.

ment commissioners who would administer the plan and persuade soldiers to participate in it.

For most of 1862 Theodore Sr. was away from his family because he was visiting troops and making his sales pitch. He received no pay from the government for his services. He traveled by train, boat, and on horseback from regiment to regiment convincing soldiers that money they had earmarked for gambling, liquor, and women should go to their families.

Sometime in the spring of 1863 Theodore Sr. was able to turn the field work over to subordinates. He returned to New York and worked as resident allotment commissioner. He also returned to his job at Roosevelt and Son. Nevertheless, he continued to take on more work, raising money for the first Negro regiment to fight for the North as well as funds to purchase medical supplies for the Union Army. He also organized a Protective War Claims Commission to benefit disabled veterans. After the war, Theodore Sr. established an unemployment bureau for army veterans.

In 1869 Theodore Sr. took his family on an extended European vacation. Theodore Sr. and Martha hoped that a change of scenery would help bring about a cure for Theodore's recurrent asthma. They also wanted to find a suitable finishing school for their daughter, Anna. Theodore Sr. mapped out an ambitious nine-country, one-year itinerary for his family. The Roosevelts left New York on May 12, 1869, and arrived in Liverpool nine days later. One of their first stops was a visit to the seashore in Hastings. That site had been recommended by their family doctor. Theodore Sr. and Theodore spent two days climbing cliffs, inspecting Saxon ruins, and walking on the beach. Theodore was so delighted at having his father's undivided attention that he wrote in his diary, "This is the happiest day that I have ever spent."

The Roosevelts' vacation lasted just over a year. They visited England, Italy, Switzerland, Austria, Germany, Belgium, and France. According to Roosevelt biographers, during their long vacation, there was only one time when Theodore Sr. was short-tempered with his four children, ages fourteen, eleven, nine, and eight. On one memorable occasion, he angrily called his children "bothers." As Edmund Morris reports in *The Rise of Theodore Roosevelt*, his father's mild scolding made Theodore Roosevelt miserable for an entire evening.

After the Roosevelts returned to America, Theodore Sr. had an important man-to-man talk with twelve-year-old Theodore. Weary of being at the beck and call of his sickly asthmatic son everytime Theodore was ailing, he lovingly but firmly told the future president: "Theodore, you have the mind but not the body, and without the help of the body the mind cannot go as far as it should. You must make your body. It is hard drudgery to make one's body but I know you will do it." Theodore responded by earnestly exclaiming: "I'll make my body!"

That event is regarded as a turning point in the life of Theodore Roosevelt. Theodore began to spend countless hours swinging dumbells, punching a bag, doing chin-ups, lifting weights, and working out on the horizontal bars. A room in the Roosevelts' house was converted into a gymnasium for Theodore. With his father's hearty approval, Theodore also began taking boxing lessons. The results of Theodore's strenuous exercising became apparent to his father when they vacationed in Africa in 1872. In a letter home, Theodore Sr. reports that he is having trouble matching his son's energy level: "I walked through the bogs with him, at the risk of sinking hopelessly and helplessly for hours. . . . I felt that I had to keep up with Teedie!"

In 1873 Theodore Sr. moved his family from their brownstone to a mansion he had constructed at 6 West Fifty-Seventh Street in New York City. The inheritance Theodore Sr. had received after the death of his father in 1871 had made him a millionaire. Now, he felt that it was time to live like one. Morris describes the mansion as having "interior furnishings that were unusually rich, with heavy Persian rugs in every hall, sumptuous furniture, and much ornamental woodwork, including a hand-carved staircase." The spacious new home also had a museum in the garret for Theodore and a fully equipped gymnasium on the top floor.

Nevertheless, even while reveling in the splendor of his new home, Theodore Sr. spent more and more of his time helping the less fortunate. He visited slums, prisons, hospital wards, and insane asylums. He lobbied for more humane treatment for the mentally ill and advocated the establishment of workhouses for vagrants. He continued to freely and generously donate his time and money to any cause he deemed worthy. Theodore Sr. once explained his inveterate altruism by telling Theodore: "All that gives me the most pleasure in the retrospect, is connected with others, an evidence that we are not placed here to live exclusively for ourselves."

His abundant wealth assured Theodore Sr. that his oldest son would have something he himself had never had—a college education. He had decided (probably without consulting Theodore) that Theodore would go to Harvard. He hired a tutor who helped Theodore cram three years of college preparatory education into two years. In the spring of 1876 Theodore Roosevelt passed his entrance examinations for attending Harvard University. On September 27, 1876, Theodore Sr. accompanied his Harvard-bound son to a Long Island railroad depot. He left Theodore with the parting advice: "Take care of your morals first, your health next and finally your studies."

Like countless other college freshmen, Theodore Roosevelt left home with no clearly defined career objective. After Theodore's freshman year, father and son discussed career plans. Theodore Sr. was no doubt aware of his son's intense interest in taxidermy, zoology, ornithology, and natural history. It was an interest the father neither encouraged nor discouraged. Theodore Sr. was well aware that Theodore had no interest in the family's plate glass business. As Morris puts it, "Theodore Sr., while sympathetic, was too wise a father to discourage his son's scientific tendencies. . . . No doubt his businessman's eye had already discerned that his absentminded and unorthodox youth would be a disaster in the world of commerce."

Theodore Sr. promised his son a small income for life if he wanted to pursue a career in science. However, Theodore Sr. emphasized that if Theodore chose that option, the income of the elder Roosevelts would be reduced. In his *Autobiography*, Theodore Roosevelt recalled the conversation as follows:

> He explained that I must be sure that I really intensely desired to do scientific work, because if I went into it I must make it a serious career; that he had made enough money to enable me to take such a career and do non-remunerative work of value if I intended to do the very best work there was in me; but that I must not dream of taking it up as a dilettante. He also gave me a piece of advice that I have always remembered, namely, that, if I was not going to earn money, I must even things up by not spending it.

Theodore was just a few weeks into his sophomore year at Harvard when he received some totally unexpected news. President Rutherford B. Hayes had appointed Theodore Sr. to replace Chester A. Arthur as the collector of customs for the port of New York. Theodore Sr. had long remained aloof from politics. However, he eagerly accepted the appointment because he felt that it symbolized the Hayes administration's commitment to civil service reform. Within two months of accepting the appointment, Theodore Sr. would become a broken, embittered, moribund man vowing to never get involved in politics again.

U.S. Senator Roscoe Conkling was the undisputed boss of the New York Republican machine. Theodore Sr. had already incurred Conkling's animosity when he had supported Hayes instead of Conkling for the 1876 Republican presidential nomination. President Hayes hoped that his appointment of Roosevelt would embarrass Conkling into withdrawing his support for Arthur's renomination as collector. That was not to be.

Conkling was an influential member of the Senate committee considering Roosevelt's appointment. Conkling used all of his parliamentary wiles to delay a Senate vote on the nomination. President Hayes refused to withdraw the nomination, and Theodore Sr. became a political pawn caught in the middle of a power struggle. Conkling ultimately had his way. On December 12, 1877, the U.S. Senate rejected Roosevelt's nomination by a vote of thirty-one to twenty-five.

On December 16, Theodore Sr. wrote to his son at Harvard:

> A great weight has been taken off my shoulders when Elliott read the other morning that the Senate had decided not to confirm me, no one can imagine the relief. . . . The machine politicians have shown their colors and not one person has been able to make an accusation of any kind against me. . . . I feel sorry for the country however, as it shows the power of partisan politicians who think of nothing higher than their own interests. I fear for your future. We cannot stand so corrupt a government for any great length of time.

What Theodore Sr.'s letter did not mention was that he was seriously ill and in great pain. Two days after writing his son, Theodore Sr. collapsed after complaining of persistent abdominal pains. His illness was diagnosed as acute peritonitis. For a brief time he seemed to recover, but it was just a temporary remission. What was thought to be peritonitis was actually cancer of the stomach. A malignant, inoperable tumor of the bowel was strangling his intestines.

Theodore spent the Christmas holidays with his family. In a diary entry written shortly after the holidays, Theodore recorded that his father had told him that he was the dearest of all his children and that he had never caused him a moment's pain. Apparently, Theodore knew that his father was ill, but the family had downplayed the illness because they did not want Theodore's academics to suffer.

While Theodore was tending to his studies, his brother, Elliott, was tending to their father. By all accounts, Theodore Sr.'s last days were spent in unspeakable, excruciating pain. His hair and beard had turned gray, and Elliott reported: "The agony in his face was awful. . . . Ether and sedatives were of no avail. He was so mad with pain that beyond groans and horrible writhes and twists he could do nothing."

On the morning of February 9, 1878, Theodore received a telegram at school instructing him to come home immediately. He arrived in New York City the next morning and saw that the flags of the city were flying at half mast. Theodore Roosevelt Sr. had died shortly before midnight on February 9 at the age of forty-six.

On the day of his father's death the only words Theodore Roosevelt could write in his diary were: "My dear Father. Born September 23, 1831." Three days later, Theodore was composed enough to express his anguish and grief:

> He has just been buried. I shall never forget these terrible three days; the hideous suspense of the ride on; the dull inert sorrow, during which I felt as if I had been stunned, or as if part of my life had been taken away, and the moments of sharp, bitter agony, when I kissed the dear, dead face and realized that he would never again on this earth speak to me or greet me with his loving smile, and then when I heard the sound of the first clod dropping on the coffin holding the one I loved dearest on earth. . . . I feel that if it were not for the certainty, that as he himself has so often said, "he is not dead but gone before," I should almost perish. With the help of my God, I will try to lead such a life as he would have wished.

Theodore's profound grief continued for several months. Morris writes, "Memories of his father surfaced in the form of dreams and hallucinations of almost photographic vividness." Sometimes the grief appeared in self-loathing diary entries: "I often feel badly that such a wonderful man as Father should have had a son of so little worth as I am. . . . How little I am worthy of such a father. . . . How I wish I could ever do something to keep up his name." Within a few months, however, the entries took on a cheerier tone. Theodore wrote that he is "astonished" at how he continues his everyday life "as if nothing had happened." Still, there were very few days when Theodore Roosevelt did not think about his dear, departed father.

Years later, Theodore's sister, Corinne recalled: "When the college boy of 1878 was entering upon his duties as President of the United States, he told me frequently that he never took any serious step or made any vital decision for his country without thinking first what position his father would have taken on the question."

Peter Collier and David Horowitz offer a final anecdote illustrating the profound influence of the father upon his namesake son in their recent book, *The Roosevelts: An American Saga*. They report that after the assassination of President William McKinley, President Theodore Roosevelt was entertaining his sisters, Anna and Corinne, at the White House. While they were seated at a table, Theodore suddenly looked up at his sisters and asked: "Do you realize that this is the birthday of our father? I have realized it as I signed various papers all day long, and I feel that it is a good omen that I begin my duties in this house on this day. I feel as if my father's hand were on my shoulder." As soon as the President had finished speaking, White House butlers served them coffee, and following a White House tradition, they gave boutonnieres to all the men present. Theodore Roosevelt picked up one of the roses. He noted that it was a Saffronia, which had been his father's favorite. He put the rose in his buttonhole and said: "I think there is a blessing connected with this."

Bibliography

Chessman, G. Wallace. *Theodore Roosevelt and the Politics of Power*. Boston: Little, Brown, 1969.

Churchill, Allen. *The Roosevelts: American Aristocrats*. New York: Harper & Row, 1965.

Collier, Peter, and David Horowitz. *The Roosevelts: An American Saga*. New York: Simon & Schuster, 1994.

Hess, Stephen. *America's Political Dynasties: From Adams to Kennedy*. Garden City, N.Y.: Doubleday, 1966.

McCullough, David. *Mornings on Horseback*. New York: Touchstone, 1981.

Miller, Nathan. *Theodore Roosevelt: A Life*. New York: Morrow, 1992.

Morris, Edmund. *The Rise of Theodore Roosevelt*. New York: Ballantine, 1979.

Roosevelt, Theodore. *The Autobiography of Theodore Roosevelt*. New York: Scribner's, 1958.

Alphonso Taft
(1810–1891)

Teacher, attorney, judge, politician, diplomat, U.S. secretary of war, U.S. attorney general, and father of President William Howard Taft

In their correspondence Alphonso Taft and his son, William Howard Taft, sound like members of a mutual admiration society. In Judith I. Anderson's book, *William Howard Taft: An Intimate History,* William is quoted as saying often, "a man never had . . . a dearer, kinder, more considerate father." In her book, *An American Family: The Tafts, 1678–1964,* Ishbel Ross describes the encounter between Alphonso Taft and world heavyweight boxing champion John L. Sullivan. Alphonso squeezed the champion's biceps, looked him up and down, and then told the great John L.: "My Will is the better man."

Despite these public displays of effusive praise, Alphonso Taft was a domineering father and William was a submissive son acutely concerned with pleasing his father. Anderson writes that as a student at Yale, William was urged by his friends to try out for the rowing crew and the football team. In both instances, Alphonso forbade it and William dutifully acquiesced. On another occasion, William was asked to join the coveted Skull and Bones secret society at Yale. Alphonso expressed his disapproval by writing that he doubted "such popularity is consistent with high scholarship."

One typical letter from Alphonso to William appears in several Taft biographies. Alphonso wrote: "I do not think that you have accomplished as much this past year as you ought. Our anxiety for your success is very great and I know that there is but one way to attain it, and that is by self-denial and enthusiastic hard work in the profession." Alphonso had high expectations for all of his children. William succeeded in fulfilling them by reaching the pinnacle of American politics. William's half-brother, Peter, may have tried too hard. Peter was valedictorian of his class at Yale, but he later suffered a physical and emotional collapse and died in a sanitarium when he was forty-three.

All of Alphonso's five sons who lived to maturity earned law degrees. When

Alphonso Taft. Courtesy of the Cincinnati Historical Society.

his youngest son, Horace, abandoned law to found a private school, Alphonso expressed his surprise and disapproval: "I cannot comprehend Horace's idea of founding a private school or what in the world he can hope from it. The law is his proper field."

The father of America's twenty-seventh president was born in East Townshend, Vermont, on November 5, 1810. Alphonso was the only child of Peter Rawson and Sylvia Taft. Robert Taft, who had emigrated from England to settle in Massachusetts in 1669, was the first of the family to live in America. Alphonso, the great-grandson of Robert, grew up on the family farm and decided early in life that his drive and ambition made him unsuitable for a life of tilling the soil. Fortunately, his parents were sympathetic and supportive.

Alphonso attended the local schools in Vermont until he was sixteen. After that, he attended Amherst for two years, traveling by boat and foot to attend school. Alphonso then returned to East Townshend and tutored for two years until he had saved enough money to attend Yale. He entered Yale in 1829, where he was a diligent scholar and graduated third in a class of ninety-three in 1833. His academic achievements earned him Phi Beta Kappa honors. Alphonso was also one of the founders of the Skull and Bones society at Yale. In later years, Presidents William Howard Taft and George Bush belonged to that secret society considered to be the nation's most influential fraternity.

After graduation, Alphonso once again returned to teaching. As usual, teaching was the means to an end rather than a career choice. Alphonso taught at Ellington Academy in Connecticut until he had the funds to return to Yale in 1837. One year later, Alphonso had earned a Bachelor of Laws degree and admission to the Vermont bar. Soon after returning to West Townshend, Alphonso realized that he had no more desire to be a small-town lawyer than he had to be a farmer. He later described Vermont as "a noble state to emigrate from." In September of 1838 Alphonso left Vermont permanently.

He first traveled to New York City and promptly decided that he had an intense dislike of the attorneys in that city. "I dislike the character of the New York Bar exceedingly," Alphonso wrote. "The notorious selfishness, or dishonesty of the great mass of the men you find in New York is in my mind a serious objection to settling there." Moving on to Philadelphia, Alphonso found that city more to his liking, but he noted that Philadelphia already had an abundance of able and experienced lawyers. He deduced that it would take many years to establish a lucrative law practice there. Pittsburgh's coal dust laden air and bleak outlook for young lawyers kept Alphonso moving further west.

The novice attorney received a warm reception in Columbus, Ohio. Alphonso was ready to settle there until he read an article in the *Toledo (Ohio) Blade* predicting that within one hundred years Cincinnati would be the greatest city in America. There were only sixty lawyers in that city and Alphonso envisioned himself soon making $3,000 to $5,000 a year. Nathaniel Wright, a transplanted Vermonter with an established practice in Cincinnati, gave Alphonso a job, and Taft began studying for the Ohio bar examination.

After having been admitted to the Ohio bar, Alphonso briefly returned to Vermont to help his parents on their farm and to begin a serious courtship of Fanny Phelps. Alphonso had started wooing Fanny when she was sixteen and he was fresh out of law school. Now she was seventeen and he was twenty-nine. After Alphonso had proposed, his future father-in-law told Taft that he would give his blessing only after he had visited Cincinnati and seen the city for himself. Fanny's father, Charles, found some undesirable aspects in Cincinnati, but he decided that the good outweighed the bad. Charles told Alphonso that they could marry in the summer of 1841, after Fanny turned eighteen. Alphonso accepted the terms. In the interim, he wrote Fanny frequently. He did not exactly pledge his undying love, but his correspondence did offer numerous self-improvement tips. Alphonso advised his fiancée on what books to read and on her spelling, syntax, and punctuation. He also asked his beloved to exchange geometry problems with him. Alphonso and Fanny were married at the bride's home on August 29, 1841. Shortly thereafter, both the bride's and the groom's parents moved to Cincinnati. All four grandparents were present when grandsons Charles Phelps Taft (1843) and Peter Rawson Taft (1845) were born.

Described as dour and industrious, Alphonso worked hard and prospered. His law practice was thriving and his political career was blossoming. Alphonso was elected to the city council, and in June of 1848 he traveled to Washington, D.C., and had his first contact with national politicians. Alphonso discussed affairs of state with President James K. Polk and Senators Daniel Webster and John C. Calhoun. Alphonso idolized Webster, and after his visit he thought that the eloquent New Englander was genuinely humble. He was less impressed with Calhoun. Taft found the South Carolina Senator's views on slavery offensive.

Ross describes Alphonso Taft at that time in his life as "an impressive figure in the courtroom, earnest and quiet in argument, slightly brooding in manner, gentle and forceful at the same time. In his city council he was constantly on the lookout for civic improvement and he did not hesitate to break away from party lines when he felt that he was in the right."

Characterizations of the personality and temperament of Alphonso are uniformly favorable. William's wife, Helen, called her father-in-law "gentle beyond anything I ever knew." According to Anderson, Alphonso had a "self-effacing and benign personality." One historian characterized Alphonso as "unostentatious, kindly and gentle." Helen Taft added that Alphonso was "just as set in his views as anyone well could be, but he was one of the most lovable men that ever lived. . . . He had a great many friends and to know him was to know why this was so." Malone's *Dictionary of American Biography* describes Alphonso's life as "marked by integrity rather than daring. He had character rather than genius."

On June 2, 1852, Alphonso became a widower. Fanny had been ill for some time with "congestion of the lungs and brain." After observing a suitable period of mourning, Alphonso began looking for a new wife. He found her during a visit to New Haven, Connecticut. Louise Maria Torrey was twenty-five years old when she met Alphonso Taft. When they met, she was staying with her uncle Samuel, a Yale classmate of Alphonso's. They were married on December 26, 1853. Alphonso was looking for a stepmother to his children more than he was looking to fall in love. According to Anderson, the union was "for both parties a matter of convenience." Louise always referred to her husband as Mr. Taft.

Four of Alphonso's and Louise's five children lived to maturity. William Howard, their second child, was born on September 15, 1857, at the family home in Cincinnati. Altogether, Alphonso sired ten children over a period of twenty-two years. After William's birth, Alphonso continued to immerse himself in politics, law, and Cincinnati culture and society. Alphonso and Louise were patrons of the arts. They were frequently seen at plays and at the opera and attended lectures.

By 1860 Alphonso had formally affiliated himself with the nascent Republican party. That year, he served as an alternate delegate to their national convention. Ross credits Alphonso with influencing the Ohio delegation to support the nomination of Abraham Lincoln. During the Civil War, Alphonso vigorously supported the Union cause by helping to sell government bonds and by making speeches denouncing slavery. Alphonso also went on the stump to urge all eligible men to enlist in the Union Army. His support for Lincoln had been tepid until the sixteenth president issued the Emancipation Proclamation.

In 1865 Alphonso was appointed judge of the Superior Court of Cincinnati. Prior to his appointment, he had dissolved his law partnership with Aaron Perry. Taft was elected to the bench twice; the second time, he ran unopposed. After leaving the judiciary, Taft was twice an unsuccessful candidate for the Republican nomination for governor of Ohio. In 1875 he lost the nomination to future President Rutherford B. Hayes. Four years later, he lost the nomination to Charles Foster.

Alphonso's failure to win higher elected office after leaving the Superior Court is directly related to a controversial decision he made in an 1869 case. Early that year, a Protestant organization sued the Cincinnati school board to prevent it from abandoning Bible reading and religious instruction in the public schools. Alphonso Taft was one of the three judges to hear the legal arguments. Alphonso dissented from the majority opinion by boldly declaring his firm belief in the separation of church and state. He argued that the school board had both an obligation and a right to keep religious instruction out of the public schools. Although the local press denounced his decision, the Supreme Court of Ohio subsequently upheld Taft's dissenting opinion and reversed the lower court's ruling. Alphonso never expressed any regret over his decision.

In spite of political defeats on the state level, Alphonso became a national political figure. In 1876 Alphonso's friend, President Ulysses S. Grant, asked him to serve as his secretary of war. Grant needed a man of Alphonso's impeccable integrity to restore public confidence in his scandal-ridden War Department. Alphonso's predecessor, William W. Belknap, had been impeached by the House for accepting bribes. Belknap's hasty resignation prevented impeachment by the Senate.

During his brief three-month tenure as secretary of war, Alphonso did what he could to curb patronage in that department and to reduce the defense budget. He left the office to become U.S. attorney general during the last ten months of the Grant administration. Taft's major accomplishment as attorney general was helping to establish the fifteen-man electoral commission that settled the disputed presidential election of 1876.

During the presidential election of 1880, Alphonso actively campaigned for his fellow Republican and Ohioan, James A. Garfield. William was now a recent graduate of Cincinnati Law School, and after having been tutored in public speaking by Alphonso, he also gave speeches urging people to vote for Garfield. In 1881 Louise's desire to travel motivated her to ask President Chester A. Arthur to appoint Alphonso to a diplomatic post. Arthur acceded by naming Alphonso ambassador to Austria-Hungary. Alphonso's major duties were ceremonial and social rather than diplomatic. Louise enjoyed the post immensely, but she was disappointed by Alphonso's inattention to protocol and his inability to speak German. She wrote, "he does not realize the embarrassment of not understanding the language."

Alphonso was never impressed with the bowing, heel-clicking, and hand-kissing of formal diplomatic dinners and receptions. He once remarked that a baron in Austria was the equivalent of a justice of the peace in Vermont. On July 4, 1884, President Arthur transferred Alphonso to St. Petersburg, Russia, where he served until August of 1885, when he retired from government services. During his tenure in Russia, he settled a number of repatriation cases involving Jews who returned to Russia after having emigrated earlier to America and becoming American citizens.

Alphonso Taft died in San Diego, California, on May 21, 1891. His funeral was held at the old Taft home in the Mount Auburn section of Cincinnati.

Shortly before Alphonso's death, U.S. Solicitor General William Howard Taft had written his wife telling her that with Alphonso's death his own career in politics and public service would likely end:

> I am not superstitious as you know, my darling, but I have kind of a presentiment that Father has been a kind of guardian angel to me in that his wishes for my success have been so strong and intense as to bring it and that as his life ebbs away and ends, I shall cease to have the luck which has followed me thus far.

After Alphonso's death, William Howard Taft was elected president of the United States and later appointed chief justice of the U.S. Supreme Court. He became the only man in the history of the United States to head both the executive and the judicial branch of government. Alphonso would have been so glad that his son's presentiment was so wrong.

Bibliography

Anderson, Judith I. *William Howard Taft: An Intimate Biography*. New York: Norton, 1981.
Burton, David H. *William Howard Taft in the Public Service*. Malabar, Fl.: Robert E. Krieger Publishing, 1986.
Duffy, Herbert S. *William Howard Taft*. New York: Minton, Balch, 1930.
Hess, Stephen. *America's Political Dynasties: From Adams to Kennedy*. Garden City, N.Y.: Doubleday, 1966.

Hess, Stephen. "Big Bill Taft." *American Heritage,* October 1968.
Malone, Dumas, editor. *Dictionary of American Biography.* New York: Scribners, 1935.
Myers, Elisabeth P. *William Howard Taft.* Chicago: Reilly & Lee, 1970.
Patterson, James T. *Mr. Republican: A Biography of Robert A. Taft.* Boston: Houghton, Mifflin, 1972.
Pringle, Henry F. *The Life and Times of William Howard Taft.* Hamden, Ct.: Archon Books, 1964.
Ross, Ishbel. *An American Family: The Tafts, 1678–1964.* Cleveland: World Publishing, 1964.
Taft, Mrs. William Howard. *Recollections of Full Years.* New York: Dodd, Mead, 1914.

Joseph Ruggles Wilson
(1822–1903)

*Printer, teacher, clergyman, professor, and father of
President Woodrow Wilson*

The father-son relationship between the Reverend Joseph Ruggles Wilson and his son Woodrow brings to mind the words of Edgar Allan Poe's poem, "Annabel Lee," for they loved each other with "a love that was more than love." A psychological study of America's twenty-eighth president coauthored by William C. Bullitt and Sigmund Freud states: "His passionate love of his father was the core of his emotional life." They cite letters between Joseph and Woodrow containing such salutations as "my beloved father" and "my precious son." They also report that the father and son "invariably kissed emotionally when they met."

Wilson biographers also write that Woodrow Wilson spoke obsessively about his father; so much so that Woodrow's frequent companions became bored with hearing the same stories again and again.

Joseph Ruggles Wilson was born in Steubenville, Ohio, on February 28, 1822. He was the seventh son and the last of ten children born to James and Anne Adams Wilson. James was a printer, newspaper publisher, and sometime politician who was elected a justice of the peace and who also served one term in the Pennsylvania General Assembly. In his book, *Woodrow Wilson,* August Heckscher writes that Joseph was marked as the scholar of the family. After learning the printer's trade, Joseph attended the local academy in Steubenville, and then he attended Jefferson College in Canonsburg, Pennsylvania. He graduated as the valedictorian at the latter institution in 1844.

For an unknown period of time, Joseph taught school. He left teaching to attend Western Theological Seminary in Allegheny, Pennsylvania. After leaving the seminary, Joseph attended Princeton Theological School. In 1846 he received his Bachelor of Divinity degree from Princeton. According to George C. Osborn's book, *Woodrow Wilson: The Early Years,* Joseph was licensed to preach in 1847. However, Heckscher records 1849 as the year of Joseph's ordination. In any case, Joseph did not become a clergyman immediately after earning his B.D. degree but opted instead to return to Steubenville and to teaching.

Joseph taught at the Steubenville Male Academy. While employed there, he met his future bride, Jessie Woodrow, a student attending a neighboring academy for women. They were married by Jessie's father on June 7, 1849, in Chillicothe, Ohio, when Joseph was twenty-seven and Jessie was twenty-two. Once married, Joseph divided his time between teaching and preaching. He joined the faculty of his alma mater, Jefferson College, as a Professor Extraordinary of Rhetoric. At the same time, he also served as the pastor of a small Pennsylvania church. Heckscher deems Joseph's first professorship important "because it developed the concern for literary composition and for public speech which were to be so marked in both him and his son."

In 1853 Joseph began teaching at Hampden-Sydney College in Virginia as a professor of chemistry and natural science. Two years later, he was named pastor of the First Presbyterian Church in Staunton, Virginia.

On December 28, 1856, in the church manse, Joseph's third child and first son was born. The boy was christened Thomas Woodrow Wilson. When he saw his plump, unusually quiet infant son, Joseph reportedly said, "that baby is dignified enough to be moderator of the (Presbyterian) General Assembly." Woodrow lived in Staunton only for about a year before his family moved.

Joseph had been establishing a reputation as a powerful and eloquent preacher. One contemporary account called him "a preacher of remarkable power, a scholar of wide learning, and an attractive personality." Joseph Wilson's physical attractiveness complemented his personality. Wilson biographers describe the Reverend Joseph R. Wilson as broad-shouldered, just under six feet tall with fiery brown eyes and a long, straight nose. On occasion, Woodrow was openly envious of his father's good looks. Bullitt and Freud's book quotes Woodrow as saying once: "If I had my father's face and figure, it wouldn't make any difference what I said."

During the summer of 1857 Joseph traveled to Augusta, Georgia, to perform the wedding of his brother-in-law, James Woodrow. While in Augusta, Joseph preached at the First Presbyterian Church. Since that congregation was without a pastor, the parishioners offered Joseph the position. Sometime in the autumn of 1857 he accepted and moved his family there.

During Woodrow's childhood Joseph became his teacher, role model, playmate, and confidant. Father and son enjoyed competing in tag, chess, and billiards. Joseph inevitably won the chess matches while Woodrow occasionally triumphed in billiards. Joseph also spent hours reading to his children, usually from works of fiction by Charles Dickens or Sir Walter Scott. Joseph also reserved time for daily prayers with his family, and the Wilsons frequently gathered to sing hymns. From his father, Woodrow Wilson learned his love of language and public speaking. As George C. Osborn writes in his biography, *Woodrow Wilson: The Early Years,* "The sound of words, the flow of language, his father's oratory were stamped indelibly upon Tommy's [Woodrow's] youthful memory."

Despite his father's good example, Woodrow Wilson remained a reluctant reader for an alarmingly long time. According to his biographers, Woodrow did not learn to read until he was eleven years old. Varying explanations have been given, among them dyslexia and other learning disabilities. Some sources blame a combination of poor eyesight and natural laziness on Woodrow's part, and yet another theory claims that Woodrow unconsciously rebelled against a demanding father who pushed him too hard.

When Joseph went to call on his Augusta parishioners at their places of business or employment, Woodrow often accompanied him. While visiting a mill, a factory, or a warehouse, Joseph usually gave Woodrow a detailed explanation of the establishment's inner workings, and upon their return home, he usually subjected Woodrow to an oral or written examination on what he had heard and seen. If there was any ambiguity in what Woodrow wrote, Joseph pointedly asked him: "What do mean by that?" Anything not meeting with Joseph's approval had to be rewritten. Joseph required Woodrow to use the dictionary to learn the precise definition of a word.

Joseph was equally exacting in his criticism of Woodrow's speech. Grammatical errors were corrected immediately; vague and incomplete statements met with quick disapproval. The only acceptable standard was precise language and speech conveying exactly what needed to be communicated. Recalling those experiences, Woodrow Wilson later said:

> When I was a boy, my father would not permit me to blurt things out or stammer a half-way job of telling whatever I had to tell. If I became excited in explaining some boying activity, he always said, "steady now, Thomas; wait a minute. Think! Think! Think what it is you wish to say, and then choose your words to say it." As a young boy therefore, even at the age of four or five, I was taught to think about what I was going to say, and then I was required to say it correctly. Before I was grown, it became a habit.

At other times, father and son would collaborate in analyzing and editing a work by one of their favorite authors. Osborn reports that after reading a speech by Daniel Webster or an essay by Charles Lamb, Joseph and Woodrow often tried to improve upon the writing, asking each other what words could be omitted without diminishing the clarity and eloquence of the work.

Joseph also had a major influence on Woodrow's attitudes toward racial issues. Although he was not a native southerner, Joseph Wilson unequivocally supported secession, slavery, and the Confederate States of America. Joseph even found a biblical sanction for the institution of slavery. During the Civil War, Joseph converted the Augusta churchyard into a military camp. Joseph was also very active in the movement that split the Presbyterian General Assembly into northern and southern branches. As Benjamin Quarles analyzes Woodrow Wilson's attitudes concerning the races in *The Negro in the Making of America:* "Indeed, he [Wilson] approved of segregation, holding the typical white Virginian's viewpoint that it was beneficial to both races." In private, Woodrow Wilson was known to refer to blacks as "an ignorant and inferior race."

Late in 1870 the Wilsons moved to Columbia, South Carolina, after Joseph

Joseph Wilson. Courtesy of the Woodrow Wilson Birthplace and Museum, Staunton, Virginia.

accepted a teaching position at the Columbia Theological Seminary. While teaching at the seminary as a professor of pastoral theology, Joseph also served as the stated supply (interim or temporary) minister of the First Presbyterian Church of Columbia. Since his election in 1865 to the office of stated clerk (chief officer) of the Southern Presbyterian Church, Joseph had become a very influential member of the church hierarchy. During their four years in Columbia, Joseph and Woodrow became even closer. Woodrow frequently accompanied his father to his classes at the seminary and raptly absorbed his lectures on theology and literature. Every

Sunday Woodrow faithfully listened to his father's sermons and discussed them with Joseph when they got home. As evidence of his father's growing influence, Osborn cites the facts that Woodrow joined his father's church in June of 1873 and left home to attend the college his father had chosen for him.

In the fall of 1873 Woodrow enrolled at Davidson College in Davidson, North Carolina. The school was a Presbyterian college, which prepared many of its students for careers in the ministry. Wilson biographers do not record that Joseph explicitly told Woodrow that he expected him to become a minister. However, it is likely that there was some kind of tacit agreement or understanding that Woodrow would enter the ministry, even though he had never expressed any desire to do so. Woodrow stayed at Davidson for only a year. He was neither physically nor emotionally ready for a prolonged absence from his parents. When he left Davidson, he was suffering from nervous indigestion and was on the verge of an emotional breakdown. Some biographers claim the illness was psychosomatic.

When Woodrow returned to Columbia, Joseph was mired in a controversy that would ultimately cause him to leave South Carolina. It all began when the congregation of the First Presbyterian Church voted to appoint a regular, full-time minister. Joseph resigned as the stated supply minister and then began engaging in some oddly vindictive behavior. He led the seminary faculty in an attempt to require the seminary students to attend Sunday services at the school chapel instead of giving them the option of attending services at the First Presbyterian Church. Seminary students made up a significant portion of the church's congregation, and naturally, Joseph's timing and motives were suspect. The students rebelled at being told where they should worship. The measure came before the church's General Assembly and it was narrowly defeated. As a result, Joseph resigned from the seminary's faculty, and so did several of his colleagues. Enrollment at the seminary declined sharply, precipitating a financial crisis that forced the institution to close temporarily. Heckscher puts the incident in perspective: "The ecclesiastical fracas in which Dr. Wilson became involved is important, not only because it affected Tommy's education, but because it displayed the combative and self-righteous style, the refusal to compromise or surrender, that in later conflicts Woodrow Wilson made his own."

Joseph's next pastoral position took him to Wilmington, North Carolina. He moved his family there in the fall of 1874. In his book, *Woodrow Wilson: World Statesman,* Kendrick A. Clements reports that Joseph disliked the city and the demands made upon him by the congregation. The church was also derelict about paying Joseph's salary on time. Nevertheless, he stayed there for eleven years. Perhaps the (for that time) generous salary of $4,000 a year kept him rooted there.

About a year after moving to Wilmington, Woodrow left home to give college another try. This time, he opted to attend Princeton. During his four years there, he continued to stay in close touch with his father. In one letter to Woodrow, Joseph cautioned his son to keep his growing ego in check: "Let the esteem you have won," Joseph urged, "be only a stimulant to fresh exertion." After Woodrow wrote a downcast letter about not doing well in an oratorical contest, Joseph tried to lift his son's spirits: "To deserve distinction is a far worthier thing than distinction itself."

When Woodrow graduated from Princeton in 1879, Joseph still tried to steer his son into a career in the ministry. Osborn reports that at times Joseph "would dramatize and emotionalize his appeal by springing up, embracing and kissing his son." However, Woodrow had already decided that being a clergyman was not for him. In September of 1879 Woodrow Wilson enrolled in law school at the University of Virginia.

Woodrow remained in law school for about one year. Once again his frail health caused him to leave school. There is also some evidence that he was an indifferent student. Clements records that he was reprimanded by the law school faculty for cutting classes. When Joseph learned of this, he sent Woodrow a letter that was a strange mixture of rebuke and affirmation: "You certainly acted most impudently . . . , and it seems to me that the faculty would be deserving of censure if they should overlook so gross a breach of discipline. But, then, I will add this—that, come what will, you possess our confidence, because we well know your character." In December of 1880 Woodrow dropped out of law school and returned to live with his parents. Under their watchful care he began regaining his health. He continued his studies during the eighteen months he lived with his parents. He received permission to take his exams at home, and in June of 1882 Woodrow Wilson received his law degree in absentia.

In October of 1882 Woodrow was admitted to the bar. After consulting with his father, he decided to set up practice in Atlanta. Woodrow soon found that a career in law was not to his liking. Clients were few, and Joseph continued to supply both moral and financial support to his disgruntled son. In one letter Joseph tried to cheer Woodrow up by telling him, "My beloved boy, you have only one thing to do: to stick to the law and its prospects be they ever so depressing." When that did not work, Joseph tried making him feel guilty: "It is a source of anxiety to me:—your law distaste." While Woodrow was brooding and sulking, Joseph was facing the realization that the best years of his life and career were now behind him. In a letter to his son, he told him: "Discouragement knocks at my door, and too often, I let him . . . in."

Following another lengthy consultation with his father, Woodrow decided to give up on a career in law and to leave Atlanta. He applied for a fellowship to study political science at Johns Hopkins University. When Woodrow's application for a fellowship was rejected, Joseph pledged to finance his further education. He also reassured Woodrow by writing: "I will not object to any decision that you may come to, and will do my utmost to secure you a position."

In the autumn of 1885 both father and son embarked upon career changes. Woodrow joined the faculty at Bryn Mawr College in Pennsylvania as a professor of history and political science. Joseph left Wilmington to teach at Southwestern Presbyterian University in Clarksville, Tennessee. Joseph had suggested to Woodrow that they join forces and found a school of their own, but Woodrow prudently declined the proposal. Also in 1885 Woodrow's first book, *Congressional Government,* was published. He dedicated the book to his father, calling him "the patient guide of his youth, the gracious companion of his manhood, and his best instructor and his most lenient critic." Joseph thanked Woodrow for the dedication in a letter: "God bless you my noble child for such a token of your affection."

By his early thirties, Woodrow was finally freeing himself from his lifelong dependence on his father. Now he was married, a professor, and a published author with a Ph.D. from Johns Hopkins University and an honorary degree from Wake Forest. Heckscher describes the change: "the father, often lonely, often depressed or in ill health accepted his fate with good grace touched faintly with melancholy. Increasingly he found his own fulfillment in Woodrow's growing success."

In 1888 Joseph became a widower. Shortly after Jessie's death, he retired from teaching. He began earning a living as an itinerant relief clergyman. After a serious illness in 1892, Joseph was forced to decline most of the preaching assignments offered to him.

According to Osborn, between 1895 and 1897, there was a profound change in the relationship between father and son. During that time, Woodrow never invited his father to his house in Princeton, New Jersey. They wrote infrequently, and Osborn characterizes their correspondence as "stilted and reserved."

Early in 1898 Joseph returned to Wilmington to live among his former parishioners. In 1902 shortly before Woodrow became president of Princeton University, Joseph moved into his son's New Jersey home. The final months Joseph spent living with Woodrow put a severe strain on his son's marriage and the domestic tranquility of the Wilson household. According to Osborn, Joseph could not stand up without assistance and was unable to feed himself. Joseph was also in such intense physical pain that he would moan, cry, or even scream for hours at a time.

Joseph Wilson died in Princeton, New Jersey, on January 21, 1903, at the age of eighty. He was buried next to his wife in a Columbia, South Carolina, cemetery. Joseph's obituary in the January 24, 1903, edition of the *Columbia (South Carolina) State* reported that as his interment scripture was read, a prayer was offered by the Reverend Dr. William Thomas Hall, moderator of the Southern Presbyterian General Assembly, and four hymns were sung. There were eight honorary and eight active pallbearers. Princeton University president Woodrow Wilson was not one of the sixteen pallbearers listed.

Bibliography

Blum, John Morton. *Woodrow Wilson and the Politics of Morality.* Boston: Little, Brown, 1956.
Bragdon, Henry Wilkinson. *Woodrow Wilson: The Academic Years.* Cambridge, Mass.: Belknap Press, 1967.
Clements, Kendrick A. *Woodrow Wilson: World Statesman.* Boston: Twayne, 1987.

Columbia (South Carolina) State. January 24, 1903.
Freud, Sigmund, and William C. Bullitt. *Thomas Woodrow Wilson: A Psychological Study.* Boston: Houghton Mifflin, 1967.
Heckscher, August. *Woodrow Wilson.* New York: Scribner's, 1991.
Link, Arthur S., editor. *The Papers of Woodrow Wilson.* Vol. 14. *1902–1903.* Princeton, N.J.: Princeton University Press, 1972.
Osborn, George C. "The Influence of Joseph Ruggles Wilson on His Son Woodrow Wilson." *The North Carolina Historical Review.* Vol. 32 (1955), pp. 519–543.
Osborn, George C. *Woodrow Wilson: The Early Years.* Baton Rouge: Louisiana State University Press, 1968.
Quarles, Benjamin. *The Negro in the Making of America.* New York: Collier, 1964.
Walworth, Arthur. *Woodrow Wilson: American Prophet.* New York: Longmans, Green, 1958.

George Tyron Harding II (1843–1928)

*Soldier, teacher, physician, insurance salesman,
realtor, merchant, farmer, and father of
President Warren G. Harding*

Charles L. Mee Jr. described George Tyron Harding II in his book, *The Ohio Gang: The World of Warren G. Harding,* as "a small, idle, shiftless, impractical, lazy, daydreaming, catnapping fellow whose eye was always on the main chance." Mee was not being malicious. The main accomplishment of Tyron's life was fathering an American president, and Tyron made the most of that accomplishment.

The father of America's twenty-ninth president was born in Blooming Grove (now Corsica), Ohio, on June 12, 1843. Tyron was the third child of Charles Alexander and Mary Anne Harding. Altogether, Charles and Mary had ten children. Only six of them lived to maturity, and Tyron was the only boy to do so. The first Harding to come to America had been a Puritan fisherman named Richard who emigrated to Braintree, Massachusetts, from England in 1623. Shortly after the Hardings had settled in Blooming Grove in 1818, the persistent rumor began circulating that the family was of Negro blood. Those charges would repeatedly dog Warren G. Harding throughout his political career. The family's explanation was that the rumor was started by a vindictive neighbor who had been caught stealing corn from the Hardings' farm.

Tyron had no aptitude or enthusiasm for being a farmer like his father. So apparently Charles decided that Tyron should enter one of the learned professions. Since Charles was more prosperous than most of the other farmers in the area, he was able to send Tyron off to school. For a time Tyron attended a subscription school run by his aunt. It was there that Tyron first noticed the girl he later married, Phoebe Dickerson. When he was fourteen, Tyron was admitted to Iberia College. He graduated from there with a bachelor's degree in 1860. In the fall of that year Tyron began teaching at a rural school four miles north of Gilead, Ohio. He lived frugally, and after teaching for two terms, he enrolled in Ontario Academy. Why a college graduate with two years of teaching experience would enroll in a secondary school seems inexplicable. However, Tyron had a reason. He was following his heart. Phoebe Dickerson was a student at Ontario Academy.

While they were attending the academy, Tyron and Phoebe became secretly engaged. Their marriage was delayed when Tyron enlisted in the Union Army. Despite his lack of height, Tyron was able to enlist as a fifer in Company C of the Ninety-Sixth Ohio Volunteer Infantry. Tyron's dreams of military glory and combat heroism were abruptly shattered when he caught pleurisy after participating in a long, rainy march. Tyron was forced to stay back in Ohio while his regiment shipped out. A few weeks later, he received his discharge.

Tyron glumly spent the next year convalescing at his parents' home in Blooming Grove. In 1864 he was able to reenlist. Tyron became a drummer boy for Company D. Before going off to war, Tyron formally proposed to Phoebe. Since Tyron was under twenty-one, he needed his father's written permission to marry. Once he had that, he procured the marriage license. On the afternoon of May 7, 1864, Tyron took the family buggy to the Dickerson farm to take Phoebe and her sister, Deb, "for a ride." In his haste to elope, Tyron broke a buggy spring with his excessive speed. After making the quick, bumpy eight-mile ride to Galion, the trio went to the home of the local Methodist minister. With sister Deb as their witness, George Tyron Harding and Phoebe Dickerson became husband and wife.

On the way back to Blooming Grove, Phoebe commemorated the nuptials by scratching four lines of verse inside Tyron's watch case.

>Phoebe Dickerson is no more
>May 7th 1864
>Phoebe Harding now it is
>Didn't we fool Mal and Liz?

The last line was a reference to Phoebe's two older sisters, Malvina and Elizabeth Ann.

The newlyweds had no honeymoon and no wedding night in the traditional sense. They kept their marriage a secret. Phoebe returned that evening to her parents' farm, and Tyron went off to war. Only after Tyron was discharged from the Union Army did the Dickersons learn that Phoebe was married.

On May 11th Tyron's outfit shipped out to Virginia. While Tyron was stationed at Fort Williams, one of his bunkmates regularly wrote to Phoebe. He unsuspectingly shared the contents of those letters with Tyron. Phoebe's replies were friendly, but impersonal. Only after the bunkmate was mustered out of the service did he learn that he had been corresponding with Tyron's wife.

While stationed in Virginia, the presidential father was able to pay a call to the president. During a furlough in Washington, D.C., Tyron and two other members of his regiment entered the White House and announced that they wished to shake hands with President Abraham Lincoln. Because of the remarkable informality of the Lincoln administration they were able to do just that. A White House servant told the three soldiers that the President could not see them immediately, but if they waited they would be able to see him in a while. After waiting about an hour, the trio was ushered into Lincoln's study. Tyron and his comrades proudly told President Lincoln that they were from the Buckeye State and that they were defending the union. President Lincoln thanked them and mentioned that Ohio had been a loyal state of the union. After shaking their hands, Lincoln joked, "now you can tell your people at home that you have seen the handsomest man in the United States." Tyron often talked about that brief encounter throughout his life.

In mid-August Tyron was stricken with typhoid fever. About two weeks later, he received an honorable discharge and a certificate of disability attesting that he suffered "an attack of typhoid contracted while in service." After being reunited in Blooming Grove, Tyron and Phoebe moved in with Tyron's parents. Tyron resumed his teaching career and began building a house. The house he built became the birthplace of Warren Gamaliel Harding on November 2, 1865. Tyron and Phoebe had seven more children (five boys and girls) over a fourteen-year period.

By 1869 Tyron was tired of teaching. He desired a career change and chose medicine. Tyron purchased a set of used medical books and began accompanying Blooming Grove physician Dr. Joseph McFarland on his rounds. In the latter part of 1870 Tyron attended medical school at the Homeopathic Hospital College in Cleveland. After one term there, Tyron received a certificate from the Northwest Medical Society enabling him to practice medicine. Attendance at an additional session of HHC in the spring of 1873 allowed George Tyron Harding to become George Tyron Harding, M.D.

Tyron's medical practice never became the passport to prosperity he had envisioned. As a country doctor, he often had to accept payment in farm produce instead of cash. Tyron was also an inveterate trader and land speculator who seldom got the best of a deal. His penchant for wheeling and dealing is aptly described by Francis Russell in his book, *The Shadow of Blooming Grove: Warren G. Harding in His Times:* "Horses appeared and disappeared in his barn like casual boarders. Carts, wagons, carriages and farm implements cluttered his yard in transit. From the day he [Tyron] arrived in Caledonia he was never out of debt." Russell also records that by 1880 Tyron's trades and land speculations had caused him to lose his home in Caledonia. The Hardings moved to a forty-acre farm. Phoebe's income as a midwife was virtually the family's only income. Somehow the Hardings scraped together the money to send Warren to college.

Iberia College, Tyron's alma mater, was now known as Ohio Central College. Warren enrolled there in the fall of 1880. Two years later, he graduated with a B.S. degree. In or around 1882 the Hardings moved to Marion, Ohio. Tyron hung up his shingle, placed an ad in the paper, and waited for the patients to come in. To supplement his meager medical practice, Tyron also sold insurance and real estate. For a brief time he also managed a hardware store in Crestline, Ohio.

There is some evidence that Tyron's medical practice was actually more lucrative than is generally believed. Randolph C. Downes in his book, *The Rise and Fall*

Dr. George Tyron Harding II. Courtesy of UPI/Bettmann.

of Warren G. Harding, 1865–1920, cites a letter written by Warren to an aunt on February 12, 1883: "Pa is very busy — making over $500 per month." However, it is quite likely that whatever money Tyron was making as a physician was just making up for his other business reverses. Still, Tyron's habitual trading finally came to some good when he became a part owner of the local newspaper, the *Marion Star.*

For a house lot he had acquired in one of his many trades, Tyron obtained a half interest in the newspaper. Eventually, Warren G. Harding would become the sole owner of the *Star*, and he would use that position as a stepping stone to a political career.

For the most part, Tyron led the quiet, uneventful, genteel life of a small-town doctor. One notable exception occurred in the fall of 1893. A man named Lewis Gunn felt that the *Star* had libeled him. Lewis and his younger brother stormed into the newspaper's editorial offices and demanded an apology from Warren. Tyron's office was across the hall. Tyron heard the commotion, and ran in the office brandishing a jackknife. As a result Tyron was pummeled by Lewis Gunn (two black eyes), and the Gunn brothers were arrested for assault.

Throughout his adult life, Warren G. Harding rendered financial assistance to his father. When the medical practice faltered and business deals turned sour, Warren paid the office rent and made the mortgage payments on Tyron's house. Watching out for his father became more burdensome for Warren after Phoebe died in 1910. The despondent Tyron lost interest in medicine and in trading. Instead, he spent his days alternately moping and napping in his empty office.

That only changed when he began courting Eudora Kelly Luvisi, a forty-three-year-old widow. After the visiting Eudora left Marion to return to her home in Indiana, a badly smitten Tyron followed here there. Tyron and Eudora were married in Anderson, Indiana, on November 23, 1911. At age sixty-eight, Tyron was a quarter century older than his second wife. Soon after his second marriage, Tyron was once again turning to Warren for money. In a letter to Warren, his sister, Abigail, wrote: "Now as to Dad and his late financial adventures. He has told me that he had purchased that farm, but how I don't know. His finances have always been a mystery to me."

Tyron was a failure at farming. He and Eudora returned to Marion and according to Russell, Eudora incessantly nagged Tyron for lack of money, ambition, and enterprise. Tyron resumed his old habit of taking naps at the office, away from the shrewish tones of Eudora's voice. They divorced in 1916.

On November 2, 1920, Senator Warren G. Harding was elected president of the United States. Ever since his son's nomination, Tyron had reveled in the resultant publicity. During the campaign, voters were reminded of Tyron's service in the Civil War. Photographs were run showing him wearing his Grand Army of the Republic regalia. The March 1921 issue of *McClure's* ran a long, rambling interview with Tyron entitled "My Boy Warren."

Along with treacly reminiscences and fulsome praise for his son, Tyron boasted that he was the first father to live to see his son elected to the presidency. Apparently Tyron and the editors of *McClure's* were unaware that John Adams and Jesse Root Grant were alive when their sons were elected president. The article concluded with Tyron pugnaciously remarking, "Now that it's all over, I've got a few scores to settle on my account. I'm just waiting around till it's time to go downtown and settle 'em."

Tyron attended his son's inauguration proudly bedecked in his GAR uniform. After returning to Marion, Tyron greeted a steady stream of journalists seeking stories about his parenting of a president. It did not take long before reporters tired of hearing Tyron tell the same old rambling anecdotes. Once again, Tyron needed something to occupy his time, and once again, he took to courting.

Alice Severns had been working part time in Tyron's office. Her putative duties were cleaning the office, typing correspondence, and assisting Tyron in attending to patients. She was twenty-six years younger than Tyron and described as buxom. On August 12, 1921, Tyron and Alice eloped. They were married in Monroe, Michigan. On the marriage license application Tyron narrowed their age difference by subtracting ten years from his age and adding ten years to hers. Following the brief ceremony at the Monroe Presbyterian Church, the newlyweds drove to Detroit. Tyron had thriftily arranged for them to spend their wedding night at the home of some relatives. En route to Marion, the newlyweds were greeted by a pack of reporters in Toledo, Ohio. At an impromptu press conference, Tyron explained his third marriage: "I was lonesome, simply unbearably lonesome."

President Warren G. Harding died in San Francisco on August 2, 1923. When he was laid to rest in Marion in August 10, Tyron once again donned his beloved GAR uniform. Warren's death made Tyron the first presidential father to outlive his son.

As news of the Teapot Dome scandal and other stories of pervasive corruption in the Harding administration dominated the nation's attention, Tyron Harding shunned the publicity he had once sought. He died at Santa Ana, California, on November 19, 1928, at the age of eighty-five. Harding's death was noted by a highly laudatory obituary in the November 19, 1928, edition of the *Santa Ana Register*. The last paragraph read:

> He undoubtedly aided his son by giving him elements of a sound body and mind and that sane, cheerful outlook on life which carried him on his remarkable success. Doctor Harding possibly would not have considered himself a great man, but he had those fine qualities of loyalty, thrift and service which are so needed in the men who bear the daily burdens of the community and who must be faithful to their friends, neighbors and citizens. This was Doctor Harding.

Bibliography

Adams, Samuel Hopkins. *Incredible Era: The Life and Times of Warren G. Harding*. Boston: Houghton, Mifflin, 1939.

Degregorio, William A. *The Complete Book of U.S. Presidents*. New York: Barricade Books, 1993.

Downes, Randolph C. *The Rise and Fall of Warren G. Harding, 1865–1920*. Columbus, Ohio: Ohio State University Press, 1970.

Edmunds, George L. "My Boy Warren: The Father's Story of the President-Elect and His Success System." *McClure's*, March 1921.

Mee, Charles L., Jr. *The Ohio Gang: The World of Warren G. Harding.* New York: Evans, 1981.
Russell, Francis. *The Shadow of Blooming Grove: Warren G. Harding in His Times.* New York: McGraw-Hill, 1968.
Santa Ana (California) Register. November 19, 1928.

John Calvin Coolidge
(1845-1926)

Farmer, soldier, carpenter, cabinetmaker, mason, blacksmith, storekeeper, public official, buggy maker, law officer, legislator, politician, teacher, magistrate, and father of President Calvin Coolidge

There is no uncertainty about how Calvin Coolidge felt about his father, John. In his *Autobiography*, Calvin Coolidge wrote: "I was exceedingly anxious to grow up to be like him." Not surprisingly, he did. The father of America's thirtieth president was thrifty, meticulous, old-fashioned, and a man of few words. All of those traits were shared by his son, Calvin.

John Calvin Coolidge was born in Plymouth Notch, Vermont, on March 31, 1845, to Galoosh and Sarah Coolidge. He was educated at the public schools of Plymouth Notch and at Black River Academy in Ludlow, Vermont. Exactly how long he attended school is not known. Available biographical information simply indicates that John Coolidge attended the academy "for a few terms." After leaving school, John alternately worked as a wheelwright, a laborer on his father's farm, and a teacher for the Pinney Hollow School District before becoming a storekeeper.

In 1868 John married twenty-two-year-old Victoria Josephine Moor. Like her husband, Victoria had attended the public schools of Plymouth Notch and the Black River Academy. Victoria bore John two children, John Calvin (who was called Calvin to avoid confusion with his father), born in 1872, and Abigail, born in 1875. Victoria's health steadily deteriorated after her marriage. She was probably suffering from tuberculosis. In the last years of her life, Calvin's mother was a chronic invalid. She died in 1885 when Calvin was twelve. Five years later, Calvin's only sibling, Abigail, died at age fifteen. The deaths of the two women in the Coolidge family certainly brought the father and son closer together. However, since they were both taciturn, their affection was implicit rather than expressed.

Coolidge biographers agree that John Coolidge was well known around Plymouth Notch as a jack-of-all-trades, and they describe him as an accomplished carpenter, brick and stone mason, and buggy maker. Epitomizing the Yankee self-reliance of a New England farmer, John Coolidge was also skilled at plumbing, welding, and veterinary medicine. Young Calvin was often a witness to his father's handiwork, and he recalled in his *Autobiography:* "From watching him and assisting him, I gained an intimate knowledge of all this kind of work. The work that he did endured. If there was any physical requirement of country life which he could not perform, I do not know what it was." Along with his skills as a handyman and farmer, John Coolidge was a successful businessman in a not particularly prosperous community. He also held several elected and appointed offices in Vermont government.

In 1868 John Coolidge embarked on a career as a storekeeper. He rented the village store in Plymouth Notch for $40 a year. Under his prudent management, the store was soon earning him $1,200 a year. An example of the thrift ethic that John passed on to Calvin is related in Calvin's *Autobiography.* Calvin recalled that his father used to travel to Boston twice a year to buy goods for his store. John usually took the midnight train to Boston from Ludlow, Vermont, and slept while traveling to save the expense of a hotel room.

From his profits as a storekeeper, John was able to buy a house across the road from the store. For $375, he received a house, two acres, several sheds and barns, and a blacksmith shop. In 1878 John's father, Galoosh, died and the inheritance of his father's property allowed John to sell the store to his brother-in-law. For the rest of his life, John lived off of his inheritance, income from his farm properties, and stipends he received as a public servant.

John held many offices. At different times he served as the township's superintendent of schools, selectman, tax collector, constable, deputy sheriff, road commissioner, and notary public. He also served three terms in the Vermont House of Representatives and one term in the State Senate. John also served on the staff of Vermont Governor William W. Stickney. In that capacity, he received the title of Colonel. That pleased him greatly, for when he had served in the Vermont National Guard, he had been only a sergeant. Given his father's background, it is not surprising that Calvin would gravitate toward a career in politics and public service. John often took his son along to sessions of the county court when it would not interfere with Calvin's farm chores or school attendance. When John served in the state legislature, Calvin occasionally traveled with him to Montpelier. Donald R. McCoy sums up the influence of the politician/father in his biography, *Calvin Coolidge: The Quiet President:* "From his father's political life, Calvin Coolidge received both valuable training in how the shrewd and discreet politician acts in search of office and a feeling of civic responsibility."

Along with lessons in practical politics, John taught Calvin the value of a dollar and that he had to work for the money he had. Planting, plowing, mending fences, and gathering firewood were but a few of Calvin's regular chores. Calvin also earned extra pocket money by selling apples and popcorn balls at town meetings. John impressed upon Calvin that money he earned was to be saved and not spent. Calvin recalled in his *Autobiography:* "Any money I earned he [John] had me put in the savings bank, because he wished me to be informed of the value of money at interest. He thought that money invested that way led to a self-respecting independence that was one of the foundations of good character."

In 1891 John remarried just before Calvin began his freshman year at Amherst College. Caroline Athelia Brown, a Plymouth schoolteacher, became the second Mrs. John Coolidge and Calvin's stepmother. Calvin Coolidge noted the marriage by writing: "My absence from home during my freshman year was more easy for me to bear because I was no longer leaving my father alone."

Throughout his college years, Calvin wrote his father on a regular basis. Claude M. Fuess's biography, *Calvin Coolidge: The Man from Vermont,* contains excerpts from those letters. In a letter dated October 15, 1891, the college freshman told his father about his trouble making friends. "I don't seem to get acquainted very fast," Calvin wrote. On January 6, 1892, Calvin confided to his father that he was homesick. "Every time I get home I hate to go away worse than before."

After graduating from Amherst in 1895, Calvin decided to pursue a career in law. Calvin and John agreed that the best way to become a lawyer was by reading law as a clerk in a law firm instead of attending law school. Naturally, it was also the most economical way to gain admission to the bar. John wrote to a political acquaintance, William P. Dillingham, who was a former governor of Vermont, asking him if he could give Calvin a clerical position in his Montpelier firm. But before Dillingham could reply, another opportunity had opened up for Calvin, and he moved to Northampton, Massachusetts, to study law at the firm of John C. Hammond and Henry P. Field. Calvin Coolidge was admitted to the bar in July of 1897. He spent the rest of his life working as a lawyer and politician.

However, it took several more years before Calvin gained complete financial independence from his father. On December 25, 1910, after having been elected mayor of Northampton, Calvin wrote his father: "Your generous Christmas letter is just received. We are very thankful for it. I could not have been Mayor without your help. The salary is $800, they may raise it to $1200. It just about pays the extra expense the office makes one."

While Calvin was serving as mayor, John was elected to the Vermont State Senate. By then Calvin considered himself a sufficiently seasoned political pro to offer his father some advice. Fuess quotes a letter Calvin wrote to his father on September 6, 1910: "You need not hesitate to give the other members your views on any subject that arises. It is much more important to kill bad bills than to pass good ones." As an afterthought, Calvin added, "It won't make any difference what you wear."

Throughout Calvin's political career, John was there to to experience his son's ascendancy. John was in Boston at Calvin's inauguration as governor of Massachusetts in 1919. He was in Washington, D.C., when Calvin took the vice-presidential oath in 1921. Most importantly, John was there when the sudden, unexpected death of Warren G. Harding made Calvin the president of the United States on the morning of August 3, 1923.

When Harding died, Calvin was on vacation visiting his father in Plymouth. The Coolidges had all retired at 9 o'clock in the evening believing that Harding was recovering from his recent illness. Sometime around midnight, John was awakened by a persistent pounding on his front door. John asked, "What's wanted?" and a telegraph messenger quickly informed him that President Harding was dead and that he had a telegram for Vice President Coolidge. John read Calvin the telegram informing him of President Harding's death. Calvin and his wife, Grace, said a prayer, got dressed, and went downstairs.

After locating a copy of the presidential oath of office, Calvin asked his father if he was still a notary. John said yes, and Calvin told his father that he wanted him to administer the oath. Acting in his capacity as a notary, John administered the oath making his son the thirtieth president of the United States. The brief ceremony took place in the sitting room of John's farmhouse at 2:47 A.M. Some years later, a reporter asked John how he could administer the presidential oath of office to his son. John replied, "I didn't know I couldn't." Just to be safe, the oath was repeated on August 21, 1923. The second time it was administered by Justice Adolph August Hoehling of the District of Columbia Supreme Court.

For the rest of his life, John Coolidge was a celebrity. He received frequent invitations to visit the White House, but he preferred to stay at home. While Calvin Coolidge was president, John visited Washington only twice. When his grandson, Calvin Coolidge Jr., died in 1924, John accompanied Calvin and Grace to the capital and stayed for thirteen days. His last visit was when he attended Calvin's inauguration on March 4, 1925.

The constant influx of visitors, sightseers, and well-wishers to John's Vermont home took its toll on him, but he endured it gracefully. Calvin wrote in his *Autobiography:* "At his advanced age, he had overtaxed his strength receiving the thousands of visitors who went to my old home in Plymouth. It was all a great satisfaction to him." An Associated Press story reported, "He was forced frequently to forsake a habit of a lifetime to remain up late into the night answering inconsequential letters which have poured in upon him and had daily been subjected to unwelcome scrutiny from motor tourists and souvenir pests who had flocked here in ever increasing numbers."

In June of 1925 John underwent an operation to clear an abscess of the prostate. The procedure took thirty-eight minutes and the *Burlington (Vt.) Free Press and Times* reported, "The sick man stood it well and felt greatly relieved." It was recommended that the prostate later be removed when John had fully recovered, but the operation was never done. In December of 1925 John lost the use of his legs. Three months later, he suffered a severe heart attack. The *Free Press and Times* reported that his pulse rate reached 140. John Coolidge died at his home on March 18, 1926, at 10:41 P.M. A Dr. Cram who attended him reported that cancer of the bladder was the cause of his death, and myocarditis (inflammation of the muscle tissue of the heart) was a secondary cause. When he died, John Coolidge was two weeks shy of his eighty-first birthday. Calvin and Grace were on a special train en route to Plymouth when they received word of the colonel's death. They arrived in Plymouth twelve hours after John had died.

Calvin Coolidge (left) with his father, John Coolidge. Courtesy of the Vermont Division for Historic Preservation, President Calvin Coolidge Birthplace.

For only the second time in the history of the presidency, the father of an American president died while his son was president. In a rare tribute to a private citizen, the U.S. Senate adjourned. The House of Representatives expressed "profound sorrow" over John Coolidge's death.

In accordance with John's instructions, the funeral service was short and simple. No hymns were sung and no eulogy was delivered. In the room where Calvin Coolidge became president, the Reverend John White recited the burial rites of the Episcopal church. The service took fourteen minutes.

A horse-drawn sleigh hearse accompanied by six soldiers from the Vermont National Guard moved the casket from the Coolidge farmhouse to the local cemetery. John Coolidge was then buried dressed in his Sunday-go-to-meeting black suit.

In his *Autobiography,* Calvin Coolidge mentioned his father more than anyone else. However, in writing about his father's death, he applied his usual economy of words. He wrote: "For my personal contact with him during his last months I had to resort to the poor substitute of the telephone. When I reached home he was gone. It costs a great deal to be president."

In his book, *A Puritan in Babylon: The Story of Calvin Coolidge,* William Allen White summed up John and Calvin's father-son relationship: "He was his father's idol. And always in his heart he sought the protecting shadow of his father's approval, even to the last."

Bibliography

Burlington (Vt.) Free Press and Times. March 19 and March 20, 1926.
Coolidge, Calvin. *The Autobiography of Calvin Coolidge.* New York: Cosmopolitan, 1929.
Crossier, Barney. "When A President Lost His Father." *Rutland (Vt.) Herald,* March 17, 1986.
Curtis, Jane Will, and Frank Lieberman. *Return to These Hills: The Vermont Years of Calvin Coolidge.* Woodstock, Vt.: Curtis-Lieberman, 1985.
Fuess, Claude M. *Calvin Coolidge: The Man from Vermont.* Boston: Little, Brown, 1940.
Greene, J. R. *Calvin Coolidge: A Biography in Picture Postcards.* Athol, Mass.: Transcript Press, 1987.
Guide to the Coolidge Homestead at Plymouth Notch, Vermont. State of Vermont Division for Historic Preservation.
McCoy, Donald R. *Calvin Coolidge: The Quiet President.* New York: Macmillan, 1967.
New York Herald. March 20, 1926.
Ross, Ishbel. *Grace Coolidge and Her Era.* New York: Dodd, Mead, 1962.
Washburn, R. M. *Calvin Coolidge: His First Biography.* Boston: Small, Maynard, 1923.
White, William Allen. *A Puritan in Babylon: The Story of Calvin Coolidge.* Gloucester, Mass.: Peter Smith, 1973.

Jesse Clark Hoover
(1846–1880)

*Blacksmith, farm implement dealer, and father of
President Herbert Hoover*

Herbert Clark Hoover never had much to say about his father, Jesse Clark Hoover, which is quite understandable since Jesse died when Herbert was six. In his *Memoirs*, Herbert Hoover merely wrote: "My recollection of my father is of necessity dim indeed." Herbert Hoover offered no insights or anecdotes about the life and values of the man who fathered America's thirty-first president. Fortunately, biographers of Herbert Hoover do provide a few glimpses into the personality and life of Jesse Clark Hoover.

Jesse was born on September 2, 1846, in the village of West Milton, Ohio, in Miami County. His father was named Eli and he was a farmer. Jesse was named for his paternal grandfather. In 1854 Grandpa Jesse, Eli, and an unknown number of Hoover children migrated from Ohio to Iowa by covered wagon. The Hoover contingent settled near the Quaker village of West Branch. According to George H. Nash's book, *The Life of Herbert Hoover: The Engineer, 1874–1914*, both of Herbert Hoover's parents attended a private "select school" near West Branch during the 1860s. The school was organized and run by Quaker missionaries. It is not known exactly how long Jesse attended that school and when his formal education ended.

When he was not going to school, Jesse worked on his father's farm. There he developed his lifelong fascination with tools, machines, and all things mechanical. According to a family history written by Herbert's wife, Lou Henry Hoover, Jesse put a clock back together after taking it apart. Jesse also tinkered with the sewing machine and farm machinery enough to learn their operating principles and details. The family history reports that Jesse made both theoretical and practical improvements on them all.

The fullest description of Jesse's personality is found in the family history penned by Mrs. Hoover: "Jesse's companions remembered him as a keen, energetic, persistent boy and young man of many friends." It is likely that Jesse could have been an engineer if he had been able to obtain the requisite education. Jesse certainly had an affinity for inventing, tinkering, and machinery. Regrettably, that opportunity did not exist for Jesse Hoover. Instead of pursuing a college engineering curriculum, Jesse learned to be a blacksmith. It is interesting to note that both of Jesse's sons trained to be engineers. Herbert became an eminent mining engineer before entering politics, and Theodore became the dean of the Stanford University School of Engineering.

Jesse was working as the village blacksmith when he married his old schoolmate Hulda Randall Minthorn in 1870. He was twenty-four and she was twenty-one. There are no records of their courtship and romance. Theodore Jesse Hoover was the first child of Jesse and Hulda. He was born on January 28, 1871. Their second child, Herbert Clark Hoover, was born around midnight on August 10, 1874, at the Hoovers' cottage in West Branch. Church records list Herbert Hoover's birthdate as August 10, but in his *Memoirs*, Hoover wrote that his birthday was August 11. Herbert was delivered by his Aunt Ellen who was a midwife. Ellen described the newborn infant as "round, plump and cordial."

Countless American fathers have dreamed of having one of their children grow up to become president of the United States. Jesse Hoover was no different. When Herbert was born, Ulysses S. Grant was seventeen months into his second term as president. Jesse announced Herbert's birth by telling his friends, "We have another General Grant at our house." Almost fifty-five years later, a father's joking boast turned into a prophecy come true.

With the addition of Herbert, there were now four people living in the Hoovers' tiny fourteen-by-twenty-foot, three-room cottage. The birth of a daughter, Mary, in 1876 made the Hoover home even more cramped and confining. Luckily by 1878 Jesse was able to provide his growing family with more spacious accommodations. On May 25, 1878, Jesse sold his blacksmith shop, cottage, and adjoining property to a man named J. C. Hill for $1,000. The sale gave Jesse the means to open his own farm implement business and to move his family to a roomy two-story house at the corner of Downey and Cedar Streets in West Branch.

Prior to the opening of his new business, Jesse's blacksmith shop had been the center of Herbert's world. Jesse's shop gave the future engineer his first knowledge of tools and machinery. Young Herbert raptly watched his bearded, muscular father shoe horses and repair plows while also keeping the customers amused with his teasing sense of humor. The blacksmith shop also gave Herbert and Theodore an escape from the staid home life of their pious Quaker mother.

In her household Hulda Hoover prohibited all the things her Quaker brethren considered to be sinful. Those sinful pastimes and practices included, but were not limited to, drinking, swearing, card playing, dancing, and wearing showy dress. Herbert Hoover recalled that the only novels allowed in their home were those "where the hero overcame demon rum." Sunday amusements of any kind were also forbidden. People were addressed as "thee" and "thou," and daily Bible readings and prayers were mandatory family activities. Another commonly told anecdote about Herbert Hoover's childhood relates that Herbert and Theodore acquired a copy of

Jesse Clark Hoover. Courtesy of the Herbert Hoover Presidential Library-Museum.

the boy's magazine *The Youth's Companion* and hid it behind Jesse's blacksmith shop lest it be discovered and they be struck down by both an angry mother and an angry God.

Jesse Hoover shared Hulda's Quaker faith and scrupulously observed their dress by donning a broad-brimmed hat, collarless coat, and plain, dark clothing. Still, Jesse maintained the personality and temperament of a member of a less restrictive faith. Richard Norton Smith in his book, *An Uncommon Man: The Triumph of Herbert Hoover*, notes that on at least one occasion Jesse was reprimanded by the ruling Quakers of West Branch. Nevertheless, Jesse was regular in his attendance at worship services and church functions. Like a good Quaker, he prayed for the inner light to enter his life to lead and guide him. However, Jesse also believed that being a good provider and a successful businessman in this life was no less important than being spiritually prepared for the next one.

In the *West Branch Local Record*, Jesse attempted to drum up business with this ad copy in 1879:

> Ho, for Kansas!
> but if you don't go there, go to
> J. C. Hoover
> and buy your farming implements.

The ad's list of implements included plows, reapers, rubber bucket pumps, sewing machines, and lightning rods. The ad concluded with: "Come and see me for I will not be beat in quality or prices. J. C. Hoover." Jesse also supplemented his income from the prospering implement business by various entrepreneurial activities. In early 1880 he and an unknown coinventor applied for a patent for a cattle turnstile and hog guard. Jesse may have also marketed a cattle pump, which was invented and manufactured by his father.

In December of 1880, Jesse became seriously ill. He died on December 13. Some Hoover biographies report that Jesse died of typhoid fever; others claim it was pneumonia. An obituary in the December 16, 1880, issue of the *West Branch Local Record* gave the cause of death as rheumatism of the heart.

The same obituary praised Jesse:

> His was a pleasant, sunshiny disposition. Ever happy and cheerful himself, he always had a kind word for all . . . thus binding the chain of love and friendship around the children, the youth and the aged. In the loss of our loved one a vacancy is left in the circle of life which never can be filled. He was a kind husband and father, a respected and useful citizen, and will be sadly missed in business circles.

Even after his death, Jesse found himself at odds with the elders of the church. His widow was rebuked by the powers that be for marking Jesse's grave with a tombstone they thought was too ostentatious.

Jesse left his wife and three children with $1,000 in life insurance and whatever money the sale of his business garnered. The funds were wisely invested and later helped to pay for the college education of Herbert and Theodore. After Jesse's death, Herbert was sent to live with a succession of uncles. Hulda died in 1884, leaving the three Hoover children parentless.

It is difficult to say how Herbert Hoover could have been influenced by a father he could barely remember. Apparently, the only thing shared was a religious faith they both found a bit too demanding. Herbert Hoover was fond of saying, "I was a Quaker, but I didn't work very hard at it." As an adult, Herbert Hoover could swear and swap stories with the coarsest of miners. He was a habitual smoker and enjoyed alcohol even during Prohibition. (He used to imbibe at the Belgian Embassy, which was technically foreign territory.) Herbert Hoover also had absolutely no qualms about fishing on the Sabbath. It is a shame that Jesse did not live to see Herbert become an adult. He might have enjoyed sharing a drink, a smoke, and a joke with his son.

Bibliography

Burner, David. *Herbert Hoover: A Public Life.* New York: Knopf, 1979.
Cedar Rapids (Iowa) Evening Gazette and Republic. August 21, 1928.
Emery, Ann. *American Friend: Herbert Hoover.* Chicago: Rand McNally, 1967.
Hoover, Herbert. *The Memoirs of Herbert Hoover: Years of Adventure, 1874–1920.* New York: Macmillan, 1951.
Hoover, Lou Henry. *Memories of a Little House and Some Later Remembrances of its Occupants.* West Branch, Iowa: Herbert Hoover Library, 1941.
Lyons, Eugene. *Herbert Hoover: A Biography.* New York: Doubleday, 1948.
McGee, Dorothy Horton. *Herbert Hoover: Engineer, Humanitarian, Statesman.* New York: Dodd Mead, 1965.
Nash, George H. *The Life of Herbert Hoover: The Engineer, 1874–1914.* New York: Norton, 1983.
Smith, Gene. *The Shattered Dream: Herbert Hoover and the Great Depression.* New York: Morrow, 1970.
Smith, Richard Norton. *An Uncommon Man: The Triumph of Herbert Hoover.* New York: Simon & Schuster, 1984.
West Branch (Iowa) Local Record. December 16, 1880, p. 1.
Wilson, Joan Hoff. *Herbert Hoover: Forgotten Progressive.* Boston: Little, Brown, 1975.

James Roosevelt
(1828–1900)

*Attorney, financier, public official,
gentleman farmer, and father of
President Franklin D. Roosevelt*

When he spoke about his father, James Roosevelt, Franklin D. Roosevelt said: "He was the most generous and kindly of men, and always liberal in outlook. . . . My father was no snob." If not a snob, James was at least selective about his associates. As a case in point, when his nouveau riche Hyde Park neighbors, the Vanderbilts, invited the Roosevelts to dinner, James politely declined on the grounds that accepting the invitation would obligate them to invite the Vanderbilts into their home.

The father of America's thirty-second president was born in Hyde Park, New York, on July 16, 1828. James was the older of two sons born to Isaac and Rebecca Aspinwall Roosevelt. Isaac was a graduate of Princeton University and the Columbia College of Physicians and Surgeons, but he spent little time practicing medicine. Reputedly, Isaac could not bear the sight of blood or of human suffering. When James was four, his family moved to a large estate Isaac had named Rosedale. Like his son Franklin, James grew up in a world of wealth and privilege. The Poughkeepsie Collegiate School was the first school James attended. The school catered exclusively to "gentlemen's sons." At the age of thirteen, James was enrolled at a school in Lee, Massachusetts, that specialized in educating unruly boys.

Roosevelt biographers do not provide any evidence that James was more unruly than any normal thirteen-year-old boy. It is highly likely that the nervous and eccentric Issac Roosevelt was worried that James was picking up bad habits from his classmates. If James had acquired any bad habits, his new school was definitely the place to lose them. Religious instruction was strongly emphasized. The school day began and ended with prayer services. Sundays were exclusively days of worship with no respite for meals. Students were allotted a quota of spice cookies to sustain them during the Sabbath.

In spite of the school's highly structured environment and pervasive religiosity,

Isaac was still deeply concerned about James's behavior. In a letter to the school's headmaster, Isaac expressed his concern about James reading fiction, tempering his worry with the comment, "I have no objection to his reading occasionally a well-written and moral or religious work of fiction." In letters to James, Isaac admonished his son, "Repent, believe in the Lord Jesus and lead a life of holy obedience to his commands," and, "I often wonder if the extent of your love is as great as mine."

James caused his worried father further distress when he went off to college. James adamantly insisted on going to New York University in Manhattan while Isaac wanted him to choose a school in a "quiet country village" locale. They compromised, and James went to college in the big city but had to live with his grandparents. James additionally agreed to take only day classes and to resist all temptations which "are mortifying to the feelings and put boys' tempers as well as their principles to a severe test."

James stayed at New York University only for one semester. Sometime in May James and three classmates were reprimanded by the school's administration for causing "disorder" in a mathematics classroom. In June James failed to take his final exams in mathematics and Latin. After leaving New York University, James attended Union College in Schenectady, New York. Apparently he had a pleasant time there. A diary entry from a classmate, Albert C. Ingham, dated June 15, 1846, reads: "I was in Charley Nott's room and found him and Roosevelt drunk. They asked me to drink but were too drunk to hand me any liquor so I got none." Another entry from Ingham's diary dated February 26, 1847, reports that he had to testify in student court that James and three of their classmates showed up at a dancing school in an inebriated condition.

A letter written by Isaac to James in the fall of 1846 admonishes James for joining a Greek letter fraternity:

> I was this morning both grieved and astonished by the reception of a letter from Dr. Nott respecting your membership in a secret society contrary to the laws of the college. I mean the society which holds its meetings at a tavern. I must request you to dissolve all connection immediately with the society. . . . Remember my dear son your promise that while at college you would not give your mother or me the least anxiety on your account.

Despite his reported drinking and carousing, James graduated from Union College with a Bachelor of Arts degree in the summer of 1847. By then James was back in the school's good graces and was even chosen to deliver the class oration at commencement.

Being a young gentleman of means, James was in no particular hurry to enter the job market. From November of 1847 to May of 1849, he leisurely toured Europe. There he received his only military training and experience when he joined the encamped army of Giuseppe Garibaldi on his travels through Italy. For about thirty days James drilled with the Italian patriot's peasant soldiers. According to some sources, James was frightened of going off to war while other sources claim that

James Roosevelt. Courtesy of the Franklin D. Roosevelt Library.

after a month of soldiering he was bored with it. In any case, James asked for and received a discharge so he could continue his travels.

After returning to the states, James enrolled in Harvard Law School. He was admitted to the New York Bar in 1851 and began working for the New York City attorney Benjamin D. Silliman. In 1853 James married his first wife, Rebecca Brien Howland. He was twenty-five and she was twenty-two. They had one child, a son they named James Roosevelt Roosevelt.

Within a year after entering the Silliman law firm, James became the director of the Consolidated Coal Company of Maryland. A short while later, he abandoned the practice of law to become a financier and gentleman farmer/country squire. At his estate, James could often be found wearing an imported tweed suit and carrying a riding crop.

James opted to avoid taking part in the Civil War. He was in his early thirties when the fighting began. He may have hired a substitute to fight in his place. During the Civil War, it was a legal and common practice for men with money to buy their way out of conscription. However, as Geoffrey C. Ward put it in his biography, *Before the Trumpet,* "Exactly what James Roosevelt did do during the war remains a mystery." Franklin Roosevelt alleged that his father worked as a member of the sanitary commission, which provided aid to sick and wounded soldiers and their families. However, there is no written evidence to support that claim.

Isaac Roosevelt died in 1863 at the age of seventy-three. As the oldest son, James received the lion's share of his father's considerable fortune. Whatever other worries James might have, lack of money would never be one of them.

In the summer of 1865, James's home at Mount Hope burned to the ground and most of the Roosevelt family papers and heirlooms were destroyed in the fire. James and Rebecca were vacationing in Europe at the time. Arson by a disgruntled servant was suspected but never proven. James sold the property to the state of New York for $45,000. The state used the land to build the Hudson River State Hospital, an asylum for the mentally ill. James used the money from the sale of his property to build a new home. He purchased 110 acres of heavily wooded land and built a house he named Springwood. The home would later become the birthplace and boyhood home of Franklin D. Roosevelt.

Prior to 1880, James engaged in two ambitious and daring business ventures. Both were failures. With his uncle, William Henry Aspinwall, James founded the Consolidation Coal Company. By 1868 the company had become America's largest bituminous coal company. James and William attempted to establish an absolute monopoly of the coal mines in the Cumberland Mountains region of Kentucky and Tennessee. Huge profits were anticipated, but those grand hopes were destroyed by the Panic of 1873. Because of the Panic, hundreds of factories were shut down. Railroad construction came to a virtual standstill. Rail traffic was drastically reduced and so was the demand for coal. In 1875 a stockholders revolt removed James and William from power.

The Panic of 1873 also thwarted an attempt to acquire monopoly control over the railroads of the southeastern United States. In 1872 James was elected president of a holding company called the Southern Railway Security Company. Through that holding company, the Pennsylvania Railroad and a group of New York investors poured millions of dollars into buying up other railroads. They accomplished their objective of obtaining a regional rail monopoly, but adverse economic conditions prevented the venture from turning any significant profits. Within a few years the Southern Railway Security Company was forced out of business.

In addition to these financial setbacks, James also had to cope with the death of Rebecca in August of 1876. At the age of forty-eight, James found himself suddenly single. After observing a suitable period of mourning, James resumed an active social life and immersed himself in his business and civic activities. Prior to Rebecca's death, James had served as a supervisor of the town of Hyde Park. He was also on the board of directors of the state hospital built on his former property and a member of the board of trustees of St. Francis Hospital in Poughkeepsie. In addition, he was a vestryman and senior warden of St. James's Episcopal Church. When he desired company, James could visit the finer New York clubs he belonged to. He was a member of the Century, the Metropolitan, and the Manhattan Clubs. James also maintained memberships in the Holland Society, Delta Phi, the Metropolitan Club of Washington, and a yacht club.

Though he kept himself busy, James was still achingly aware that club memberships, business deals, and civic involvement were no substitute for female companionship. Ward writes that sometime in 1877 James fell in love with Theodore Roosevelt's sister, Anna. In 1880, he proposed to her. Anna was disturbed that James had misread her, mistaking friendship for love. Anna's mother, Mittie was able to tactfully rebuff James. Fortunately, the closing of one door opened another for the lonely widower. On an April evening in 1880 Mittie Roosevelt held a dinner party at her Manhattan home. Twenty-five year old Sara "Sallie" Delano was one of the guests. James was quickly smitten. The hostess later said, "He never took his eyes off her!" Roosevelt biographers describe the young, dark-haired, dark-eyed Sara Delano as a woman of aristocratic beauty. Her haughty and aloof manner had been known to intimidate would-be suitors. James Roosevelt was different. He was too much in love to be intimidated.

Now in his early fifties, James Roosevelt was still a strikingly handsome man. His rust-colored muttonchops were now speckled with gray, and his waist was thickening, but his deep-set eyes, firm jaw, and poised, dignified, and urbane manner compensated for what age had taken away.

In May of 1880 Sara visited James at Springwood. Mittie Roosevelt and her two daughters came along as chaperones. During her week-long stay, Sara became convinced that James would propose to her. She later wrote, "If I had not come then; I should now be 'old Miss Delano' after a rather sad life!" Sometime in June of 1880 James traveled to Warren Delano's country home seeking the father's permission to marry Sara. However, Warren had some serious doubts and reservations. At age fifty-two, James was more than twice Sara's age. Using his charm and powers of persuasion, James got Warren to change his mind. Warren later said of James, "He is the first person that has made me realize that a Democrat can be a gentleman."

On October 7, 1880, James Roosevelt and Sara Delano were married at Warren's Algonac estate in the presence of 125 guests. Sara's neck was adorned by a five-strand pearl necklace James had given her as a wedding gift. One month later, the Roosevelts left for a ten-month European vacation/honeymoon. By mid–September of 1881 the Roosevelts were back at Hyde Park and were preparing for the birth of a child in January.

The birth of Franklin Delano Roosevelt was a genuine ordeal for Sara. She was in labor for more than thirty-seven hours before Franklin was born. The birth occurred only after the attending physician had given Sara an overdose of chloroform, which made her unconscious. When Franklin left his mother's body, he was blue-skinned, limp, and in a respiratory trance. The traditional spankings failed to awaken the newborn baby. After the doctor administered artificial respiration, Franklin bellowed a loud, but welcome, cry. In Sara's diary James wrote: "At quarter till nine my Sallie had a splendid large baby boy. He weighs 10 lbs., without clothes." Sara remained bedridden for the next thirty days after Franklin's birth. It is believed that she was advised not to have any more children and that after Franklin's birth, James and Sara practiced the severest and most successful method of birth control — total abstinence.

Since James was fifty-four when Franklin was born, he has sometimes been depicted as a doting but distant father, too old and frail to engage in the rough and tumble horseplay of male bonding. In fact, however, James spent considerable time with Franklin. He taught his son to sled, swim, skate, fish, hunt, and ride horses. Franklin often accompanied his father when James made the rounds of his estate. From his father, Franklin received much of his knowledge in forestry, farming, and land management.

Between the ages of two and fourteen, Franklin made eight trips to Europe with his parents. Most of the visits were undertaken so James could go to various hot springs; he was a firm believer in the healthful effects of soaking in mineral waters. As Ted Morgan puts it in his book, *FDR: A Biography,* "The pattern of Franklin's childhood was determined by his father's health."

There is no mention of James ever using corporal punishment or physical force to discipline Franklin. On the rare occasions when Sara thought James needed to punish their son, James would tell Franklin, "Consider yourself spanked."

In contrast to Franklin, James was only slightly interested in politics. A life-long Democrat, James left his party to vote for his distant relative Theodore in 1898 and 1900. President Grover Cleveland once offered James a foreign diplomatic post, but James turned it down. When Franklin was five, he accompanied his father to the White House to meet President Cleveland. As James and Franklin were leaving, President Cleveland patted Franklin on the head and told him, "My little man, I am making a strange wish for you. I hope that you may never be President of the United States."

Franklin's carefree days of playing with the man he affectionately called "Popsie" ended when the future president was eight years old. James suffered a serious heart attack, which made him a virtual invalid for the last ten years of his life. In her book, *No Ordinary Time,* Doris Kearns Goodwin explains that James's heart attack had a profound influence on the development of Franklin's personality: "From that point on, the boy's built-in desire to please his parents by being a 'nice little boy' was amplified by the fear that if he ever appeared other than bright and happy it might damage his father's already weakened heart."

The only recorded conflict between father and son after the heart attack occurred when Franklin wanted to go to school at the U.S. Naval Academy. Franklin had become immensely interested in naval history, and he told James that he wanted to go to Annapolis and become a naval officer. James sternly told Franklin that since he would eventually inherit a large estate, he needed to stay closer to home. He advised Franklin: "Study law as I did. It prepares a man for any profession." Aware of his father's wishes and frail health, Franklin acquiesced.

In the twilight of his life, James saw one more attempt at amassing great wealth become another shattered dream. James had backed a project to build a canal through Nicaragua. The project collapsed shortly before James's death when Panama was chosen as the canal site.

By November of 1900 James was seriously ill. To be closer to his doctors, Sara and James moved from Springwood to an apartment in New York City. As James grew weaker, Franklin was summoned from his classes at Harvard University to be by his father's bedside. Franklin arrived at their apartment on December 5 and did all he could to comfort his moribund father. By the afternoon of December 9, there was nothing more Franklin could do. James Roosevelt was dead at the age of seventy-two. Sara and his two sons were with him when he died. James's last words to Sara were: "Only tell Franklin to be a good man."

His obituary in the December 9, 1900, issue of the *New York Herald* reported: "Death was due to heart failure and while not unexpected was quite sudden.... He was taken so suddenly with the fatal attack which ended his life that there was not sufficient time in which to summon a physician before he expired.... He leaves a widow and two sons, J. Roosevelt Roosevelt and Franklin Delano Roosevelt."

Bibliography

Churchill, Allen. *The Roosevelts: American Aristocrats*. New York: Harper & Row, 1965.
Collier, Peter, and David Horowitz. *The Roosevelts: An American Saga*. New York: Simon & Schuster, 1994.
Davis, Kenneth S. *FDR: The Beckoning of Destiny, 1882–1928. A History*. New York: Putnam's, 1971.
Freidel, Frank. *Franklin D. Roosevelt: The Apprenticeship*. Boston: Little, Brown, 1952.
Freidel, Frank. *Franklin D. Roosevelt: A Rendezvous with Destiny*. Boston: Little, Brown, 1990.
Goodwin, Doris Kearns. *No Ordinary Time*. New York: Simon & Schuster, 1994.
Hess, Stephen. *America's Political Dynasties*. Garden City, N.Y.: Doubleday, 1966.
Larsen, Rebecca. *Franklin D. Roosevelt: Man of Destiny*. New York: Franklin Watts, 1991.
Lash, Joseph P. *Eleanor and Franklin*. New York: Norton, 1971.
Morgan, Ted. *FDR: A Biography*. New York: Simon & Schuster, 1985.
New York Herald. December 9, 1900.
Ward, Geoffrey C. *Before the Trumpet: Young Franklin Roosevelt, 1882–1905*. New York: Smithmark, 1994.

John Anderson Truman (1851–1914)

Farmer, livestock dealer, watchman, public official, and father of President Harry S Truman

Harry S Truman expressed how his father, John Anderson Truman, influenced his life when he told his biographer William Hillman,

> My father was a very energetic person. He worked from daylight to dark, all the time. And his code was honesty and integrity. His word was good. When he told us that something was a fact . . . that was just what it was: it was the truth. And he raised my brother and myself to put honor above profit. He was quite a man my dad was. . . . He was not a talker. He was an acter. He lived what he believed, and taught the rest of us to do the same thing.

The father of America's thirty-third president was born in Platte County, Missouri, on December 5, 1851. John was one of five children (three girls and two boys) born to Anderson Shippe Truman and Mary Jane Holmes Truman. John had little formal education. He attended a rural school for a few years and presumably left school to work on the family farm.

John was in his late twenties when he first met Martha Ellen Young. How and when they first met is unknown. In his biography, *Truman*, David McCullough speculates that they may have met at an informal dance. At five feet, four inches, John was at least two inches shorter than Martha. Obviously, that did not matter. John Truman always made a good first impression. His thin, reddish-brown hair was always neatly trimmed and combed. He was fastidious about his appearance and was cheerful and eager to please. John was also industrious, ambitious, and sincere. In short, he was a very likable person. John and Martha were married in the parlor of Martha's Grandview, Missouri, home on December 28, 1881. John was thirty and Martha was twenty-nine. Shortly after their wedding, John and Martha settled in Lamar, Missouri.

In November of 1882 John acquired a twenty-by-twenty-eight feet, six-room house for $685. For an additional $200, he purchased a barn and went into the

John Anderson Truman. Courtesy of the Harry S Truman Library, Deane Photography Studies.

business of buying, selling, and trading horses and mules. In terms of prestige and community esteem, a mule trader was the nineteenth century equivalent of a used car salesman. Anderson Shippe Truman was surprised by his son's career choice. He noted that no one believed a horse trader even when he was telling the truth. Undaunted, John placed an ad in the *Lamar Democrat* proclaiming: "Mules bought and sold. I will keep for sale at the White Barn on Kentucky Avenue a lot of good mules. Anyone wanting teams will do well to call on J. A. Truman."

In the autumn of 1882 John and Martha had their first child, an unnamed son who was stillborn. On May 8, 1884, Harry S Truman was born in their small Lamar home at four in the afternoon. The attending physician received a $15 fee. To celebrate Harry's birth, John planted a pine seedling in his front yard. Several Truman biographies also report that John also nailed a mule shoe over his front door for good luck, but according to McCullough that story is apocryphal.

According to Richard Lawrence Miller's book, *Truman: The Rise to Power,* John's mule trading business was "adequate," and dozens of animals passed through the Truman sale barn every week. However, John must have felt that he could do better in another town because in March of 1885 he sold his house for $1,600 and moved his family to Harrisonville, Missouri. Exactly why John left Lamar remains unknown. He did not leave as a failed businessman. He came to Harrisonville with enough money to reestablish himself in the horse and mule trading business.

John's time in Harrisonville was even shorter than his stay in Lamar. This time, business failure may have been his reason for moving. After less than two years in Harrisonville, John made another move and a job change. John rented seventy-one acres of farmland from Isaac P. Dye, a farmer turned prospector, and he began raising corn. John must not have done too well as a tenant farmer. In 1887 he moved his family to the farm of his father-in-law, Solomon Young. Martha may have persuaded her father to take John in as a partner. At the age of thirty-six, John may have been feeling the pangs of a midlife crisis. He was a failed businessman and farmer with a wife and two children to support. Despite years of initiative, enterprise, and hard work, John Truman was utterly dependent on his father-in-law for bed, board, and income.

John and his family stayed on the Young farm from 1887 to 1890. McCullough describes those years as "a time of self-contained security and plenty, such as the Trumans were not to know again." "Never, never give up," was one of John's favorite adages. He believed in those words and lived by them. Now nearly forty and with a family numbering five, John detested his dependence on Solomon Young. An inheritance from his recently deceased father gave John one more opportunity to achieve financial independence.

John moved his family to Independence, Missouri, and resumed the trade of livestock dealer and trader. Along with horses and mules, John began dealing in hogs, sheep, goats, and cattle. He also started dabbling in real estate. According to Richard Lawrence Miller, in December of 1890 John purchased several adjoining lots on Crysler Street in Independence for $4,000. He made a $1,000 down payment and mortgaged the other $3,000. Three months later, he sold the property to a brother-in-law for $4,300. About a year after that, John bought two lots for $600.

John and Harry shared several common traits and interests: a passionate interest in politics, a pugnacious personality and an explosive temper, a love of books and reading, and a belief that one had to make good on one's debts. As quoted in

Plain Speaking, Harry S Truman told interviewer Merle Miller that his father "never liked to miss a political meeting and he often took me along with him." The year Harry was born, John won a $75 bet that Grover Cleveland would be elected president.

The first Democratic National Convention Harry attended was the one in 1900 when he accompanied his father to Kansas City. The Trumans witnessed the renomination of William Jennings Bryan. John also served as a delegate to the Missouri State Democratic Convention in 1908, and his political connections got him the job of road overseer for Jackson County, Missouri.

Anecdotes and recollections about John Anderson's bellicose behavior appear in *Plain Speaking*. Harry S Truman told Merle Miller a story about a man called Colonel Crisp who tried to welsh on paying John a $27 debt for nine cords of wood. When Crisp balked at paying, John Truman told him, "all right I'll take it out of your hide then." After hearing that, Crisp promptly paid up. Truman also told Merle Miller, "My father was a fighter, and if he didn't like what you did, he'd fight you . . . he'd whip anybody up to two hundred [pounds] if they got in his way."

Richard Lawrence Miller reports that John engaged in fistfights with political opponents and once beat up a man who had criticized a candidate he was supporting. Richard Lawrence Miller also quotes an anecdote about John striking a man in the face with a whip.

Despite his father's penchant for violence, Harry S Truman said that his father never spanked him. He told Merle Miller, "He could give you a scolding that would burn the hide off of you. I'd rather have taken a licking." One anecdote about John punishing Harry is related in some of the Truman biographies. John had bought Harry a Shetland pony, which Harry would ride alongside his father's mount. During one of their rides Harry fell off the pony. John refused to slow down so his son could remount. He told his son that he should stay on foot if he could not stay on a pony at a walk. Harry had to walk half a mile to get home. He later wrote: "I learned a lesson."

The father and son's shared love of books and reading is also illustrated in *Plain Speaking*. Harry S Truman talked to Merle Miller about his father reading to him from Plutarch's *Lives*. Harry credited the works of the ancient Greek biographer with giving him insights in understanding modern politicians: "He [Plutarch] knew more about politics than all the other writers I've read put together. When I was in politics, there would be times when I tried to figure somebody out, and I could always turn to Plutarch, and nine times out of ten I'd be able to find a parallel in there."

When Harry was in his teens, John took one final gamble at the big deal and the reward of financial security. Using his life savings and the liquid assets from a farm Martha had inherited, John started speculating in grain futures at the Kansas City Board of Trade. The man who had dreamed of having it all, lost it all. Charles Robbins in his biography of Truman, *Last of His Kind,* reports that John's total losses were "about $30,000, and most of his landed property, including his pleasant home in Independence and a 160-acre farm his wife had recently inherited from her father." John's devastating financial losses forced Harry Truman to abandon his dream of going to college.

According to Cabell Phillips's book, *The Truman Presidency,* John and his family moved to Kansas City in 1902. McCullough writes that "In April 1903, John was once again in the livestock business, but this seems to have fared poorly. The next year he was a watchman for Missouri Elevator." During this time, Harry supplemented John's income by working in the mailroom of the *Kansas City Star* and then as a timekeeper for a railroad contractor. In or around 1905 John had to accept the humiliation of another financial rescue by his in-laws. The Youngs offered John the job of managing the Grandview farm he had left fifteen years earlier. John returned knowing he would probably spend the rest of his life there. In 1906, Harry left Kansas City to live with his parents at the Youngs' farm. Solomon Young was dead, and John was getting too old to run the place by himself. Evidently, Harry was also one of the few people who could put up with working for John. In her book, *Bess W. Truman,* Margaret Truman recalls that John "demanded as much work from his sons as from his hired hands who frequently quit in exasperation at his sharp tongue and minimal wages."

However, the years Harry and John spent working together on the farm greatly strengthened the bond between father and son. In his biography, *Harry S. Truman: Fair Dealer and Cold Warrior,* William E. Pemberton points out: "He [Harry] worked with his father and established himself as a man of worth in John's eyes, while proving to himself that he could do the physical and mental labor required to run a diverse enterprise of six hundred acres, with several hundred more of rented land." McCullough concurs with that conclusion: "The time with his father had also brought an important change. Working together in all seasons they had grown closer than either had ever supposed they might. Indeed, John Truman had come to depend on Harry and to respect his judgement."

According to Phillips, there were some years when the Grandview farm had annual profits as high as $15,000 and John was able to pay off his debts. However, Harry S Truman offers a differing account: "We never did catch up with our debts. We always owed the bank something — sometimes more, sometimes less, but we always owed the bank."

After an election that was held in either 1910 or 1912 (different sources give different dates), John Truman was appointed road overseer of district thirty in Jackson County. John became responsible for the repair and maintenance of county roads and bridges in that district. The job paid a mere two dollars a day, and the work never really ended. Filling mudholes and potholes, fixing culverts and bridges was just one aspect of the job. The position also entailed performing political duties. The overseer had to collect the poll tax from every registered voter in the district. The voter had the option of paying the three dollar tax or working on a county road crew for three days. John was also empowered to hire and fire workers, so he could reward political allies and punish political foes. John was as hard on his road crews as he had been on his farm workers. Harry S Truman recalled that road workers would "beef about it on the job [but] they'd go home and brag about how old man Truman gave the taxpayers a fair break. I was taught the expenditure of public money is a public trust."

While working as road overseer, John Truman fatally injured himself. In his typically stubborn and independent manner, John tried to single-handedly move a boulder. He developed a severe hernia, which caused an intestinal blockage. In October of 1914 John underwent surgery to relieve the blockage. The operation was successful, but John never fully recovered. John Truman died on the morning of November 2, 1914. Harry was at his father's bedside when John died at the age of sixty-two.

A headline on the front page of the November 3, 1914, edition of the *Independence Examiner* lauded John S. Truman as "An Upright Citizen Whose Death Will Be a Blow to His Community." His obituary reported: "Mr. Truman became dangerously ill about two months ago. Later he was taken to the Swedish Hospital in Kansas City, where an operation for a disorder of the stomach was performed. About a week ago he was taken back home." The obituary also added, "he stood high in the esteem of his fellow members of the Jackson County Road Overseers Association and of the County officials with whom he had dealings." The death of John Truman gave Harry S Truman his first public office. Harry was appointed to replace John as road overseer.

Many years after John's death, Merle Miller asked Harry S Truman: "Would you say that your father was a success?" The ex–President gave an answer that made the question seem superfluous: "He was the father of a president of the United States, and I think that is success enough for any man."

Bibliography

Ferrell, Robert H., editor. *The Autobiography of Harry S. Truman*. Boulder, Co.: Colorado Associated University Press, 1980.
Hillman, William. *Mr. President*. New York: Farrar, Straus & Young, 1952.
Independence (Missouri) Examiner. November 3, 1914, p. 1.
McCullough, David. *Truman*. New York: Simon & Schuster, 1992.
Miller, Merle. *Plain Speaking: An Oral Biography of Harry S. Truman*. New York: Berkley Books, 1973.
Miller, Richard Lawrence. *Truman: The Rise to Power*. New York: McGraw-Hill, 1986.
Pemberton, William E. *Harry S. Truman: Fair Dealer and Cold Warrior*. Boston: Twayne, 1989.
Phillips, Cabell. *The Truman Presidency: The History of a Triumphant Procession*. New York: McMillan, 1966.
Robbins, Charles. *Last of His Kind*. New York: Morrow, 1973.
Truman, Harry S. *Memoirs*. Vol. 1, *Year of Decisions*. Garden City, N.Y.: Doubleday, 1955.
Truman, Margaret. *Bess W. Truman*. New York: Morrow, 1973.
Underhill, Robert. *The Truman Persuasions*. Ames, Iowa: Iowa State University Press, 1981.

David Jacob Eisenhower (1863-1942)

Merchant, engine wiper, mechanic, gas company plant manager, director of employee savings plan, and father of President Dwight D. Eisenhower

In his diary, Dwight D. Eisenhower was able to unabashedly write: "I loved my Dad." That was no easy feat, for David Jacob Eisenhower was not an easy man to love. Stern, autocratic, moody, reserved, and aloof, the father of America's thirty-fourth president was more likely to engender fear rather than love in the hearts of Dwight and his other five sons. In his autobiography, *At Ease,* Dwight Eisenhower maintained that his parents had a "genuine partnership," but he was quick to add, "Father was the breadwinner, Supreme Court and Lord High Executioner." Whatever was good for the father was good for the rest of the family.

David Jacob Eisenhower was born in Elizabethville, Pennsylvania, on September 23, 1863, to Jacob and Rebecca Eisenhower. Jacob and Rebecca had fourteen children and Eisenhower biographers do not record how many were born before and after David. Jacob was a farmer and a leader in the River Brethren sect of the Mennonites. The sect's name derived from their practice of river baptisms. In 1878 Jacob sold his Pennsylvania farm for $8,500 and moved his family and about three hundred fellow members of the sect to Kansas. They formed a colony in Dickinson County. Jacob purchased a 160-acre farm, and apparently he did quite well financially. Jacob was able to give each of his children $2,000 in cash and a 160-acre farm as wedding gifts.

David openly detested the mundane, repetitive farm chores he had to do. The only aspect of farm life he enjoyed was tinkering with machinery. David wanted to escape the farm by becoming an engineer. However, his father had other plans. Being a devout member of the River Brethren, Jacob was firmly convinced that farming was God's work and engineering was not. Nevertheless, David persisted until Jacob relented. In the fall of 1883 David enrolled at Lane University in Lecompton, Kansas.

The curriculum of the now defunct school was a mixture of classical education

David Jacob Eisenhower. Courtesy of the Dwight D. Eisenhower Library.

and vocational training. David took courses in mechanics, penmanship, rhetoric, mathematics, Greek, and engineering. Eisenhower biographers do not record anything about David's grades, but they agree that David's desire to get his degree greatly lessened after Ida Elizabeth Stover enrolled at Lane University in the fall of 1884.

David and Ida fell in love even though their personalities were quite different.

David was quiet, shy, somber, and he seldom smiled. Biographers characterize Ida as outgoing with a hearty laugh, a twinkle in her eyes, and an ever-present grin. Despite his gloomy nature, David was still physically attractive. David was swarthy with thick black hair, thin lips, deep-set eyes, and muscular, broad shoulders. David married Ida on his twenty-second birthday (September 23, 1885) at the chapel of Lane University. She was twenty-three at the time.

For a wedding gift, Jacob gave David the customary $2,000 cash and the 160-acre farm. David was still dead set against being a farmer, so he mortgaged the farm to his brother-in-law, Chris Musser, and used the money to purchase a general store in Hope, Kansas. David went into partnership with Milton Good, an experienced salesman and retailer. Their plan for success was for David to provide the capital and for Good to supply the business acumen. If names meant much, a store in Hope with a partner named Good would have been quite profitable. However, the store went bankrupt in just two years for a number of reasons. The price of wheat fell to fifteen cents a bushel, and farmers could not pay their bills. A grasshopper invasion had also decimated farm crops. In addition, David had overextended credit to many customers. There was also talk that David and Ida simply lived beyond their means.

Moreover, Good had also absconded with most of the store's inventory, leaving David to deal with the creditors. David hired a lawyer to settle the debts. David's store was sold, his mortgage on the farm was foreclosed and the money left after paying off the debts was pocketed by the lawyer as his fee. David was left with his wife's piano and a lifelong distrust of lawyers. In his later years, David was quite unhappy when his son Edgar became a lawyer. After having satisfied his creditors, David temporarily left his pregnant wife and infant son to go looking for work away from Hope. Some friends in Hope housed and fed Ida and her infant son, Arthur. David was not with his wife when their second son, Edgar, was born in January of 1889.

David found work in Denison, Texas, as a $10-a-week engine wiper for the Missouri-Kansas-Texas Railroad. By March of 1889 he was able to send for Ida and his two sons. They moved into a tiny, rented frame house described as not much more than a shack. The time David spent working for the MKT must have been the bleakest and most depressing time of his life. He was stuck in a menial, low-paying job with no prospect of upward mobility. Only in his late twenties, David was a college dropout and a failed businessman who had squandered a considerable inheritance.

During this time of despondency David turned to mysticism and became an avid student of pyramidology. He drew a large chart (ten feet high and six feet wide) depicting the three Egyptian pyramids. David became convinced that the dimensions of the pyramids confirmed biblical events and that the three structures contained the answers to all things, past, present, and future. In his book, *Ike the Soldier: As They Knew Him*, Merle Miller reports that David "seemed to withdraw even farther from the real world."

The birth of a third son named David Dwight on October 14, 1890, did little to raise David's spirits. Another child was another mouth to feed and another drain on his meager income. The same day David Dwight was born (the first two names would later be transposed), David's mother died, but David did not have the money to travel to Abilene for her funeral.

Because of his family's intervention, David was finally able to escape the mind-numbing drudgery of scouring soot and grease from engines, twelve hours a day, six days a week. In the spring of 1891 Jacob came to David with a job offer. David's brother-in-law, Chris Musser, had become foreman of the Belle Springs Creamery, which was owned by the River Brethren. Jacob persuaded Musser to offer David a job as a mechanic/"engineer." On March 11, 1892, David signed a contract to work as a "refrigerating engineer." In other words, he was responsible for keeping the machinery running.

David's new job paid a paltry $340 a year. The job paid less than his engine wiper's position, but it was probably more fulfilling. In the spring of 1891, David, Ida, and their three sons arrived in Abilene. According to Eisenhower biographers, when they arrived, David had exactly $24 to his name. During their first seven years in Abilene, the Eisenhowers lived in a very small house just south of the railroad tracks. During that time, three more sons were born: Roy in 1892, Paul in 1894 (he died as an infant), and Earl in 1898. The yard was much too small for five energetic boys to play in. Ida complained that too much of her time was taken up keeping her sons out of other people's yards.

When the family was able to move to a larger home, it was due to the generosity of relatives and not because David was making substantially more money. David's brother, Abraham, had decided to move further west. Jacob had been living with Abraham, and he required a caretaker. David and Ida were offered Abraham's house at nominal rent with an option to buy in exchange for looking after Jacob. They readily accepted the offer. Compared to their previous homes in Denison and Abilene, the new home was positively palatial. It had 818 square feet of living space with an attic and basement and was located on a three-acre plot. There was also a barn with a hayloft and stalls for the farm animals. The three acres also allowed the family to have an orchard, a vegetable garden, and a smokehouse.

Life in the Eisenhower home centered around David's whims, wishes, and commands. Since David rose shortly after 5 A.M., so did the rest of the family. Arthur Eisenhower recalled: "We never dared to stay out after nine o'clock at night." All the boys had numerous chores to perform. Failure to do chores resulted in quick punishment. David had no qualms to energetically use a maple switch or a leather strap on his sons. David never took his lunch to work with him. Instead, Ida unfailingly prepared a hot lunch for one of the boys to deliver to the creamery. Like staying out late, failing to deliver the hot lunch was something the Eisenhower boys did not dare to do.

The Eisenhower family also placed a strong emphasis on worship. There were daily prayers (morning and evening) and Bible readings. David and Ida did not smoke, drink, swear, play cards, or gamble. However, Dwight and all of their other children would indulge in those activities as adults. Eisenhower biographers report that the children never heard their parents raise their voices to each other or argue. The reason was simple: Ida went along with everything David wanted.

In the first volume of his mammoth biography of Dwight D. Eisenhower, Stephen E. Ambrose characterizes Dwight's father: "David was something of a stranger and a terror to his children. He was aloof, paying little attention to their youthful successes or disappointments, seldom discussing with them their activities, hopes or dreams." Merle Miller in his book, *Ike the Soldier,* comes to essentially the same assessment of David's relationship with his children: "David never played with his sons; he never taught them games. He did not take them hunting or fishing; he did not swim with them; he showed no interest in who their friends were."

Dwight Eisenhower devoted a seventeen-page chapter of his autobiography, *At Ease,* to his mother, but his father did not get such lengthy treatment. The longest anecdote he related about his father is a chilling account of David thrashing his son Edgar with a leather harness strap. Edgar had been skipping school to work for the town doctor. When David learned that Edgar had been deceiving him, he surprised him by being present when Edgar came home for lunch. Dwight Eisenhower recalled: "I never before or after saw him so angry. . . . Father in a surprise visit from the creamery, found us in the barn. His face was black as thunder. With no pause for argument, he reached for a piece of harness, a tug it was called, at the same time grabbing Ed by the collar he started in."

The flogging ended only after Dwight intervened by telling his raging father, "I don't think that anyone should be whipped like that, not even a dog." Dwight then justified his father's behavior: "Had it not been for the application of leather, prolonged and unforgettable, my brother might well have become an unhappy handyman in Kansas. . . . Undoubtedly fear that this boy would seriously damage all the years of life ahead provoked my father to a violent display of temper and temporary damage."

The year 1916 was a landmark year in David's life. He changed jobs and religions. In the summer of that year David attended the national convention of Jehovah's Witnesses in Washington, D.C. It is not known why he went and how he got there. However, it is recorded that news of his attendance there caused the River Brethren to summarily fire him from his job at the creamery. David then began working as a mechanic for the Abilene Gas Company, where he stayed until his retirement in 1931. While working there, David advanced from mechanic to plant manager to director of employee savings. In the latter position, David was responsible for making sure that eight hundred employees saved or invested at least ten percent of their salary every month.

Although he could advise others on how to save, David was not very good at it himself. In fairness to him, it must be remembered that he never made more than $200 a month. After his business failure, he never took any more financial risks or bought anything on credit. Edgar Eisenhower recalled that shortly before his death,

David told him: "I got something that has bothered me for a long time. I am not going to leave you boys anything. That breaks my heart." Edgar remembered, "Dad cried, the first time I ever saw him cry in his life."

David Eisenhower died at Abilene, Kansas, on May 10, 1942, at the age of seventy-nine. His obituary in the March 11, 1942, edition of the *Abilene Daily Chronicle* read in part: "Mr. Eisenhower was one of the community's most respected citizens and was active in business until around 1931 when he retired. . . . The six Eisenhower sons have distinguished themselves in their chosen fields and the community has watched their careers with great interest." Topping the list of the six sons that followed was Brigadier General Dwight D. Eisenhower, assistant chief of staff, war plans division, Washington, D.C.

When his father died, Dwight Eisenhower was routinely working sixteen hours a day, seven days a week. He was too busy to attend his father's funeral in Abilene. On March 10 Dwight wrote in his diary: "Dad died this morning. Nothing I can do but send a wire." The next day he wrote: "I'm quitting work now, 7:30 p.m. I haven't the heart to go on tonight." On March 12, the day of his father's funeral, Dwight mourned his father by closing his office for thirty minutes and by penning an eloquent eulogy:

> My father was buried today. I've shut off all business and visitors for thirty minutes, to have that much time, by myself, to think of him. He had a full life. . . . He was a just man, well liked, well educated, a thinker. He was undemonstrative, quiet, modest, and of exemplary habits — he never used alcohol or tobacco. He was an uncomplaining person in the face of adversity, and such plaudits as were accorded him did not inflate his ego.
>
> His finest monument is his reputation in Abilene and Dickinson County, Kansas. His word has been his bond and accepted as such; his sterling honesty, his insistence upon the immediate payment of all debts, his pride in his independence earned him a reputation that has profited all of us boys. . . . I'm proud that he was my father. My only regret is that it was always so difficult to let him know the great depth of my affection for him.

Bibliography

Abilene (Kansas) Daily Chronicle. March 11, 1942.
Ambrose, Stephen E. *Eisenhower: Soldier, General of the Army, President-Elect, 1890–1952.* New York: Simon & Schuster, 1983.
Beschloss, Michael R. *Eisenhower: A Centennial Life.* New York: Burlingame, 1990.
Brendon, Piers. *Ike: His Life and Times.* New York: Harper & Row, 1986.
Burk, Robert F. *Dwight D. Eisenhower: Hero and Politician.* Boston: Twayne, 1986.
Burke's Presidential Families of the United States of America. London: Burke's Peerage Ltd., 1975.
Childs, Marquis. *Eisenhower: Captive Hero.* New York: Harcourt, Brace, 1958.
David, Lester, and Irene David. *Ike and Mamie: The Story of the General and His Lady.* New York: Putnam's, 1981.

Davis, Kenneth S. *Soldier of Democracy: A Biography of Dwight Eisenhower.* Garden City, N.Y.: Doubleday, 1952.
Eisenhower, David. *Eisenhower: At War, 1943–1945.* New York: Vintage Books, 1986.
Eisenhower, Dwight D. *At Ease: Stories I Tell My Friends.* New York: Avon, 1967.
Ferrell, Robert H., editor. *The Eisenhower Diaries.* New York: Norton, 1981.
Hatch, Alden. *General Ike: A Biography of Dwight D. Eisenhower.* Cleveland: World Publishing Company, 1944.
Lyon, Peter. *Eisenhower: Portrait of a Hero.* Boston: Little, Brown, 1974.
Miller, Merle. *Ike the Soldier: As They Knew Him.* New York: Putnam's, 1987.
Neal, Steve. *The Eisenhowers: Reluctant Dynasty.* Garden City, N.Y.: Doubleday, 1978.

Joseph P. Kennedy Sr. (1888–1969)

Bank examiner, banker, businessman, public official, diplomat, and father of President John F. Kennedy

Historian Arthur M. Schlesinger Jr. reports in his book *A Thousand Days,* that John F. Kennedy summed up his father's influence on the Kennedy children by saying: "My father wasn't around as much as some fathers when I was young; but whether he was there or not, he made his children feel that they were the most important thing in the world to him. He was so terribly interested in everything we were doing. He held up standards for us, and he was very tough when we failed to meet those standards." When America's thirty-fifth president spoke of his father being terribly interested in their lives, he was understating the situation. A more common view of Joseph P. Kennedy's influence and dominance over the lives of his children is expressed by Doris Kearns Goodwin in her book, *The Fitzgeralds and the Kennedys*: "Joe Kennedy, having achieved an almost primitive dominion over his children's youthful souls, would rule his boys and girls for the rest of their lives."

Joseph Patrick Kennedy (hereinafter called Joe) was born in Boston, Massachusetts, on September 6, 1888. Joe was the first of four children (two boys and two girls) born to Patrick Joseph and Mary Augusta Hickey Kennedy. P. J., as Joe's father was commonly called, was a stevedore turned saloonkeeper. He bought his first tavern when he was twenty-two, and he helped to make the enterprise a profitable one by being a steadfast teetotaler. Profits from his saloons later allowed P. J. to branch out into coal, banking, and real estate.

P. J. had a natural affinity for politics. He naturally saw politics as a means of allowing himself and his fellow Irish immigrants to make economic inroads into the closed Boston society. One of Joe's early childhood memories was an election day when he heard two of his father's ward heelers proudly report that they had voted 128 times.

Even though his family was moderately well off, Joe began working part-time jobs before he was in his teens. Earning money helped to satisfy his competitive urges, and it showed his less well-to-do Irish friends that he was one of the gang.

Joseph P. Kennedy Sr. Courtesy of the John F. Kennedy Library.

Joe sold newspapers, delivered hats, sold candy on an excursion steamer, and ran errands for his father's bank. Joe's cousin, Joseph Kane, recalled that whenever they met, Joe would always ask, "How can we make some money?"

Coupled with a keen interest in money was a fierce desire to succeed, which was nurtured by parents who had high expectations of their firstborn son. When Joe was thirteen, his parents enrolled him in the prestigious Boston Latin School. In her book, *The Kennedy Neurosis*, Nancy Gager Clinch writes: "We can see the familiar pattern of a parent projecting his own thwarted ambitions onto his son, a pattern that Joe Kennedy repeated with his own children." Although a poor student (he graduated one year behind his class at the Latin School), Joe was quite popular with his classmates. He was senior class president and captain of the baseball team for two years. During his senior year, Joe won the Mayor's Cup for having the highest batting average (.667) in the city high school league.

In the fall of 1908 Joe fulfilled his parents' desires by enrolling at Harvard. The snobs and snubs he encountered there he would remember for the rest of his life. In *The Founding Father*, Richard J. Whalen describes that social setting: "For the grandson of an immigrant and the heir of a saloonkeeper, Harvard could be a hard experience. There would be no crude discrimination of the bullying sort, but a subtle, cruel exclusion, to remind one that he was an intruder in a place to which others were born." At Harvard, Joe was more concerned with making the grade socially than academically. Because of his religion and economic status, Joe was automatically excluded from the "best" undergraduate clubs. However, as Whalen puts it, Joe "held his own socially at Harvard, he took fun where he found it." Clubs he was elected to include the Institute of 1770 and Hasty Pudding.

According to Whalen, the social snubs at Harvard were less damaging to Joe's psyche than to his ability to excel at a higher competitive level of baseball. Joe made the freshman team without much trouble, but he did not make the varsity squad until his junior or senior year. He won his varsity letter only because he played first base during the final out of the Harvard-Yale game. Whalen reports that it was only because of his father's influence that Joe even got into the game. Team captain "Chick" McLaughlin claimed that he asked his coach to put Joe into the game because he wanted to obtain a license to operate a movie theater after he graduated. McLaughlin said that friends of Joe's father told him that the license would be unobtainable unless Joe won his varsity letter. An unidentified teammate later told Whalen, "Joe was the kind of guy who, if he wanted something bad enough, would get it, and he didn't much care how he got it. He'd run right over anybody."

Joe graduated with a B.A. degree from Harvard in 1912. Thanks in part to his father's influence, he quickly obtained a job as a state bank examiner. By studying bank records and books, Joe soon learned how banks made their money and how they were connected to other businesses. In the fall of 1913 the Columbia Trust Company was in imminent danger of being bought out by the First Ward National Bank. P. J. Kennedy, who was a major shareholder, scraped up all the money he could and left it to Joe to stop the merger. By calling on friends, calling in favors, and borrowing to the hilt, Joe thwarted the planned merger. In appreciation, the directors of Columbia Trust elected Joe president. At the time it was widely reported that twenty-five-year-old Joe Kennedy was the youngest bank president in the United States. However, that claim was false; historian John H. Davis called it "pure Kennedy hype." Nevertheless, it clearly marked Joe Kennedy as a young man on the rise. Joe boldly and bluntly told a local newspaper reporter that he wanted to be a millionaire by his thirty-fifth birthday.

Wealth was not the only thing Joe had his mind set on. Shortly after becoming the president of the Columbia Trust Company, the Boston newspapers announced Joe's engagement to Rose Fitzgerald, daughter of Boston Mayor John Francis "Honey Fitz" Fitzgerald. Joe and Rose had first met during summer vacations in Old Orchard Beach, Maine, when they were children. They had dated as teens although Rose's father did not approve of Joe. It was only after Joe had become a Harvard graduate and a bank president that Honey Fitz grudgingly acquiesced to his daughter's romance.

In her autobiography, *Times to Remember*, Rose Fitzgerald Kennedy revealed that Joe never formally proposed. She recalled: "I don't think he ever did ask me, not just straight-out.... It was less a matter of 'Will you marry me?' than of 'When we get married.'" Rose also did not recall exactly when Joe gave her an engagement ring and what he said to her when he presented it. However, she described the ring in detail as "a two-carat stone, pure white, flawless, superb." Flawless jewelry was not the only thing Rose liked about Joe. She described him as a man who "smiled and laughed easily, and had a big, spontaneous, and infectious grin that made everybody in sight want to smile too. Even then, he had an aura of command, an attitude of being competent to take charge of any situation."

On October 7, 1914, they were married in a small private ceremony. The wedding was performed by Cardinal William O'Connell in his private chapel. Joe would later boast, "I always wanted to be married by a Cardinal and I was." After a two-week honeymoon, Joe and Rose moved into a $6,500 house in the predominantly Protestant Boston suburb of Brookline. Already deeply in debt from his purchase of Columbia Trust stock, Joe borrowed an additional $2,000 for a down payment on the house. Whalen sums up Joe's financial situation at that time: "Success, formerly a matter of pride with Kennedy was now an urgent necessity."

Less than ten months after their wedding day, the first of Joe and Rose's nine children (four boys and five girls) was born. Joseph P. Kennedy Jr. was born in Brookline on July 25, 1915. The parental expectations for Joe Jr. would be even more stringent than they had been for his father.

Due in part to Mayor Fitzgerald's influence and connections, Joe was able to boost deposits and add new business for the bank. The mayor also helped Joe by appointing him city director of the Collateral Loan Company. In his book, *Joseph P. Kennedy: A Life and Times*, David E. Koskoff calls the Collateral Loan Company "a large semipublic pawnshop established by the city to protect the poor from loansharks." After taking office and examining the books, Joe found evidence of large-scale embezzling. When the irregularities were exposed, five months of hearings, charges, and countercharges followed. The end result was that Joe disgustedly resigned his position.

In 1917 Joe was elected to the board of trustees of the Massachusetts Electric Company. He was named to the board on May 29, 1917, the same day that his second son, John Fitzgerald Kennedy, was born in Brookline.

On April 6, 1917, the United States entered World War I. Joe did not choose to enlist in any branch of the armed services. His decision was not well received by many of his Harvard classmates who enlisted and served. During the war Joe served as assistant general manager of the Fore River Shipyard in Quincy, Massachusetts. Joe turned the management of Columbia Trust over to his father and immersed himself in the supervision of 2,200 workers feverishly turning out ships for the war effort. Under Joe's management Fore River set new production records, but they came at a price. According to Koskoff, Joe worked himself into ill health, and his dealings with Assistant Secretary of the Navy Franklin D. Roosevelt also put him under great emotional strain. Joe later recalled, "Roosevelt was the hardest trader I ever ran up against. When I left his office, I was so disappointed and angry that I broke down and cried."

When the war and the shipbuilding boom ended, Joe went to work for the investment firm of Hayden, Stone and Company. In the wide open, unregulated bull market of the 1920s, Joe Kennedy learned the fine points of stock manipulation and began amassing his considerable fortune. One common practice of the time was for an operator to stimulate interest in a stock by buying and selling a large number of shares. "You simply advertised the stock by trading it," Joe once explained. When interest peaked, the operator would unload the stock and its value would drop.

Joe's profile in the 1940 annual edition of *Current Biography* highlights his years as a stock manipulator: "Until 1924 Kennedy moved in the 'intense secretive circles of operators in the wildest stock market in history, with routine plots and pools, inside information and wild guesses'—and he learned market operations thoroughly." Joe showed his considerable knowledge of the market and his ability to foresee future events when he told an associate, "It's easy to make money in this market. We'd better get in before they pass a law against it." In *A Question of Character,* Thomas C. Reeves describes how easily Joe achieved his stated goal of becoming a millionaire by the age of thirty-five: "By 1924, at thirty-five, Joe was a millionaire several times over. He drove a Rolls-Royce, hired a corps of servants and sent his family to New York two years later in a private railroad car that completed its trip at a private siding near the Kennedy's new home."

Recognizing the vast moneymaking potential of motion pictures, Joe entered that business in 1926. The owners of Film Booking Office of America (FBO) had been forced to sell out because they could not avoid taking short term loans at high rates of interest. Joe soon organized a syndicate to buy them out. FBO produced low budget westerns and melodramas for small-town audiences. Under Joe's leadership the studio began cranking out about one movie a week at an average cost of $30,000 a feature. During Joe's first year as head of the studio FBO generated an income of nearly $9 million. Anticipating the demise of silent movies, Joe entered into a partnership with David Sarnoff's Radio Corporation of America (RCA) in the fall of 1927. That partnership paved the way for Kennedy and Sarnoff to buy into a chain of movie theaters. In 1928 they gained control of the KAO theater chain with a $4.2 million stock purchase. The following fall, Joe was named head of the newly created RKO (Radio Keith Orpheum) studio. Whalen reports that when Joe left the movie business thirty-two months later, he was $5 million richer and more than thirty pounds underweight.

During his reign as a movie mogul, Joe had an extramarital affair with Hollywood legend Gloria Swanson. In her autobiography, *Swanson on Swanson,* she chronicles their affair and claims that Joe had sought permission from church officials to live apart from his family so they could live together. She writes that their affair ended after she discovered that Joe had charged many items to her account. The affair with Swanson was just one of Joe's many marital infidelities. George Smathers, who served in the U.S. Senate with John F. Kennedy, remarked about how the father and son had a propensity for chasing women: "Jack liked girls. He liked girls very much. He came by it naturally. His daddy liked girls. He was a chaser." Goodwin also notes the similarity: "Jack seemed to be imitating the pattern his father had established after the near-disaster of his affair with Gloria Swanson, a pattern of keeping his relationships with women both superficial and numerous. It appears that the Kennedy children not only knew about their father's womanizing but fully accepted it, so long as their mother was protected from public embarrassment."

Though he was often an absentee father, Joe remained a presence in his children's lives even when he was away. In her autobiography, Rose accurately labeled Joe "the architect of our lives." All of the Kennedy children received frequent letters from their father. Every Sunday the Kennedy children would line up in order of their ages (oldest first, youngest last) to speak to their father on the phone.

In *The Kennedys: Dynasty and Disaster, 1848–1983,* John H. Davis paints a grim picture of the Kennedy household: "Joe Kennedy ran a tense, Spartan household at Hyannis Port. The children were expected at meals five minutes ahead of time. . . . When father Joe spoke to a child at meals he expected to receive an intelligent answer back, no small talk or wisecracks. . . . The Kennedy children were never allowed to relax and be themselves." Whalen concurs with that characterization of Joe and quotes Eunice Kennedy Shriver: "Daddy was always very competitive. The thing that he always kept telling us was that coming in second was just no good. The important thing was to win—Don't come in second or third—that doesn't count—but win, win, win."

Joe's obsession with winning is cited as the reason he found it so difficult to accept his daughter Rosemary's mental retardation. Joe had refused to institutionalize her, saying, "What can they do for her that her family can't do better? We will keep her at home." However, by early adulthood Rosemary had become too difficult to control. Her tantrums, rages, and verbal abuse had become more than an embarrassment and an inconvenience. Rose's sister, Agnes Fitzgerald Gargan, described Rosemary as having "the body of a twenty-one-year-old yearning for fulfillment with the mentality of a four-year-old."

Without consulting Rose, Joe eventually had Rosemary lobotomized. He kept the operation a secret from his family and simply told Rose that it was time to institutionalize Rosemary and that the family should forego visiting her. According to Goodwin, it was not until 1961 that Rose finally learned the truth about her daughter's condition.

Joe had the uncommon good sense to get out of the stock market before the 1929 crash. When one of his friends expressed surprise at seeing him withdraw from the market, Joe said, "Only a fool holds out for top dollar." With his fortune safely intact, Joe was now free to turn his attention to politics.

Joe believed that Franklin D. Roosevelt was the man to back for president in 1932. It is not clear exactly when he decided to back Roosevelt, but he believed that the New York governor was a winner, and Joe had no use for losers. According to *Current Biography 1940*, Joe gave $15,000 to Roosevelt's 1932 campaign fund, loaned an additional $50,000, and contributed another $100,000 indirectly. Joe did not expect his generosity to go unnoticed and unrewarded. However, President Roosevelt was in no particular hurry to appoint Joe to any office. His first offer was to make him New York director of the National Recovery Administration. For a man of Joe's ambition, the offer was insulting. In June of 1934 President Roosevelt took everyone by surprise by proclaiming that Joe Kennedy was his choice for chairman of the newly created Securities and Exchange Commission.

To many it seemed incongruous to appoint the ultimate Wall Street insider to a position where he would be responsible for reforming and even abolishing the very practices that had made him a multimillionaire. John Flynn in the *New Republic* castigated Kennedy's appointment: "Had FDR's dearest enemy accused him of an intention of making so grotesque an appointment as Joseph Kennedy to the Chairman of the SEC, the charge might have been laid to malice. Yet the President has exceeded the expectations of his most ardent ill-wishers."

Joe served as SEC chairman for fifteen months. Goodwin calls Joe's tenure as chairman "his finest hours of public service." When Joe resigned as chairman in February of 1935, there were numerous newspaper and magazine editorials praising him for a job well done. The *Kansas City Star* wrote: "It was a real achievement for the administration to find a wizard who was able to take what was regarded as an unworkable act and make it work and make the moneyed interests like it." Joe's greatest vindication came from the man who had once been his harshest critic. In the October 1935 issue of *New Republic* John Flynn wrote:

> When Joseph Kennedy was named by President Roosevelt as a member of the SEC and in effect made its chairman I expressed in this department a sharp criticism of the appointment.... I ventured some criticisms of his record in a business which, I thought, made his appointment unwise. Now Mr. Kennedy has resigned as Chairman of the Commission. And I think it but fair to him to say that he disappointed the expectations of his critics. He was, I firmly believe, the most useful member of the Commission.

Shortly after leaving the SEC, Joe embarked on a European vacation with Rose and their daughter Kathleen. Before sailing off to England he told the press,

"I am going to feel that I am out of politics — if this is politics — for the rest of my natural life. I'm all through with public life." Nothing could have been further from the truth. Whalen reports that Joe served as an informal adviser and confidential emissary for President Roosevelt. He also did consulting work for Paramount Pictures, RCA, and William Randolph Hearst's publishing empire. Joe had also anticipated the inevitable end of Prohibition. He obtained the rights to become the exclusive American agent for several scotch and gin distillers. Reeves quotes FBI files estimating that after Prohibition Joe made an additional million dollars a year from his liquor franchises.

In 1936 Joe offered President Roosevelt his wholehearted support in the president's bid for reelection. He gave speeches, contributed money, and published a book entitled *I'm for Roosevelt*. The book was largely ghostwritten by journalist Arthur Krock and was an utterly uncritical endorsement of the New Deal. In the book Joe declared: "I have no political ambitions for myself or for my children as I put down these few thoughts about our President." In appreciation of Kennedy's support, President Roosevelt first appointed Joe Chairman of the U.S. Maritime Commission, but a much more prestigious post soon followed. In December of 1937 the President named Joe American ambassador to the Court of St. James's. The appointment was a public relations coup for the president. Joe was the first Irishman appointed to that important diplomatic post. Paper after paper reported how the grandson of an immigrant had fulfilled the American dream by acquiring great wealth and a vital political and diplomatic position.

Joe assumed the ambassadorial post with high hopes and great expectations. When he left it in the autumn of 1940, his career in public service was irrevocably over. He never received another government appointment. Whalen sums up Joe's tenure as ambassador: "the mission to London took Kennedy onto unfamiliar terrain; the acuity shown in business politics deserted him in diplomacy." By temperament and personality, Joe was unsuited to be a diplomat. He greeted visitors to his office with his feet propped up on his desk. He was constantly chewing gum, swore often, lost his temper in public, and he once referred to the queen as "a cute trick."

Those transgressions and social blunders were minor compared to his failure to correctly assess Hitler's intentions in Europe, which led him to urge President Roosevelt to adopt isolationist policies. Mere hours before the Nazis occupied Vienna, Kennedy wired the President that he believed Hitler was bluffing. After Hitler had annexed Austria and made it part of the Third Reich, Kennedy continued to misread the situation. He said: "I am sure I am right that none of these various moves has any significance for the United States, outside of general interest." He even publicly predicted that there would be no war in Europe. When Chamberlain capitulated to Hitler, Kennedy endorsed the action by saying that neither Britain nor France were militarily ready to fight Germany over Czechoslovakia. Eventually, Roosevelt and Churchill began conducting secret diplomatic talks, and they completely ignored Kennedy.

Despite their apparent falling out, Kennedy supported Roosevelt for a third term in 1940. After the Japanese attack on Pearl Harbor, Joe sent a telegram to the President:

DEAR MR. PRESIDENT
IN THIS GREAT CRISIS ALL AMERICANS ARE WITH YOU. NAME THE BATTLE POST. I'M YOURS TO COMMAND.

The only response from the White House was a form letter from the President's secretary acknowledging receipt of the telegram.

Joe did not serve in the armed forces in World War II, but three of his sons (Joe Jr., John, and Robert) did. Two of them survived the war. Joe Jr. did not, and his death sent Joe Kennedy into a profound and prolonged depression. Kennedy biographers concur that Joe Jr. had been Joe's favorite son and the son who was most like Joe. Joe Kennedy outlived four of his nine children, but none of their deaths affected him as deeply as Joe Jr.'s. For months Joe often sat alone for hours listening to classical music. According to Arthur Krock, the death of Joe Jr. "was one of the most severe shocks to the father that I've ever seen registered on a human being." When one of Joe Jr.'s former roommates visited the grief-stricken father, Joe burst into tears and said, "I feel bad that I was away so much when the boy was growing up. I didn't know him like I should have. I cheated him."

The political aspirations Joe once harbored for Joe Jr. were now transferred to John. According to Reeves, on Christmas of 1944 Joe bluntly told his oldest surviving son that he was to take Joe Jr.'s place and go into politics. John initially resisted, but Joe had his way. John later recalled: "It was like being drafted. . . . He demanded it. You know my father." In 1957 Joe boasted: "I got Jack into politics; I was the one. I told him Joe was dead and that it was therefore his responsibility to run for Congress." From John's election to the House of Representatives in 1946 to his ascendancy to the presidency in 1960, Joe orchestrated and bankrolled his son's political career. However, Joe always downplayed his role in his son's success. When asked what he did to help his son, he replied, "I just called people. I got in touch with people I knew. I have a lot of contacts. I've been in politics in Massachusetts since I was ten."

After getting John started in politics, Joe divided his time between New York and Palm Beach. He dabbled in real estate, oil, and gas and became even wealthier. He told one friend, "I really began to make money when I came down here [Palm Beach] to sit on my butt and think."

After John F. Kennedy was elected president of the United States in 1960, a friend telephoned Joe and asked him how it felt to be the father of the president. Joe candidly answered: "Hell, I don't know how it feels. Of course I'm proud, but I don't feel any different. I don't know how I feel." During the campaign Joe had stayed in the background, but after the election, he was constantly seen with his son. Joe explained it by saying: "There are no accidents in politics. I can appear with him any time I want to now." During the first year of the Kennedy administration Joe spent only one afternoon at the White House. However, father and son conversed on the phone as much as six times a day. White House aides said that the calls dealt mostly with family matters. But as Whalen points out, "politics was very much a family matter."

On December 19, 1961, while golfing in Palm Beach, Joe was stricken by a severe stroke. The stroke paralyzed the right side of his body, and Joe never recovered. Summoning his immense will to live, Joe Kennedy still lived long enough to see John and Bobby assassinated and to witness Teddy's Chappaquidick disgrace.

Joseph P. Kennedy Sr. died on November 18, 1969, at his home in Hyannis at the age of eighty-one. After a small, private funeral at the Hyannis Catholic Church, Joseph P. Kennedy Sr. was laid to rest at the Holyhood Cemetery in Brookline.

Joe's death was front page news in the November 19, 1968, edition of the *New York Times*. A full-page, eight-column, obituary chronicled his remarkable life. An editorial expressed how the *Times* viewed his place in history:

> Joseph Patrick Kennedy will go down in history primarily as the father of a distinguished and powerful family. Solely as a public official it is doubtful that he would rate more than a footnote, and that not more than half favorable. . . . He inculcated in his sons a passion for public affairs — business was a forbidden topic in the family circle — a devotion to each other, and a competitive spirit that had no use for defeat or even for "moral victories."
>
> The result was a family of spectacularly successful political leaders who owed the elder Kennedy much of their zest, some of their tactics, and happily little of their political philosophy.

Bibliography

Clinch, Nancy Gager. *The Kennedy Neurosis*. New York: Grosset & Dunlap, 1973.
Collier, Peter, and David Horowitz. *The Kennedys: An American Drama*. New York: Summitt, 1984.
Current Biography 1940. New York: H. W. Wilson, pp. 450–453.
Davis, John H. *The Kennedys: Dynasty and Disaster, 1848–1983*. New York: McGraw-Hill, 1984.
Goodwin, Doris Kearns. *The Fitzgeralds and the Kennedys: An American Saga*. New York: Simon & Schuster, 1987.
Hamilton, Nigel. *JFK: Reckless Youth*. New York: Random House, 1992.
Kennedy, Rose Fitzgerald. *Times to Remember*. Garden City, N.Y.: Doubleday, 1974.
Koskoff, David E. *Joseph P. Kennedy: A Life and Times*. Englewood Cliffs, N.J.: Prentice-Hall, 1974.
New York Times. November 19, 1968, pp. 1, 50–51, 54.
Reeves, Thomas C. *A Question of Character: A Life of John F. Kennedy*. New York: Free Press, 1991.
Schlesinger, Arthur M. Jr. *A Thousand Days: John F. Kennedy in the White House*. Boston: Houghton Mifflin, 1965.
Swanson, Gloria. *Swanson on Swanson*. New York: Random House, 1980.
Whalen, Richard J. *The Founding Father: The Story of Joseph P. Kennedy*. New York: New American Library, 1964.

Sam Ealy Johnson Jr.
(1877–1937)

Barber, teacher, farmer, rancher, magistrate, legislator, politician, realtor, laborer, public servant, and father of President Lyndon B. Johnson

Lyndon B. Johnson got his passion for politics from his father. Sam Ealy Johnson Jr. served twelve years in the Texas House of Representatives. America's thirty-sixth president often quoted his father's advice: "If you can't come into a roomful of people and tell right away who is for you and who is against you, you have no business in politics."

Sam Ealy Johnson Jr. was born in Buda, Texas, on October 11, 1877. Sam was the fifth of nine children born to rancher/farmer Sam Johnson Sr. and Eliza Bunton Johnson. Their first four children were girls, so Sam Sr. was especially pleased with the birth of a son.

Johnson biographers Robert Dallek and Robert A. Caro both report that Sam was a precocious child who impressed others with his quick mind and amazing memory. They relate that as a preschooler, Sam astonished an older sister by reciting a thirty-two stanza poem he had overheard her rehearsing for a school recital. They describe Sam as having some of the same character traits Lyndon would be known for: ambition, competitiveness, determination, and a desire to dominate. Dallek and Caro also report that as an adult Sam displayed the same coarseness, crudeness, and vulgarity that tarnished Lyndon Johnson's persona. Besides having similar personalities, Sam and Lyndon Johnson looked a lot alike. Both father and son were over six feet tall, with black hair, pale skin, a large nose, and oversized ears with prominent lobes.

When Sam was ten, his family moved from Buda to a farm on the banks of the Pedernales River. The nearby town of Johnson City, Texas was founded by Sam Sr. Growing up on the farm, Sam was driven by an intense desire to "ride faster, plow longer, straighter rows; and pick more cotton than his companions." By the time he was a teenager, Sam was determined that he would not spend his life toiling on the Johnson farm. He knew that education was the way out. However, that took

Sam Ealy Johnson Jr. Courtesy of the LBJ Library and Museum.

more money than a farm family of eleven had. Sam's parents could not even afford the modest tuition fee required by the public schools. According to a family history, when Sam was in high school, Sam Sr. gave him some cattle and told him: "This is all I can do on your schooling this year." Sam learned how to butcher and sold steaks and soup bones to pay for his schooling.

When the meat and bones money had run out, Sam took to barbering. After the town barber in Johnson City retired, Sam bought his barber's chair and tools on credit. He began by practicing on his friends until he became adept enough to charge for his services. In his desire to get ahead, Sam pushed himself too hard. He was stricken with what has been termed indigestion or a nervous condition. The affliction forced Sam to drop out of high school. Sam's parents sent him to live with his uncle, Lucius Bunton, at his west Texas ranch.

After a few months there, Sam regained his health. He left with a resolve to become self-supporting by becoming a teacher. In Texas in the late 1800s, it was possible to become a state certified teacher by passing an examination. Applicants did not need a college degree or even a high school diploma. Sam acquired a library of thirteen books covering the test material. He moved in with his grandmother, Jane Bunton, a former teacher, who became his tutor. After a few weeks of intensive study, Sam passed the exam. On the subjects of Texas and United States history, Sam achieved a score of 100 percent.

Sam Johnson spent the next two to three years teaching in tiny rural schools in the Texas hill country. However, the ambitious young man was still not content. He wanted more materially than a teacher's salary could afford him. In 1898 Sam returned to his father's farm on the Pedernales and did well enough at farming and ranching to make some money. Apparently, he accumulated enough to permit him to dabble in politics. In 1902 Sam was elected justice of the peace in Gillespie County. According to Dallek, Sam's bargain five-dollar weddings had him marrying more couples than any pastor in Gillespie County. After serving two years as justice of the peace, Sam was elected to the first of his six terms in the Texas House of Representatives.

In the cloakrooms and corridors of Austin, Sam truly found his niche. Dallek reports that Sam "quickly established himself as a practical legislator," and according to Caro, "He seemed, in fact, born to the Roll Call and the Rules of Order. And he had the unteachable gift for the persuasion that is so integral a part of the legislative life." During his freshman term, Sam authored bills to purchase and restore the Alamo and to ban calf-roping contests. Both proposals were signed into law. However, there were more losses than victories. Sam also supported unsuccessful measures to tax insurance and telephone companies and to give railroad workers an eight-hour day. The *Gillespie County News* lauded Sam's first-term legislative performance in its editorial: "Hon. S. E. Johnson . . . has succeeded in passing more bills, probably, than any other member of the present Legislature. Mr. Johnson accomplishes his ends by quiet and consistent attention to duty, by unfailing attendance on committee meetings and the sessions of the House, and consistently refraining from the making of speeches."

The year 1906 brought both great successes and great failures for Sam Johnson. He won the Democratic primary by such a large margin that he ran unopposed for a second term in the November general election. The great failure was financial ruin caused by the collapse of the market for cotton futures. From 1902 to 1904, Sam had made money gambling on the price of cotton. In 1905 he lost money, and in 1906 he lost everything. Lyndon Johnson later mentioned his father's fiasco by remarking, "My daddy went busted waiting for cotton to go up to twenty-one cents a pound, and the market fell apart when it hit twenty."

When the Texas State Legislature convened in 1907, Representative Sam Johnson was several thousand dollars in debt. As a legislator, Sam received five dollars a day during the sixty-day session, and two dollars a day whenever the session ran longer. Clearly, staying in Austin was not going to get him out of debt. Sam could have eased his financial woes by shaking down lobbyists or selling his vote to the highest bidder. However, that was not his way. According to Caro, Sam's steadfast refusal to accept gifts and favors from lobbyists set him apart from his legislative colleagues. Like his fellow legislators, Sam Johnson frequented the bars and brothels of Austin. But unlike them, Sam paid his own way. As Caro puts it, "if he was foolish, he was foolish on his own money."

While he was serving his second term in the legislature, Sam was interviewed by a stringer for an Austin newspaper. Her name was Rebekah Baines and she married Sam in 1907 when she was twenty-six and he was twenty-nine. She later recalled that interview in these words: "I asked him lots of questions, but he was pretty cagey and I couldn't pin him down; I was awfully provoked with that man!" The marriage of Sam and Rebekah would produce five children (two boys and three girls). Their first child, Lyndon Baines Johnson, was born in the Johnson's three-room farmhouse near Stonewall, Texas, on August 27, 1908.

The same year Lyndon was born, Sam declined to seek a third term in the legislature. Sam did not seek office again for almost a decade. During that hiatus from politics, Sam earned his living as a rancher, realtor, and land speculator. Those years were the most prosperous time of his life. Sam bought and sold cattle, profited in cotton futures, and invested in a local bank. In one of his real estate deals, Sam made over $12,000 from the sale of a ranch. During this period of affluence, Sam displayed the vanity his son, Lyndon, later also became noted for. He bought a new Hudson and hired a local teenager to chauffeur his family. Sam also started wearing hand-tooled boots and expensive Stetson hats.

One of Lyndon Johnson's earliest memories of his father is a secret haircut he received from him. Johnson recalled:

> When I was four or five, I had long curls. He hated them. "He's a boy," he'd say to my mother, "and you're making a sissy of him. You've got to cut those curls." My mother refused. Then, one Sunday morning when she went off to church, he took the big scissors and cut off all my hair. When my mother came home, she refused to speak to him for a week.

According to Caro's biography, Sam appears to have been an abusive father. Caro reports that Lyndon was "slapped and spanked repeatedly by Sam." In an interview, Lyndon Johnson said: "My father, he'd take a razor strap and just whip the hell out of us." In fairness to Sam, however, it should be remembered that Lyndon Johnson has been known to exaggerate. Dallek's version of Sam disciplining Lyndon presents a kinder, gentler view of the man: "Sam Johnson's spankings were not usually severe; quite the opposite in fact." Dallek also reports that Lyndon outfoxed his father by screaming hysterically the first time his father struck him and telling his partners in punishment: "When he hits the first lick, scream like it's killing you, and he'll go easy."

Biographers of Johnson agree that at times Lyndon was genuinely afraid of his father, for example, when Lyndon was seventeen and wrecked his father's car. He abandoned the vehicle and took a bus to New Braunfels, Texas, to hide out at an uncle's house. Sam telephoned Lyndon there and told him that he had traded in his old car for a new one. Sam told Lyndon that he needed someone to pick it up and drive it home. Sam further instructed Lyndon to slowly drive the new car around the courthouse square because "there's some talk around town this morning that my son's a coward, that he couldn't face up to what he'd done, and that he ran away from home. Now I don't want anyone thinking that I produced a yellow son." Lyndon did as his father asked, but a short while later he was once again taking the car without his father's knowledge or consent.

In his book, *My Brother Lyndon*, Sam Houston Johnson writes that there was a constant competitiveness and tension between Sam and Lyndon that often occurs between a father and his oldest son. He also writes that Lyndon objected to his father's drinking.

Sam's second stint in the legislature began after being elected in November of 1917. Two of his most notable legislative achievements of that time were his opposition to the anti–German hysteria generated by World War I and his advocacy of stronger consumer protection laws. House Bill 15, introduced in February of 1918, made it a criminal offense for anyone in Texas to criticize the American military, the flag, or America's participation in World War I. In an eloquent speech, Sam reminded his fellow lawmakers that patriotism should be tempered with common sense and justice. Although the bill passed overwhelmingly, Sam was able to delete a provision that would have given any Texas citizen the power of arrest.

In 1923 Sam sponsored and secured passage of what he regarded as his most notable bill. It became known as the "Johnson Blue Sky Law." The bill regulated the advertising and sale of oil stock and created a Securities Division of the State Railroad Commission to enforce its provisions. The bill protected consumers from the hordes of unscrupulous salesmen who had invaded Texas selling phony oil stocks. The bill got its nickname from a legislator who said that these salesmen were selling everything but the blue sky to their victims.

There are also other, less publicized examples of Sam's effectiveness as a lawmaker. The hill country of Texas became more accessible because Sam worked tirelessly for the construction of State Highway 20 from Fredericksburg to Austin. Elderly constituents who had served as army scouts or as Texas Rangers obtained badly needed pensions they did not know they were entitled to. So did veterans of the Spanish-American War and their widows. As his son would do four decades later, Sam Johnson worked on behalf of the elderly and the poor. Sam also earned a reputation as an outspoken foe of the Klu Klux Klan. Sam Houston Johnson recalls that his father once fended off a group of Klansmen with a baseball bat and that a speech Sam gave on racial tolerance caused the KKK to issue death threats. Sam Houston also claims that he had heard his father use the epithet "Kukluxsonofabitch" so often that he was in high school before he learned that "sonofabitch" was a separate designation.

Unfortunately for Sam, once again his financial failures eclipsed his legislative triumphs. Sam still had ambitions and visions of amassing great wealth. Following the death of his mother in 1917, Sam sold all property he owned and borrowed heavily so he could buy the 433-acre family farm. Succumbing to his gambler's instincts, Sam invested heavily in planting a cotton crop. However, adverse soil, weather, and economic conditions knocked the price of cotton down from forty cents to six cents a pound. By then, Sam's indebtedness was between $30,000 to $40,000. For a second time, financial ruin caused Sam to quit politics. Dallek reports that Sam's final days as a lawmaker were spent living in a tent with thirty other legislators.

After leaving the legislature, the only job Sam could find was as a part-time game warden for two dollars a day. Other low-paying, menial jobs followed between periods of idleness and unemployment. Sam worked on the road grading crew building the highway he had fought for in the legislature. Sam's last known job was as a state bus inspector.

The financial decline also marked a deterioration in Sam's relationship with Lyndon. The headstrong teen was shirking his household chores and ordered his younger siblings to do them, and Lyndon regularly took his father's car without getting permission. Sam Houston Johnson recalls, "No one could boss him or persuade him to do anything he didn't want to do."

In July of 1937 Sam suffered a massive heart attack. Two months later, freshman Congressman Lyndon Johnson visited his hospitalized father during a congressional recess. Sam convinced his son to check him out of the hospital, pleading: "I want to go home where people know when you're sick and care when you die." On October 23, 1937, Sam Johnson died at the age of sixty.

The next day, Sam was buried at the family burial grounds on the banks of the Pedernales. Texas Governor James V. Allred and Texas Secretary of State Ed Clark were among the mourners. Hundreds of other people lined the river banks. Uniformed veterans of the Civil War, the Spanish-American War, and World War I paid their final respects to the man who had once represented them and secured their pensions. The service began with the assembled throng singing: "Shall We Gather at the River." It ended with Railroad Commissioner Lon Smith reciting from *Hamlet:* "He was a man, take him for all in all, I shall not look upon his like again."

Sam Johnson was buried beneath a red granite marker with an epitaph written by his wife, Rebekah: "Of purest gold from the Master's hand/a man who loved his fellow man."

Bibliography

Caro, Robert A. *The Years of Lyndon Johnson: Means of Ascent.* New York: Knopf, 1990.
Caro, Robert A. *The Years of Lyndon Johnson: The Path to Power.* New York: Knopf, 1982.
Cormier, Frank. *LBJ: The Way He Was.* Garden City, N.Y.: Doubleday, 1977.

Dallek, Robert. *Lone Star Rising: Lyndon Johnson and His Times, 1908–1960*. New York: Oxford University Press, 1991.
Johnson, Sam Houston. *My Brother Lyndon*. New York: Cowles, 1969.
Kearns, Doris. *Lyndon Johnson and the American Dream*. New York: Harper & Row, 1976.

Francis Anthony Nixon
(1878–1956)

*Farmhand, glass worker, potter, house painter, farmer,
telephone lineman, carpenter, bricklayer, barber,
handyman, oilfield roustabout, steeplejack, streetcar
motorman, citrus worker, merchant, and father of
President Richard M. Nixon*

Francis Anthony Nixon is not any easier to know than his famous son, Richard. In his *Memoirs*, Richard Nixon lauds his father as "a man of ambition, intelligence and a lively imagination." However, he also acknowledges that his father "had tempestuous arguments with my brothers. . . . I tried to follow my mother's example of not crossing him when he was in a bad mood. . . . He often argued vehemently on almost any subject with the customers he waited on in the store." In a subsequent book, *In the Arena*, Richard Nixon paid homage to his father by writing, "I have never known anyone who worked longer and harder than he did."

Stephen E. Ambrose in his book, *Nixon: The Education of a Politician*, describes Frank as being "boisterous" and "argumentative," but he tempers his judgment of the man by explaining, "His father frightened him [Richard] sometimes, and appalled him at others, but he never had cause to doubt Frank's love or protection. No one in Yorba Linda would have dared to touch one of Frank Nixon's boys." The harshest judgment of the father of America's thirty-seventh president comes from Fawn M. Brodie. In her book, *Richard Nixon: The Shaping of His Character*, she writes: "We know that he was often full of fun, irrepressibly proud of his sexuality, responsible, and honest, but also gruff, bad-tempered, and tight-fisted — a yelling man, a hollering man. He was a great hater, and he seems to have felt pride rather than guilt about his hates."

Frank Nixon was born on December 3, 1878, in Vinton County, Ohio. He was the second of five children (two girls and three boys) born to Samuel Brady Nixon and Sarah Ann Wadsworth Nixon. When Frank was seven, his mother died of tuberculosis. For a time, Frank was sent to live with an uncle. While Frank was away, Samuel alternately worked as a teacher, a mailman, and a laborer in a pottery factory. Eventually Samuel was able to save enough money to buy a forty-acre farm and bring Frank back home. Frank's younger brother, Ernest, recalled a time when their father's only assets were a five dollar bill and a hen sitting on a nest of eggs.

In 1890 Samuel married Lutheria Wyman. Frank left home shortly after his father's remarriage. The few extant descriptions of Frank's stepmother characterize her as cruel, harsh, hateful, and physically abusive toward Frank. Her reputed abuse was most likely a major factor in Frank quitting school and leaving home when he was thirteen or fourteen.

Frank's first job was as a farmhand for 25¢ a day plus the right to fatten and sell a calf. According to Jonathan Aitken's biography, *Nixon: A Life*, after selling the calf, Frank spent the proceeds on new clothes, quarreled with his employer, and quit his job. Aitken notes: "That set the pattern for Frank's nomadic lifestyle for the next fourteen years." Nixon biographers enumerate about twenty different jobs Frank worked before he settled in California. A few of them were: potato farmer, barber, potter, bricklayer, glass-blower, and streetcar motorman. Aitken quotes a letter of reference written for Frank by a former employer named H. A. Cramp. It reads: "He has no bad habits that I know of. He does not smoke tobacco or drink . . . he does his work fully and well. He is a good man and you will make no mistake in employing him." Despite such a glowing recommendation, Frank never stayed with any one job for long. Ambrose explains Frank's wanderings and constant changes in employment as follows: "He knew a great deal about machines and tools, little about people. He was argumentative, cantankerous, opinionated; he shouted a great deal; he was critical of his bosses; small wonder that every spring found him working a new job."

While working as a streetcar motorman in Columbus, Ohio, Frank became involved in politics. Motormen were required to work in an open air vestibule. During the winter of 1906, Frank suffered from frostbitten feet. His complaints to his employer were ignored, so Frank organized the other motormen and conductors to stage a protest. Frank's efforts resulted in the state legislature passing a bill mandating closed vestibules for the motormen. Frank won the battle, but he lost the war. After the bill passed, the streetcar company summarily fired him.

In 1907 Frank permanently left Ohio. He moved to California and found employment as a streetcar motorman of the Pacific Electric line running from Los Angeles to Whittier. Early in 1908, while attending services at the Friends (Quaker) church in Whittier, Frank found himself attracted to a young lady singing in the choir. The lady was Jane Milhous, and Frank quickly managed to get someone to introduce him to her. The introduction led to an invitation to the church's Valentine's Day social. Taking Jane to the social led to Frank meeting Jane's sister, Hannah Milhous. Frank came to the social with Jane, but he left with Hannah. Just over four months later (June 25, 1908), Frank and Hannah were married. He was twenty-nine and she was twenty-three.

Nixon biographers concur that Hannah's family was at best ambivalent about Hannah marrying Frank. He was not a Quaker; he had little education; he had an

Frank Nixon. Courtesy of the Richard Nixon Library & Birthplace, Yorba Linda, California.

erratic and unstable work history, and he had no apparent prospects. By all accounts and appearances, their marriage was a union of opposites. In his *Memoirs,* Richard Nixon recalls: "The principle that opposites attract aptly describes my father and my mother." When he married Hannah, Frank was making a living as a laborer in the citrus groves. A collision between Frank's streetcar and an automobile trying to cross the tracks had led to Frank being fired from his second motorman position. Frank and Hannah were living with her parents when their first child, Harold Samuel Nixon was born on June 1, 1909.

Frank and Hannah's first permanent home was a house in Yorba Linda that Frank built from a do-it-yourself kit he had ordered from the Sears Roebuck catalog. His father-in-law, Franklin Milhous, had advanced Frank and Hannah $3,000 for the home and twelve acres of land. On January 9, 1913, the house Frank had built became the birthplace of Richard Milhous Nixon.

Using seedlings obtained from his father-in-law's nursery, Frank attempted to start a lemon grove on his twelve acres. Ambrose reports that bad luck or poor judgment doomed the project to failure. Frank's acreage did not drain well, had a layer of clay subsoil, and produced lemons of inferior quality. Frank earned an additional income by performing whatever odd jobs he could find. The first years of Frank and Hannah's marriage were a time of economic deprivation. Like Eisenhower's father, David Jacob, Frank refused to go into debt. When friends told Frank that his lemon groves would increase both in yield and in quality if he fertilized the soil with manure, Frank always replied, "I won't buy fertilizer until I raise enough lemons to pay for it." But with unfertilized soil he could never raise enough lemons.

When Richard was nine, Frank finally gave up on the lemon grove. By that time his family numbered six (four boys). Frank had also changed his mind about going into debt and borrowed $5,000 to open a gas station and general store in East Whittier, fifteen miles north of Yorba Linda. Before leaving Yorba Linda, Frank had rejected a proposition that would have substantially improved his financial status. In 1919 there was an oil boom in Yorba Linda. An oil speculator offered Frank $45,000 for his property, but Frank had turned it down. He felt that if someone offered him that much, the property was worth holding on to. Subsequently, no oil was found on the land, and Frank ended up selling the property for less than one-tenth of the original offer.

Frank ran the new family business with the energy, drive, and zeal of a true workaholic. The business was a genuine "mom and pop" operation. The whole family worked at the store. Frank worked his boys hard because he expected as much from them as he expected of himself. Richard Nixon recalls in his *Memoirs* that he had to rise at four in the morning so he could get to the Los Angeles vegetable and fruit market by five. There he selected the produce, delivered it to the store, and had it washed, sorted, and displayed before catching the school bus at eight. After school, Richard usually returned to the store to take inventory and perform other chores. Frank kept the store and service station open seven days a week. On Sundays, he left the store only long enough to attend Quaker services and to teach Sunday school. Frank had converted to the Quaker faith shortly after marrying Hannah.

Frank showed the same ardor in teaching Sunday school that he displayed in running the family business and acquired a reputation as a no-nonsense teacher who adeptly controlled the rowdy boys in his class. Nixon cousin and author Jessamyn West said: "Frank was certainly ardent in his Sunday school teaching. His cheeks flamed and his voice trembled."

By his late forties, Frank was finally enjoying some financial success. Ambrose records that by 1925 Frank's service station was selling $5,000 worth of tires every month. Eventually, Frank was able to lease the service station to a neighbor and concentrate on running the general store. In his *Memoirs,* Richard Nixon recalls that "had it not been for the illness that struck our family, we would have been modestly well off by the standards of those times." The illness he alludes to is tuberculosis, which killed his brother Harold in 1933. When Harold was stricken, Frank had already outlived one of his sons. Arthur, his fourth son, had died of encephalitis in 1925. After that tragic death (Arthur was only seven), Frank believed his son's demise was a punishment from God, and Frank never again kept his store open on Sundays.

Arthur's death had also made Frank even more religious. Frank became a regular listener of radio evangelists Billy Sunday, Aimee Semple McPherson, and the Reverend "Fighting Bob" Shuler. Once a week, he used to take his sons to Los Angeles to hear McPherson or Shuler preach. One fellow Quaker recalled Frank testifying his faith by shouting: "We must have a reawakening! We've got to have a revival! We have got to get the people back to God!"

When Harold became ill, Frank could have sent him to the Los Angeles County Hospital for free treatment, but he was philosophically opposed to socialized medicine. Aitken explains: "He decided it was his duty as a citizen and taxpayer to have nothing to do with the state hospital service on the grounds that it would be taking charity." Instead, he opted to send Harold to expensive private sanatoriums. To pay for Harold's medical care, Frank sold some of the land around his store. For a short time, Harold's health improved enough for him to live at home. After that he became weaker, and Frank and Hannah took him to a sanatorium in Prescott, Arizona. Frank had no more land to sell, so Hannah paid for Harold's treatment by renting a cabin in Prescott and caring for Harold and three other tuberculosis patients. Meanwhile, Frank, Richard, and Don continued to run the store. Frank took over Hannah's cake baking and pie making enterprises. When he could get a weekend off, Frank made the eight-hundred-mile round trip to Prescott to visit his wife and ailing son.

An unexpected occurrence caused Hannah and Harold to leave Prescott and move back to California. At the age of forty-four, Hannah became pregnant. Frank's initial reaction was to exclaim: "The doctor doesn't know what he's talking about!" The doctor was right, however, and Frank was wrong. Frank and Hannah's fifth and last son, Edward Calvert, was born on May 3, 1930, at the Whittier Hospital.

In February of 1933 Frank took a rare "vacation." Harold, knowing that death was near, asked his father if he could see the Mojave Desert. Frank rented a trailer and told his family that they would be gone for a month. They returned home three days later after Harold suffered a severe hemorrhage. Harold Nixon died on March 7, 1933. In his *Memoirs*, Richard Nixon remembers arriving home from Whittier College to see Harold's lifeless body being carried out of the house while both parents sobbed uncontrollably. Aitken writes that Frank and Hannah were so grief-stricken that Richard had to assume responsibility for notifying relatives, escorting mourners to the funeral home, and making the burial arrangements.

With the death of Harold, Richard became Frank's oldest surviving son. Frank had always taken a keen interest in Richard. Now that interest was intensified. Frank faithfully attended practices of the Whittier College football team to encourage Richard as he gamely struggled to make the squad. He also accompanied Richard to his college debate meets. During the drives home, Frank and Richard used to analyze the arguments and the judge's decisions. In his book, *In the Arena*, Richard Nixon writes: "His encouragement and advice were the primary factors that led me to develop any talents I may later have had as a debater."

Was Frank Nixon an abusive father? By today's standards of child rearing, yes. Was he also an abused child? Yes, again, but that does not absolve him of his own physical abuses. For his time he may not have been considered excessively harsh. Brodie quotes Hannah as saying that Frank "would not hesitate using the strap and the rod on the boys when they did wrong." Jessamyn West tells an anecdote of Frank throwing his sons into an irrigation ditch after he found them openly defying his orders not to go swimming in it. Apparently, Richard was punished less than his brothers, but he told his former law partner, Thomas Bewley, "I got the strap." Undoubtedly, Frank's reputation for arguing and yelling supports the characterization of him as a harsh parent.

When Richard Nixon attended law school at Duke University, Frank only loaned him money for school expenses rather than giving it to him. Since Richard was a college-educated adult, Frank apparently believed that he should be receiving loans instead of handouts. After Richard finished school, he repaid the loans. However, when Richard Nixon entered politics, Frank took a keen interest in his career. In his *Memoirs*, Nixon recalls: "My father's interest in politics made him the most enthusiastic follower of my career from its beginnings. My success meant to him that everything he had worked for and believed in was true: that in America with hard work and determination a man can achieve anything. During the years that I was in Congress, I sent home copies of the daily *Congressional Record*. He read them cover to cover—something that no congressman or senator that I knew took the time to do."

Frank Nixon lived to see Richard elected vice president of the United States in 1952. He attended his son's inauguration and grudgingly donned the required formal attire. In his book, *Richard Milhous Nixon: The Rise of an American Politician*, Roger Morris reports that Frank strenuously objected to having to wear tails and called the formal clothing "a monkey suit." After relenting, Frank told the gathered friends and relatives, "They made me do it."

Frank Nixon died at his California home on September 4, 1956, at the age of seventy-seven. His obituary in the September 5, 1956, edition of the *New York Times* reported that he had been in ill health for the past three years. For much of his adult life, he had suffered from bleeding ulcers. He was becoming progressively deaf, and, in all probability, he was shouting more than ever. In his late seventies he had sustained a fractured hip and broken ribs from a fall.

In his autobiography, *In the Arena,* Richard Nixon recalls the last time he saw his father alive. Frank told him: "I don't think I'll be here in the morning." Richard replied, "Dad, you've got to keep fighting." Frank's last words to Richard were: "Dick, you keep fighting."

Funeral services for Frank Nixon were held on September 7, 1956, at the East Whittier Friends Meeting House. To avoid any photographers scattered among the five hundred mourners, Vice President Nixon, Pat, and Hannah Nixon and Richard's brothers, Edward and Francis Donald Nixon, sat behind a curtain. U.S. Secretary of Labor James P. Mitchell attended the services as President Eisenhower's personal representative.

Aitken analyzes Frank's influence on Richard as follows:

> Frank created deep insecurities in his sons because of the unpredictability of his temper and the mean streak in his character. Too often he bore grudges against those he imagined to be his adversaries and too easily he hurt feelings among those whom he loved. These behavior patterns may have contributed to the psychological complexities that were later to appear in his famous second son.

In his acceptance speech for the 1968 Republican nomination for president, Richard Nixon recalled his childhood dreams and his life influences:

> I see another child. He hears the trains go by at night and dreams of faraway places he would like to go. It seems like an impossible dream. But he is helped on his journey through life. A father.... A gentle Quaker mother.... A great teacher.... A courageous wife and two loyal children.... Tonight he stands before you — nominated for President of the United States.

Hannah is characterized as a gentle Quaker mother, Pat as courageous, Tricia and Julie Nixon as loyal. But when it came to describing Frank Nixon, even Richard Nixon was unable to come up with a suitable adjective.

Bibliography

Abrahamsen, David, M.D. *Nixon vs. Nixon: An Emotional Tragedy.* New York: Farrar, Straus and Giroux, 1976.

Aitken, Jonathan. *Nixon: A Life.* Washington, D.C.: Regency, 1993.

Ambrose, Stephen E. *Nixon: The Education of a Politician, 1913-1962.* New York: Simon & Schuster, 1987.
Brodie, Fawn M. *Richard Nixon: The Shaping of His Character.* New York: Norton, 1981.
"Condolences for Nixon." *New York Times.* September 6, 1956, p. 25.
DeToledano, Ralph. *One Man Alone: Richard Nixon.* New York: Funk and Wagnalls, 1969.
"Father of Nixon Dies at Age 77." *New York Times.* September 5, 1956, p. 27.
"500 Attend Service for Nixon's Father." *New York Times.* September 8, 1956, p. 17.
Mazlish, Bruce. *In Search of Nixon: A Psychohistorical Inquiry.* Baltimore: Penguin, 1972.
Morris, Roger. *Richard Milhous Nixon: The Rise of an American Politician.* New York: Holt, 1990.
Nixon, Richard. *In the Arena: A Memoir of Victory, Defeat, and Renewal.* New York: Simon & Schuster, 1990.
Nixon, Richard. *RN: The Memoirs of Richard Nixon.* New York: Grosset & Dunlap, c. 1978.
Parmet, Herbert S. *Richard Nixon and His America.* Boston: Little, Brown, 1990.

Leslie Lynch King Sr. (1882–1941)

Wool merchant and biological father of President Gerald R. Ford Jr.

Leslie King was a father to Gerald Ford only in the biological sense. The way King led his life effectively prevented the development of any filial affection in America's thirty-eighth president for his biological father.

Leslie Lynch King Sr. was born in Chadron, Nebraska, on July 25, 1882. His father, Charles King, had migrated to Nebraska from Pennsylvania. Charles King established a stagecoach line from Omaha to Wyoming, and he also helped the Burlington Railroad expand into the Wyoming Territory. Following the arrival of the railroad, Charles King set up banks, general stores, and warehouses in towns along the railroad's route. His shrewd investments and business expertise made King a multimillionaire.

Leslie King first met his future wife, Dorothy Ayer Gardner, in the spring of 1912 when he was visiting his sister, Marietta, who was a college classmate and close friend of Gardner. Despite a ten year age difference, there was an immediate and mutual attraction. Leslie King has been described as tall, handsome, blonde, blue-eyed, and broad-shouldered. Ford's various biographers have described Dorothy Gardner as pretty, vivacious, and gregarious. After a short courtship, they were married at Harvard, Illinois, on September 7, 1912. They were a strikingly attractive couple, but they were not a happy couple. In his memoirs, *A Time to Heal*, Gerald Ford reports that they quarreled frequently and that he had heard that King was physically abusive. Betty Ford writes in her book, *The Times of My Life*, that King was so jealous and insecure, he would not let the milkman make deliveries to their home. Most recently, James Cannon in his book, *Time and Chance: Gerald Ford's Appointment with History*, writes that beginning with their honeymoon, King was both physically and verbally abusive to Ford's mother. Cannon writes that Dorothy left Leslie King shortly after Gerald was born. According to Cannon, when Gerald was an infant, King threatened his wife, mother-in-law, and infant son with a butcher knife.

The only child of the Kings' marriage, Leslie Lynch King Jr., was born in

Omaha, Nebraska, on July 14, 1913. At King's insistence, the boy was named for his father. The Kings divorced in December of 1913 after an Omaha court found Leslie King "guilty of extreme cruelty." King was ordered by the court to pay alimony and child support, but he refused to pay anything. When the court attempted to seize his assets, it found that King was bankrupt. Charles King then assumed responsibility for paying Dorothy Gardner King twenty-five dollars a month for child support.

For over a decade, Gerald Ford was unaware of his biological father's existence. In his memoirs, Ford reveals that when he was about twelve or thirteen, his mother told him that Gerald R. Ford Sr. was not his real father. Ford said, "It didn't make a big impression on me at the time."

In 1929 or 1930 (Ford's memoirs and Cannon's book differ on the date), Leslie King unexpectedly reentered Gerald Ford's life. Ford later called the unpleasant encounter "the first major shock of my life." When they were reunited, Ford was a student at South High School in Grand Rapids, Michigan, and he was working at a local restaurant across the street from the school. Ford noticed that for about fifteen or twenty minutes, a stranger had been standing by the candy counter staring at him. The stranger finally approached Ford and said, "I'm Leslie King, your father. Can I take you to lunch?" A stunned Ford politely told King that he was busy working. King still persisted and told Ford, "Ask your boss if you can get off." Ford received the necessary permission. King introduced Ford to his wife, Margaret, and then he drove them to a nearby local restaurant.

King had stopped off in Grand Rapids after taking a train from Wyoming to Detroit to pick up a new automobile. King explained to Ford that he had located him by visiting the local high schools and asking if they had a Leslie King enrolled. When King got to South High and was told there was no Leslie King enrolled there, he had asked if there was a Junior Ford attending school there. King was told that Junior Ford could be found working in the restaurant across the street.

Ford recalls that the lunch conversation was superficial small talk about the football team at South High. King did ask Ford if he would like to live with him in Wyoming. Ford told him that he was happy in Michigan. Throughout the meal, Ford resisted the impulse to ask his father why he had waited all these years to look him up. The visit ended with King giving Ford twenty-five dollars and telling him to buy himself something he could not normally afford. Apparently King believed that the small sum would make up for years of neglect and unpaid alimony and child support. Ford summed up his feelings about the surprise reunion in his autobiography: "Nothing could erase the image that I gained of my real father that day: a carefree, well-to-do man who didn't really give a damn about the hopes and dreams of his firstborn son."

When Ford returned home from work, he told his mother and stepfather that he had met his real father that day. His parents were comforting and consoling, but that still did not keep Gerald Ford from weeping tears of anger and resentment before falling asleep that evening.

The child support payments from Charles King had ended in 1929 when he lost most of his fortune in the stock market crash. After Charles King died, Dorothy Ford learned that Leslie King had inherited fifty thousand dollars. She got a judgment from a Nebraska court to force Leslie King to pay $100 a month for Gerald Ford's college education. However, Leslie King was one step ahead of the law. He had moved to Wyoming and was no longer under the jurisdiction of the Nebraska court. Characteristically, King refused to pay anything.

In his memoirs, Ford's last mention of his biological father concerns his own bleak financial situation when he was a junior at the University of Michigan. In spite of a partial football scholarship, part-time job, and money received from donating blood, Ford lacked sufficient funds to stay in school. Ford wrote Leslie King in Wyoming and asked for a loan, but he never received a reply.

According to Lloyd Shearer's article, "President Ford's Other Family," which appeared in the September 15, 1974, issue of *Parade*, Leslie King continued to visit Gerald Ford after the Grand Rapids encounter. Ford's half-sister, Patricia King, said: "Whenever he [Leslie King] got to Michigan he made a point of looking Jerry up, or so at least he told us." Leslie King's widow, Margaret Atwood King, added: "If I recall correctly, we even visited him at Yale one time when Jerry was assistant football coach there." Assuming that Leslie King was telling the truth and that Margaret Atwood King's memory is accurate, the visits must have been strained occasions for Gerald Ford.

Leslie Lynch King died in Tucson, Arizona, on February 13, 1941. He was fifty-nine years old and had suffered from acute asthma the last ten years of his life. He was buried at Forest Lawn Cemetery in Glendale, California. When King died, Gerald Ford was in his final year at Yale Law School. If Gerald Ford felt any grief, sorrow, or sense of loss at the death of his biological father, he kept it to himself.

Bibliography

The Ancestry of Gerald R. Ford. Gerald R. Ford Library, Ann Arbor, Michigan.
Cannon, James M. *Time and Chance: Gerald Ford's Appointment with History*. New York: Harper Collins, 1994.
Ford, Betty and Chris Chase. *The Times of My Life*. Harper and Reader's Digest Association, 1978.
Ford, Gerald R. *A Time to Heal*. New York: Harper and Reader's Digest Association, 1979.
"G. R. Ford, Executive Dies at 72." and "Death Ends Long Career." *Grand Rapids Press*. January 26, 1962.
"Nebraska Man Is Claimed by Death." *Tucson Citizen*. February 19, 1941, p. 1A.
Randolph Sallie G. *Gerald R. Ford, President*. New York: Walker, 1987.
Shearer, Lloyd. "President Ford's Other Family." *Parade*, September 15, 1974.
terHorst, Jerald R. *Gerald Ford and the Future of the Presidency*. New York: Third Press, 1974.
Vestal, Bud. *Jerry Ford Up Close: An Investigative Biography*. New York: Coward, 1974.

Gerald R. Ford Sr. (1889–1962)

Paint salesman, businessman, and adoptive father of President Gerald R. Ford Jr.

Gerald R. Ford Sr., the adoptive father of America's thirty-eighth president, is the man Gerald Ford always regarded as his father. Gerald Ford once summed up their relationship by saying: "He was the father that I grew up to believe was my father, the father I loved and learned from and respected. He was my dad."

Gerald R. Ford Sr. was born in Grand Rapids, Michigan, on December 9, 1889. Little has been written about his early life. It is known that Ford Sr. had adult responsibilities thrust on him when he was a teen. Ford Sr.'s father, George Ford, was killed in a train accident when the boy was only fourteen. That is when Ford Sr.'s formal schooling ended; he quit school to help support his mother and three sisters.

Ford Sr.'s first jobs were with the electric railroad company in Grand Rapids and then with the Grand Rapids Wood Finishing Company. Ford Sr. was working for the latter employer as a paint salesman when he met a young divorcee named Dorothy Gardner King at an Episcopal church social.

In Gerald R. Ford Sr., Dorothy found some important qualities that had been lacking in her first husband. Ford Sr. was even-tempered, respectful toward women, and a man of great integrity. The tall, black-haired, amiable bachelor was also openly affectionate toward Dorothy's baby son. Gerald Sr. and Dorothy were married in Grand Rapids on February 1, 1916. The marriage produced three half brothers for Gerald Ford: Thomas G. Ford, born in 1918; Richard A. Ford, born in 1924; and James F. Ford, born in 1927.

In 1919 Ford Sr. was working as a paint salesman and had become affluent enough to buy a home on Rosewood Avenue in East Grand Rapids. His reputation for honesty and integrity contributed to his success. Ford Sr. was known to guarantee the quality of the paint he sold even when the manufacturer would not. Unfortunately, by 1921 business had taken a downturn. Paint sales were down and the bank foreclosed on Ford Sr.'s mortgage. The Fords had to move to a rented house. The move meant additional chores for young Gerald Ford. He had to tend the fur-

Gerald R. Ford Jr., Dorothy Ford and Gerald R. Ford Sr. Courtesy of Gerald R. Ford Library.

nace in the winter and mow the lawn in the summer, along with the customary chores of cleaning his room, making his bed, and doing kitchen duties when it was his turn.

Living in the home of Gerald R. Ford Sr. meant that everyone worked and did his share. Along with working there was a strictly enforced code of conduct that Ford Sr. expected his children to live up to. Gerald Ford has written that his parents had three rules: "tell the truth, work hard and come to dinner on time." Ford also added, "Woe to any of us who violated his rules."

In 1929 Gerald Ford Sr. went into business for himself by founding the Ford Paint and Varnish Company. His timing could not have been worse. Three weeks after Ford Sr. began his new venture, the stock market crashed, precipitating the Great Depression. However, since Ford Sr. had an impeccable reputation for paying his bills, the DuPont Corporation extended him credit at a time when many businesses and banks were failing. Ford Sr. called his employees together and told them that there would be no layoffs. The employees agreed to work for $5.00 a week until times got better and management could pay them the difference between the five-dollar weekly wage and their regular salary.

To show his sincerity, Ford Sr. also worked for five dollars a week until he could afford to pay his workers more. Ford Sr.'s business was able to survive the Great Depression without laying anyone off. When times finally got better, Ford Sr. made good on his pledge. Besides being a businessman who was genuinely concerned about his employees, Gerald Ford Sr. was active in civic organizations and the Grace Episcopal Church. Ford Sr. was one of the first directors of a program for economically disadvantaged youth in Grand Rapids called Youth Commonwealth. Ford Sr. also helped to establish a summer camp for underprivileged children.

Gerald Ford Sr. was both a joiner and a doer. He belonged to the Grand Rapids Exchange Club, the Elks, the Masonic Lodge, and the Shrine. Ford Sr. was 33rd degree Mason and an active supporter of the Boy Scouts. In civic affairs, Ford Sr. was twice the director of civil defense in Kent County and also served as director of the Grand Rapids Chamber of Commerce. Ford Sr. served four years as chairman of the Kent County Republican Committee. He left that position in 1948 when Gerald Ford ran for his first term in the U.S. House of Representatives. From the example set by his adoptive father, Gerald Ford learned the importance and value of trust, honesty, and integrity, and the importance of being actively involved in civic affairs.

Gerald Ford Sr. died at his home in Grand Rapids on January 26, 1962, at the age of seventy-two. Cannon reports that Ford Sr. died after slipping on some ice and sustaining a concussion. Newspaper obituaries list a heart attack as the cause of death.

A standing room only crowd squeezed into Grace Episcopal Church to pay final respects to a well-liked and much respected businessman and civic leader. Gerald Ford Sr.'s obituary in the January 26, 1962, issue of the *Grand Rapids Press* described the deceased as a lifelong local resident and father of U.S. Representative Gerald R. Ford Jr. The obituary also stated: "The family suggests those wishing to pay tribute to the memory of Mr. Ford may do so in the form of gifts to Youth Commonwealth."

One of the greatest tributes to the life and memory of Gerald R. Ford Sr. came from ex-President Ford. A man who had conferred and conversed with monarchs, prime ministers, presidents, and premiers said: "Dad was one of the truly outstanding people I ever knew in my life."

Bibliography

The Ancestry of Gerald R. Ford. Gerald R. Ford Library, Ann Arbor, Michigan.

Cannon, James M. *Time and Chance: Gerald Ford's Appointment with History.* New York: Harper Collins, 1994.

Ford, Betty and Chris Chase. *The Times of My Life*. Harper and Reader's Digest Association, 1978.
Ford, Gerald R. *A Time to Heal*. New York: Harper and Reader's Digest Association, 1979.
"G. R. Ford, Executive Dies at 72." and "Death Ends Long Career." *Grand Rapids Press*. January 26, 1962.
"Nebraska Man Is Claimed by Death." *Tucson Citizen*. February 19, 1941, p. 1A.
Randolph Sallie G. *Gerald R. Ford, President*. New York: Walker, 1987.
Shearer, Lloyd. "President Ford's Other Family." *Parade*, September 15, 1974.
terHorst, Jerald R. *Gerald Ford and the Future of the Presidency*. New York: Third Press, 1974.
Vestal, Bud. *Jerry Ford Up Close: An Investigative Biography*. New York: Coward, 1974.

James Earl Carter Sr. (1894–1953)

Soldier, cowboy, merchant, businessman, farmer, politician, legislator, and father of President Jimmy Carter

In his autobiography, *Why Not the Best?*, former President Jimmy Carter described his relationship with his father by writing:

> I never even considered disobeying my father, and he seldom if ever ordered me to perform a task; he simply suggested that it needed to be done, and he expected me to do it. But he was a stern disciplinarian and punished me severely when I misbehaved. From the time I was four years old until I was fifteen years old he whipped me six times and I've never forgotten any of those impressive experiences.

James Earl Carter Sr., the father of America's thirty-ninth President, was the fourth of five children (two boys and three girls) born to William Archibald and Nina Pratt Carter. James Sr. (hereinafter called Earl) was born on September 12, 1894, in Arlington, Georgia. When Earl was around nine years old, his father was shot and killed by a business partner. Reputedly, he was murdered in a dispute over the ownership of a desk. His former partner was never convicted. In 1904 Earl and his family moved to Plains, Georgia.

Earl's formal education ended after he completed the tenth grade at Riverside Academy in Gainesville, Georgia. In *Why Not the Best?*, Jimmy Carter notes that Earl received the most advanced education of any Carter male since the family had first moved to Georgia in the 1700s. In her book, *Brother Billy*, Ruth Carter Stapleton records that Earl left Plains when he was seventeen and worked as a cowboy in Texas for two years. Apparently two years of riding and roping convinced Earl that a home in Plains was preferable to a home on the range. With the money he had saved, Earl invested in an ice house in Plains. He later opened a laundry and dry cleaning business. According to Stapleton, "Earl soon proved to be the best businessman in Plains."

Earl Carter. Courtesy of Jimmy Carter Library.

When the United States entered World War I in 1917, Earl enlisted in the army. According to Jimmy Carter, Earl's extremely poor eyesight kept him out of the infantry. Earl served in the Quartermaster Corps and was discharged with the rank of lieutenant. Earl used his mustering out pay to bankroll some new business ventures when he returned to Plains. In their book, *Jimmy Carter: A Character Portrait,* authors Bruce Mazlish and Edwin Diamond recount that not all of Earl's ventures were successful, but they do not provide any specific details. At any rate, Earl Carter had impressed the people of Plains as a young man of energy, drive, and ambition. Among the most impressed was a young lady named Lillian Gordy.

Earl and Lillian first met at a dance sometime in 1921 when she was a nurse in training at a local private hospital. According to Mazlish and Diamond, Lillian was dating someone else at the time, but her employer told her that he preferred if she would date Earl. Ruth Carter Stapleton describes Earl's courtship of Lillian: "Earl began to court her with the same thoroughness that he showed in business: flowers, notes, constant attention with cautious but warm displays of affection." Ruth also reports that Lillian wanted to get married right after their engagement, but the ever practical Earl told her to wait until after she had completed her nursing internship. They were married on September 27, 1923, at the parsonage of the Baptist minister in Plains. Earl was twenty-nine and Lillian was twenty-five. Earl had hoped that a potato crop he had planted would pay for their honeymoon. Apparently, the yield was poor, and the honeymoon was postponed.

James Earl Carter Jr., the first of Earl and Lillian's four children, was born on October 1, 1924, at the Wise Hospital in Plains. Jimmy Carter was the first American president to be born in a hospital. When Jimmy was born, Earl had already purchased his first farm on credit. That farm generated enough income to allow Earl to pay off the loan and to begin buying additional properties. After a while, Earl was doing so well in land speculation that he could afford to loan money to other Sumter County farmers. Mazlish and Diamond report that at one time or another, most of the six hundred white farmers in Sumter County came to Earl for a loan. Eventually, Earl would own four thousand acres, which were farmed by two hundred black tenant farmers.

Jimmy Carter was around four years old when his family moved to the predominantly black community of Archery, Georgia. Earl opened a general store next to his farmhouse. The store sold work clothes, tobacco, seed, animal feed, and other rural staples. Products produced on the Carter farm such as ham, sausage, lard, and syrup were also sold. Despite Earl's growing affluence, the Carters lived in a manner typical of rural, white Southerners of the time. Their home lacked electricity and indoor plumbing. Lillian Carter said, "We lived very, very well in terms of having what we wanted." According to *Why Not the Best?*, the lack of electricity was a factor in Earl becoming interested and involved in politics. Jimmy Carter recalls, "With the advent of the Rural Electrification Program, when I was about thirteen years old, my father became one of the first directors of our local REA organization. He then began to learn the importance of political involvement on a state and national basis to protect the program that meant so much in changing our farm life-style."

Carter biographers characterize Earl's politics as conservative. Apparently Earl ran for office as a Democrat, and he usually supported the Democratic ticket. Jimmy Carter does point out that after Franklin D. Roosevelt's agricultural production control programs forced his father to slaughter some of his hogs and plow up some of his cotton crop, Earl never again voted for a Democrat for president. He also adds, "he [Earl] was quite conservative, and my mother was and is a liberal, but within our family we never thought much about trying to define such labels."

One Democrat Earl Carter always supported was former Georgia Governor Gene Talmadge. Talmadge served as Georgia's governor from 1933–37 and 1941–43. Mazlish and Diamond label Talmadge "one of the great demagogues and race baiters of the twentieth century." In *Turning Point,* Jimmy Carter acknowledges his father's racial attitudes: "Certainly by today's standards my father was segregationist, as were nearly all of the white citizens of the area, so far as I knew. It was a way of life that in the early 1950s had rarely been challenged in Georgia."

Carter biographers report that Earl and Jimmy had a close and loving father-son relationship. According to Stapleton, "They spent many hours together walking through the fields, inspecting one of our many farms, hunting quail, or walking the dogs." On different occasions, Jimmy Carter has called his father "always my best friend" and his only "close friend."

Biographers also point out that Earl had a special nickname for Jimmy: "Hot" or "Hot Shot." Most Carter biographers regard the nickname as a term of endearment, but Lloyd deMause and Henry Ebel in their book, *Jimmy Carter and American Fantasy: Psychohistorical Explorations,* speculate that the nickname could have been a sarcastic one Earl used as a put-down. Nicknames aside, there is agreement among Carter biographers that Earl had high standards and expectations for all of his children, but especially for Jimmy. Since Jimmy was the firstborn child and also the only Carter male child for thirteen years, he occupied a special place in Earl's life.

There is some evidence that no matter how hard Jimmy tried, Earl was sparing with his approval. Jimmy's sister, Gloria Carter Spann, has said: "No matter how well Jimmy did, Daddy always said that he could do better." According to deMause and Ebel, "Earl Carter was a concerned, rather intrusive father, who demanded very high standards of his firstborn son, while generally showing preference to the younger children." As Mazlish and Diamond put it, "The perfectionist Mr. Earl had special standards — he expected a 'performance that was exemplary' — for his namesake."

After leaving Plains for the Naval Academy in 1943, Jimmy rarely saw his father. According to Mazlish and Diamond, while serving in the navy Jimmy Carter visited his parents an average of once every two years. Jimmy Carter claims that naval regulations prevented him from visiting more frequently. However, Mazlish and Diamond point out that as a naval officer Jimmy Carter was entitled to thirty days of leave every year. Apparently, Jimmy Carter opted to spend his leave time away from Plains. One reason for this may have been a quarrel Jimmy and Earl had because of their differing views on race relations. The incident is cited in several Carter biographies. When Jimmy was serving on the submarine USS *K-1,* the ship docked in Jamaica for some shore leave. The British governor-general of the island invited the crew members to attend a party in their honor. After the crew accepted, the governor-general told them that the ship's black crewmen were not invited. The crew responded by unanimously voting to skip the party.

When Jimmy Carter proudly told his parents of their refusal, Earl sharply disagreed with their action. According to one account of the incident, a heated discussion ensued between Earl and Jimmy. In *Turning Point,* Jimmy Carter reports that

Earl simply said: "The governor of Jamaica was absolutely right," and then left the room without further comment. Jimmy Carter also recalls: "There was simply no way that I could explain the reasons to my father. After that, he and I agreed to avoid racial subjects on my rare and brief visits home." According to Stapleton, Earl Carter "refused to even discuss the idea of integration." Mazlish and Diamond speculate that Earl may have been a believer in white supremacy, but they point out that Earl never joined the Ku Klux Klan or the White Citizens' Council. Reportedly Earl usually left the house whenever Lillian entertained a black guest in the Carter home.

Both physically and philosophically, Earl had more in common with Billy than with Jimmy Carter. Various Carter biographies describe Earl as short (5'8"), stocky, jowly, with a ruddy complexion and wearing thick eyeglasses over his blue-gray eyes. By contrast, Jimmy Carter is five feet, nine-and-one-half inches tall, trim (circa 155 pounds) and has hazel eyes. The few published photos of Earl Carter do not show him displaying Jimmy's well-known toothy grin.

In November of 1952 Earl was elected to serve as the Sumter County representative in the House of Representatives of the Georgia General Assembly. Earl had previously been elected to the Sumter County school board. When he was elected to the state legislature, Earl was already suffering from the cancer that would eventually take his life. Jimmy Carter writes in *Turning Point* that a steady stream of visitors, black and white, came to see his dying father, leaving behind many gifts of flowers and food. Carter recalls: "Even my mother was surprised to learn of his secret acts of kindness and generosity." Stapleton recalls that Earl "supplemented the incomes of many families of both races or helped pay for college expenses."

Earl Carter died at his home in Plains on July 22, 1953, when he was fifty-nine years old. A one-column obituary on the front page of the *Americus (Georgia) Times Recorder* reported that: "Mr. Carter was one of Plains' leading farmers and businessmen, and his death here today brought sorrow to the whole community." The obituary also mentioned that the deceased state representative was a member of the Plains Baptist Church, the Plains Lions Club, the Americus Elks and the American Legion.

Ruth Carter Stapleton recalled that when she and Jimmy went to notify friends and neighbors of Earl's death, Jimmy began reviewing his life and told her, "I want to be a man like my father." Jimmy's desire to emulate his father returned him to his Georgia home and put him on a path that would take him from Plains, Georgia, to 1600 Pennsylvania Avenue.

Bibliography

Americus (Georgia) Times Recorder. July 22, 1953, p. 1.
Carter, Jimmy. *Turning Point: A Candidate, a State, and a Nation Come of Age.* New York: Times Books, 1992.

Carter, Jimmy. *Why Not the Best?* Nashville, Tn.: Broadman Press, 1975.
deMause, Lloyd and Henry Ebel. *Jimmy Carter and American Fantasy: Psychohistorical Explorations.* New York: Two Continents/Psychohistory Press, 1977.
Lasky, Victor. *Jimmy Carter: The Man and the Myth.* New York: Marek Publishers, 1979.
Mazlish, Bruce and Edwin Diamond. *Jimmy Carter: A Character Portrait.* New York: Simon & Schuster, 1979.
Richman, Daniel A. *James E. Carter: Thirty-Ninth President of the United States.* Ada, Okla.: Garrett Educational Corporation, 1989.
Smith, Betsy Covington. *Jimmy Carter President.* New York: Walker, 1986.
Stapleton, Ruth Carter. *Brother Billy.* New York: Harper & Row, 1978.

John Edward Reagan
(1883–1941)

*Store clerk, shoe salesman, public official, and father of
President Ronald Reagan*

Ronald Reagan writes about his father, Jack, with a mixture of admiration, filial love, and respect, and just a dash of pity. In his first autobiography, *Where's the Rest of Me?*, Reagan recalls his father as "a man who might have made a brilliant career out of selling but he lived in a time — and with a weakness — that made him a frustrated man." The time was the Great Depression and the weakness was alcohol. Jack Reagan was an alcoholic. None of the Reagan biographies or autobiographies indicate that Jack was ever abusive to his wife and two sons. The worst thing any of them record is that his excesses sometimes made him surly. However, the sad fact is that liquor all too often got the best of him.

The father of America's fortieth president was born on July 13, 1883, in Fulton, Illinois. Jack was the second son and third child of John Michael Reagan and Jennie Cusack Reagan. John Michael worked as a farmer and as a laborer in a grain elevator. Jack was orphaned at the age of six when his parents died six days apart. John and Jennie were both victims of tuberculosis. Jack's brother and sister went to live with an uncle named Bill. Jack was sent to Bennett, Iowa, to live with his Aunt Margaret and her husband, Orson G. Baldwin. Working in his uncle's store gave Jack his first experience in clerking and salesmanship. Jack's formal schooling ended after he completed the sixth grade and became a dropout at the age of twelve. The Cedar County, Iowa, census of 1900 lists Jack Reagan as a resident of Bennett and gives his occupation as "dry goods salesman."

Sometime before the Baldwins sold their store and moved to Waterloo, Iowa, in 1902 Jack Reagan began clerking at the J. W. Broadhead dry goods store in Fulton, Illinois. In her book, *Early Reagan*, Anne Edwards reports that Jack's relationship with his uncle had "greatly deteriorated." Hotel registers verify that when Jack came back to Bennett for a visit, he stayed at the local hotel (fifty cents a night) rather than with his aunt and uncle.

Jack's charming manner, muscular frame, and dark-haired good looks did not

Jack Reagan. Courtesy of Ronald Reagan Library.

go unnoticed by the young ladies of Fulton. Unfortunately for Jack, neither did his fondness for alcohol. In a town that small Jack's reputation as a hard drinker made parents cautious about letting their daughters date the young bachelor. That ceased to matter after petite, perky, auburn-haired Nelle Clyde Wilson began working with Jack at Broadhead's. When Jack met Nelle has been lost to history, but they were married on November 8, 1904, at the Immaculate Conception Church in Fulton. Jack and Nelle's first son, John, was born on September 3, 1909. Ronald Wilson Reagan was born at his family's home in Tampico, Illinois, of February 6, 1911. According to *Where's the Rest of Me?,* Jack gave Ronald his lifelong nickname of Dutch the first time he heard his newborn son crying. Jack remarked, "For such a little bit of a fat Dutchman, he makes a hell of a lot of noise, doesn't he?" In his second autobiography, *An American Life*, Ronald Reagan revised the quote to: "He looks like a little fat Dutchman. But who knows, he might grow up to be president some day."

Despite his family's poverty, constant moving and his father's alcoholism, Ronald Reagan has steadfastly maintained that his childhood was the happiest time of his life. The Reagans lived in at least six different Illinois towns and cities (Tampico, Chicago, Galesburg, Dixon, Monmouth, and Fulton) before Ronald left home in 1928 to attend Eureka College. According to Gary Wills' book, *Reagan's America: Innocents at Home*, between the ages of six and ten, Ronald Reagan attended a different school every year. Wills also reports that the Reagans had five different addresses in Dixon, four in Tampico, and two in Galesburg. Jack never owned a house he lived in until after he was retired and Ronald bought his parents a house in California.

In *An American Life*, Ronald Reagan writes about the transience of his early years, but he offers no insights or speculations on how it affected him. He merely explains, "My father was constantly searching for a better life and I was forever the new kid in school.... We moved to wherever my father's ambition took him.... I'm sure that the fact that our family moved so often left a mark on me."

When he was eleven, Ronald Reagan was unforgettably confronted with his father's alcoholism. On a winter evening, Ronald came home and found his father passed out on the front porch. He writes that his father reeked of whiskey, and he considered pretending he had not seen him. After vainly attempting to awaken his dad, Reagan grabbed his father by the overcoat and dragged him off to bed. Reagan biographer Lou Cannon writes that the experience left Reagan with a lifelong aversion to alcohol. Ronald Reagan's biographers all describe him as a moderate to light drinker.

One thing Jack apparently passed on to Ronald was a talent for storytelling. Ronald Reagan has been quoted as calling his father "the best raconteur I ever heard." Jack Reagan is usually described as having had a salesman's gift for glibness and an affinity for skillfully telling off-color stories—but never in mixed company. During his public years, Ronald Reagan, too, became well known for his seemingly endless supply of anecdotes about his Hollywood days and nights.

Aside from stories about his drinking, the most commonly told tales about Jack Reagan concern his abhorrence of religious and racial bigotry. In *Where's the Rest of Me?*, Ronald Reagan tells of his father refusing to allow his children to see the movie *Birth of a Nation*, because Jack believed that the film glorified the Ku Klux Klan. Another recurring anecdote relates that traveling salesman Jack Reagan once stormed out of a hotel when the desk clerk told him: "You'll like it here Mr. Reagan. We don't permit a Jew in the place." Jack reportedly replied: "I'm a Catholic, and if it's come to the point where you won't take Jews, you won't take me either." Ronald Reagan writes that his father slept in his car that evening and contracted near-pneumonia, which later led to his first heart attack. In *An American Life*, Reagan adds, "There was no more grievous sin at our household than a racial slur or other evidence of religious or racial intolerance."

By his late forties, Jack Reagan's days of selling shoes were over. Several Reagan biographies report that Jack was fired from a sales job on Christmas Eve 1931. However, Wills disputes this because it would mean that Jack was unemployed from December of 1931 to June of 1933. During that time both of his sons were in college. It is doubtful that Jack could have afforded to keep them in school. Wills claims that the correct date must have been Christmas Eve of 1932. Sometime after his firing, Jack found work as a clerk/manager of a small discount school store in Springfield, Illinois. It is not clear exactly how long Jack worked there, but it could not have been for a long time because according to Reagan biographers Jack was back in Dixon in the fall of 1932 and working very hard to get Franklin D. Roosevelt elected president.

Jack's hard work was rewarded after Roosevelt's election. Jack was placed in charge of the welfare office in Dixon. As with most of Jack's jobs, there is no record of exactly how long he worked in the welfare office. Reagan biographers report that a series of heart attacks forced Jack into early retirement, for which the likely date would have been 1936 or 1937. By then Ronald Reagan was making a comfortable living as a radio announcer and was regularly sending his parents money. Cannon writes that Ronald's financial support enabled his mother to quit working.

The last four years of Jack's life were spent in California as the father of an up-and-coming movie star. Shortly after signing a movie contract with Warner Brothers in 1937, Ronald Reagan moved his parents to California. Ronald also got his father a twenty-five-dollar-a-week job at the studio answering his son's fan mail and photo requests.

In 1940 Jack traveled with Ronald, Pat O'Brien, Jane Wyman, Bob Hope, and Kate Smith to South Bend, Indiana, for the premiere of *Knute Rockne—All-American*. A star-struck Jack Reagan was able to spend three glorious days hob-nobbing with celebrities. As an added bonus, Jack finally saw the beloved Fighting Irish of Notre Dame play a football game. Ronald Reagan later mentioned, "He was an Irishman who really worshiped from afar; he'd never seen a Notre Dame team play. He thought that Pat O'Brien was the greatest man since Al Smith." The Fighting Irish did not disappoint. Jack watched them defeat the College of the Pacific. Jack later told Nelle: "I think that afternoon was worth dying for." One regrettable side effect of the trip was that Jack Reagan once again fell off the wagon. Apparently, he was swept away by the festiveness of the occasion and the opportunity to go bar-hopping in South Bend with his hero, Pat O'Brien.

Jack Reagan died at his Hollywood home on May 18, 1941, at the age of fifty-seven. His death was noted by a one-paragraph obituary in the May 20, 1941, issue of the *Los Angeles Times*. The obituary simply reported the places and times for the requiem mass and interment for John Reagan, father of Ronald Reagan, film actor, and added that he was also survived by a widow and another son, Neil Reagan.

Almost half a century after Jack's death, President Ronald Reagan was back in California campaigning for Vice President George Bush to succeed him. During his speech, President Reagan told his audience that he was not just campaigning for his party, he was also campaigning for his late parents. President Reagan described his father by saying: "He was the best storyteller I ever heard and the strongest man of principle I've ever known. He believed in honesty and hard work. He was filled with a love of justice and a hatred of bigotry. . . . We called him Jack." Even allowing for campaign rhetoric and hyperbole, Ronald Reagan sounds like a man who genuinely loved and admired his father.

Bibliography

Boyarsky, Bill. *Ronald Reagan: His Life and Rise to the Presidency.* New York: Random House, 1981.
Cannon, Lou. *President Reagan: The Role of a Lifetime.* New York: Simon & Schuster, 1991.
Cannon, Lou. *Reagan.* New York: Perigee, 1982.
Edwards, Anne. *Early Reagan.* New York: Morrow, 1987.
Los Angeles Times. "John Reagan." May 20, 1941.
Reagan, Ronald. *An American Life: The Autobiography of Ronald Reagan.* New York: Simon & Schuster, 1990.
Reagan, Ronald. *Speaking My Mind: Selected Speeches.* New York: Simon & Schuster, 1989.
Reagan, Ronald, with Richard G. Hubler. *Where's the Rest of Me?* New York: Karz Publishers, 1965.
Sullivan, George. *Ronald Reagan.* New York: Messner, 1985.
Vaughn, Stephen. *Ronald Reagan in Hollywood: Movies and Politics.* Cambridge: Cambridge University Press, 1994.
Wills, Gary. *Reagan's America: Innocents at Home.* New York: Penguin, 1988.

Prescott Sheldon Bush
(1895-1972)

Soldier, businessman, investment banker, politician, U.S. senator, and father of President George Bush

In his autobiography, *Looking Forward,* George Bush writes about the strong and lasting influence his father, Prescott Sheldon Bush, has had on the life of America's forty-first President. At the same time, Bush even-handedly gives credit to his mother's influence: "Our father had a powerful impact on the way we came to look at the world. But the writer who once described Dad as 'the greatest influence on my life' was only partly right. Our mother's influence and example were equally strong. Dad taught us about duty and service. Mother taught us about dealing with life."

Like his most famous son, Prescott Bush fought in a world war, graduated from Yale, enjoyed a career as a successful businessman/politician, and served in Congress. Bush biographers customarily describe Prescott Bush as tall (6'4"), athletic, robust, and handsome. Physical descriptions usually mention a trim physique, thick black hair, deep set blue-gray eyes, and prominent eyebrows. From his father, George Bush inherited his height, blue eyes, trim build, love of sports (particularly golf), and much of his political philosophy and political acumen.

Prescott Bush was born in Columbus, Ohio, on May 18, 1895, to Samuel Prescott and Flora Sheldon Bush. The first Bushes to come to America had settled in Cape Cod, Massachusetts, after emigrating from England in the mid-1600s. Samuel was a mechanical engineer who served as the president of the Buckeye Steel Casting Company in Columbus for over twenty years. Samuel was sufficiently affluent to finance Prescott's education at St. George's School in Newport, Rhode Island, and at Yale University.

At Yale, Prescott was an all-around athlete participating in varsity baseball, football, and golf. He was also president of the Yale Glee Club and a member of the prestigious Skull and Bones Society, which his son George later also joined. During his junior year, Prescott briefly dropped out of school after enlisting in the Connecticut National Guard. For a few weeks in 1916 Prescott served as a private in

Prescott Bush. Courtesy of the Connecticut Historical Society, Hartford, Connecticut.

the army commanded by John J. Pershing, which futilely pursued and hunted Pancho Villa and his band of rebels.

After receiving his B.A. from Yale in 1917, Prescott enlisted in the army. He served with the 158th Field Artillery Brigade in France during the Meuse-Argonne offensive and with the Army of Occupation in Germany after the signing of the armistice ending World War I. When he left the army in 1919, Prescott had risen to the rank of captain.

Settling in St. Louis after the war, Prescott began working as a salesman for the Simmons Hardware Company. While working for them, Prescott was sent to a plant in Tennessee that manufactured bridles and saddles. He examined the operation and advised the home office to sell the plant. His advice was acted upon, and Prescott's reputation as a shrewd businessman was firmly established.

While living and working in St. Louis, Prescott met his future wife, Dorothy Walker. Bush biographers do not describe their courtship or when, where, and how they first met. Prescott and Dorothy were married on August 6, 1921, at the Episcopal Church of St. Ann in Kennebunkport, Maine, when he was twenty-six and she was twenty. They had five children (four boys and one girl) over a period of sixteen years. George Herbert Walker Bush, their second son, was born at the Bushs' home in Milton, Massachusetts, on June 12, 1924.

Sometime after the Simmons Hardware Company was bought out by the Winchester Repeating Arms Company, Prescott moved his family to Columbus, Ohio, so he could help Samuel run the Buckeye Castings Company. Unfortunately, that business failed after a few months. Prescott's next job was with the Hupp Products Company, a floor covering firm. He was hired for the express purpose of straightening out the firm's financial affairs. Prescott did his job too well when he found the financial difficulties came from illegal profit skimming. That earned him the permanent wrath of Mr. Hupp, and Prescott took to keeping a loaded gun in his desk. Ultimately, Hupp was convicted of swindling, and Prescott was hired by Hupp's creditors to take over the business. Following a series of mergers, Hupp's former business was acquired by the U.S. Rubber Company, which became Prescott's next employer.

Prescott left U.S. Rubber in 1926 and began working for the Wall Street brokerage house of the W. A. Harriman Company. Prescott's old school ties worked to his advantage here. Both Averell Harriman and E. Roland Harriman were Yale alumni and members of the Skull and Bones. In 1930 the Harriman organization merged with the private banking firm of Brown Brothers and Company. The merger was mutually advantageous. The Harrimans gained the prestige of the Brown Brothers' long respected name. The Brown Brothers, who had suffered financial reverses because of the recent stock market crash, gained some sorely needed capital from the Harrimans. Prescott became a partner in the new firm.

As the firm prospered, Prescott Bush began serving on the boards of directors of several large corporations. Some of them were: the Columbia Broadcasting System, Prudential Insurance Company, the Pennsylvania Water and Power Company, and Pan American Airways.

In addition to his business activities, Prescott Bush was very active in the U.S. Golf Association. He served as its president in 1935, and he also won the national senior golf championship in 1951 by shooting a 66. Bush biographers also record that Prescott lobbied to eliminate the stymie rule in golf, which required a golfer to putt around an opponent's ball if it blocked a clear shot at the cup. Prescott was also a longtime supporter of the United Negro College Fund, and he served as a trustee of Yale University and the Episcopal Church Foundation of the United States.

Because of his affluence, Prescott was able to raise George and his other children in an environment of wealth and privilege that few people know. The Bushes lived in a nine-bedroom home on a two-acre wooded lot in Greenwich, Connecticut. A staff of four servants (a cook, two maids, and a chauffeur) attended to the family's needs. The family chauffeur drove the children to their private school classes. The Great Depression never directly touched their lives.

In his autobiography, *Looking Forward,* George Bush acknowledges that his family lived comfortably but adds, "not ostentatiously." He also recalls that "my brother, Pres, John and Buck, my sister Nancy, and I — all grew up understanding that life isn't an open-ended checking account. Whatever we wanted, we'd have to earn. From an early age we knew that if an illness or something really serious occurred, our folks would be there to help, but once we left home, we'd make it on our own."

When writing about how Prescott raised his children, Bush biographers describe him as a "no nonsense," "strict," "firm," but also "just" and "affectionate" parent. In his book, *Flight of the Avenger: George Bush at War,* Joe Hyams reports that Prescott "brandished a belt" as a means of discipline. Hyams also points out: "Even today George admits that his father was 'pretty scary' and his brother Johnathan recalls, 'We were all terrified of Dad as boys.'" In *Looking Forward,* George recalls that both of his parents "believed in an old-fashioned way of bringing up a family — generous measures of both love and discipline."

Clearly, Prescott Bush always expected his children to listen to him and to obey him. At the family dinner table there was a dress code of jackets and ties for the sons. At breakfast Prescott or Dorothy usually read a lesson from the Bible. Every Sunday, the family attended worship services at the Episcopal church, and no one was excused.

Prescott's career in politics began with his interest in civic and national affairs. For several years, Prescott was the presiding officer of the Greenwich town meeting. He also served as director of the Greenwich Hospital Association, the Greenwich Defense Council, and the Greenwich Boys Club.

In 1942 Prescott helped the war effort by serving as national chairman of the U.S.O. War Fund Campaign. During his tenure as chairman, over 33 million dollars were raised for the U.S.O. In 1943 and 1944 he headed the fund-raising campaigns of the National War Fund, Inc., an organization of over six hundred war relief agencies. Because of World War II, George Bush took his first steps at being on his own. In June of 1942 George was graduating from Phillips Academy in Andover, Massachusetts. Secretary of War Henry Stimson was the commencement speaker and told the class of '42 that even though there was a long war ahead, the graduates could better serve their country by furthering their education. George had already told his parents that he planned to enlist and become a navy pilot. After commencement, Prescott asked George if Stimson's speech had changed his mind. George told his father: "No sir, I'm going in." Prescott knew when to let go. He acquiesced to his son's decision with a handshake.

The book, *George Bush*, gives George's explanation for forgoing college to fight in World War II: "'I had a very powerful father,' Bush once said. 'Very much a leader, admired by everybody. I had a kind of— not really a competitive thing with him — but I wanted to get out on my own.'"

After the war, the Connecticut Republicans began utilizing Prescott's fundraising abilities. In 1947 he was named chairman of the Connecticut State Finance Committee of the Republican party. One year later, he served as a delegate-at-large to the Republican national convention. Two years after that (1950), he was the Republican's nominee for the U.S. Senate seat held by William Benton. *Current Biography 1954* describes Prescott's campaign as "brisk, aggressive, and, at times, a highly unconventional campaign." At political rallies Prescott sang bass in a quartet composed of former Yale Whiffenpoof singers. He also hired a musical group called the Brooklyn Sym-phoney to play at his campaign stops. Prescott accompanied the group by strumming a guitar. Hitting on the standard 1950 alliterative, anti-Truman campaign issues of "Korea, communism, confusion and corruption," Bush lost to Benton by approximately 1,000 votes out of 862,000 cast.

Two years later Bush again ran for the Senate. This time he won. He defeated Congressman Abraham Ribicoff by a margin of 559,586 to 529,213. Prescott was an obvious beneficiary of Eisenhower's lopsided presidential election victory. Eisenhower carried Connecticut by approximately 130,000 votes. Four years later, Senator Bush had the good fortune to be running for reelection with President Eisenhower. Eisenhower carried Connecticut by 306,000 votes and Senator Bush won reelection by a margin of 138,000 votes.

Prescott Bush served in the U.S. Senate from November 4, 1952, to January 2, 1963. Senator Bush supported the Eisenhower administration on most issues. He was a fiscal conservative who supported a strong national defense as a deterrent to war. Senator Bush also gained national attention for his opposition to the headline-hunting sensationalism of Wisconsin Senator Joseph McCarthy. Prescott is also credited with being the coauthor of the Federal Aid Highway Act, which created America's present-day system of interstate highways.

In an editorial in the June 5, 1954, issue of *Business Week*, Senator Bush is quoted describing the McCarthy-army hearings as an "unpleasant spectacle." As a solution, the senator proposed that the Senate adopt a uniform code of fair procedures for its investigating committees. The July 1959 issue of *Reader's Digest* ran an article written by Senator Bush expressing his advocacy of peace through a strong national defense: "Our expressed policy, the aim and purpose of our entire defense system, is to deter the Kremlin from starting a war. What better way to deter than to show? What we could show is nothing more than the greatest military might ever assembled in the history of the world."

Senator Bush declined to seek reelection in 1962, but he remained politically active. He drew national attention in the summer of 1963 when he withdrew his support for New York Governor Nelson Rockefeller for the 1964 Republican presidential nomination. The action was triggered by Governor Rockefeller's divorce and remarriage. An article in the June 24, 1963, issue of *U.S. News & World Report* quotes Bush asking how Rockefeller "can desert a good wife, mother of his grown children, divorce her, then persuade a young mother of four youngsters to abandon her husband and their four children and marry the Governor."

After George Bush was elected to Congress in 1966, Prescott was still around to help his son. According to Sullivan, Prescott's influence enabled George, the freshman congressman, to receive an appointment to the important House Ways and Means Committee. During the last years of Prescott's life, George served as U.S. ambassador to the United Nations, a position that allowed George to stay in close contact with his father. In her book, *Barbara Bush: A Memoir,* the former First Lady writes that she and George felt "very fortunate" to be living so near to Prescott at that time.

Prescott Bush died at the Memorial Hospital for Cancer and Allied Diseases in New York City on October 8, 1972, at the age of seventy-seven. His three-column obituary in the October 9, 1972, edition of the *New York Times* listed his many achievements and accomplishments both in and out of politics. The October 11, 1972, edition of the *Times* mentioned that flags in the state of Connecticut flew at half-mast that day in honor of the deceased former senator. New York Mayor John Lindsay, former New York Governor Averell Harriman, U.S. Senator Lowell Weicker, and Yale University President Kingman Brewster were among the dignitaries attending the funeral services for Prescott Bush.

The name of Prescott Bush drew national attention again almost twenty years after his death during the 1992 presidential election campaign. In the first debate between President George Bush and Arkansas Governor Bill Clinton at St. Louis in October 11, 1992, the president attacked Governor Clinton for his college involvement in antiwar protests. The governor promptly responded by reminding President Bush how his father, Prescott, had the courage to oppose Senator Joseph McCarthy. Clinton declared: "You were wrong to attack my patriotism." Under the rules of the debate, the governor had the floor. At that moment, all President George Bush could do was look on and listen.

Bibliography

Biographical Directory of the U.S. Congress, 1774–1989. Washington, D.C.: U.S. Government Printing Office, 1989.
Bush, Barbara. *Barbara Bush: A Memoir.* New York: Scribner's, 1994.
Bush, George, with Victor Gold. *Looking Forward: An Autobiography.* New York: Doubleday, 1987.
Bush, Prescott. "To Preserve Peace Let's *Show* the Russians How Strong We Are!" *Reader's Digest,* July 1959.
Congressional Digest. June 1953, February 1957, and November 1959.
Current Biography 1942. New York: H. W. Wilson, 1942, pp. 116–117.
Current Biography 1954. New York: H. W. Wilson, 1954, pp. 140–142.
"Ex-Senator Prescott Bush Dies: Connecticut Republican Was 77." *New York Times,* October 9, 1972, p. 34.

"Ex-Senator Bush Eulogized at Services at Greenwich." *New York Times,* October 11, 1972, p. 46.
"Fair Play in the Senate." *Business Week,* June 5, 1954, p. 164.
Green, Fitzhugh. *George Bush: An Intimate Portrait.* New York: Hippocrene Books, 1991.
Hyams, Joe. *Flight of the Avenger: George Bush at War.* San Diego: Harcourt Brace Jovanovich, 1991.
King, Nicholas. *George Bush: A Biography.* New York: Dodd Mead, 1980.
Stefoff, Rebecca. *George H. W. Bush: Forty-First President of the United States.* Ada, Okla.: Garrett Educational Corporation, 1990.
Sullivan, George. *George Bush.* Englewood Cliffs, N.J.: Messner, 1989.
"Rockefeller Under Fire: Bush Urges That He Withdraw." *U.S. News & World Report,* June 24, 1963, p. 20.

William Jefferson Blythe III (1918?–1946)

Dairy worker, soldier, salesman, and biological father of President Bill Clinton

In his biography of President Bill Clinton, *First in His Class,* David Maraniss sums up William Jefferson Blythe III: "everything about Bill Blythe was contradictory and mysterious." Exactly how many times he was married, how many children he fathered, and even his date of birth are matters of dispute.

According to most accounts, the biological father of America's forty-second president was born near Sherman, Texas, on February 27, 1918. However, Maraniss reveals that Blythe's military records list February 21, 1917, as his birthdate. There is no explanation given for the discrepancy.

There is agreement that William was the sixth of nine children born to William Jefferson "Willie" Blythe and Lou Birchie Ayers Blythe. The Blythes were hard working farmers with little education and little money. They eked out a living raising what have been called the four C's — corn, cattle, chicken, and cotton. Whatever formal education William received ended sometime in his early teens. After his father was stricken with colon cancer, William quit school to begin working full-time in a local dairy. Biographers differ as to whether William was thirteen, fourteen, or fifteen at the time. "Willie" died two years after William quit school. Since he was the oldest child without a family of his own, William became the main financial support for his widowed mother and three younger siblings.

In 1936, one year after "Willie's" death, the struggling Blythe family lost their forty-acre farm to foreclosure. Lou Blythe then moved her family to a small apartment in Sherman. By then William had entered into his first marriage, having married in or around December of 1935 seventeen-year-old Virginia Adele Gash, the daughter of a Sherman tavern owner. The marriage lasted about one year.

In a 1993 interview with a reporter from the *Washington Post,* Adele said that she married William because she wanted a home of her own and William's job with the dairy was going to provide them with company-owned living quarters. When the housing did not materialize, William and Adele moved into his mother's already cramped apartment. Unhappy with the arrangement, Adele went to Dallas to visit an aunt. She never returned, and William never came to Dallas to ask her back. He sent Adele her possessions via parcel post, and they were divorced in December of 1936. "Young and dumb was what we were," Adele told the *Post* reporter.

William never worried about complicating his life. He continued to see Adele after they were divorced. Adele claims that during one of those visits, William fathered her son, Henry Leon. Henry was born on January 17, 1938, and he adopted the surname of Ritzenthaler from his mother's second husband. A birth certificate filed in Austin, Texas, on January 17, 1938, names W. J. Blythe as the father of Adele Gash's son, Henry Leon Blythe. When Henry Leon was born, William was working as a traveling salesman. He sold auto parts and heavy equipment in Texas, Oklahoma, Louisiana, Tennessee, Arkansas, and California. By all accounts, William was a natural salesman. Affable, engaging, hard-working, and persuasive, William was able to make a modest, middle-class living in sales.

While he was on the road making sales calls, William was also calling on the ladies. A marriage license filed in Ardmore, Oklahoma, on August 11, 1938, documents the marriage of W. J. Blythe to twenty-year-old Maxine Hamilton. Maraniss reports that the marriage only lasted nine months and that the divorce judge ruled William "guilty of extreme cruelty and gross neglect of duty . . . in that he refused to provide for her a place to live, and within two weeks after the marriage he refused to furnish her transportation to her parents in Oklahoma City, Oklahoma." An article in the September 13, 1993, issue of *People Weekly* claimed discovery of a marriage license recording the marriage of W. J. Blythe to Minne Fave Gash in Durant, Oklahoma, on December 29, 1940. Minne was the younger sister of William's first wife, Adele. Both Maraniss and Adele claim that William married her to avoid marrying another woman he had impregnated. It is not known how long this alleged marriage lasted. There is no record showing when — if ever — William divorced Minne.

Maraniss also reports that a birth certificate filed in Kansas City in May of 1941 names W. J. Blythe as the father of a baby girl born to a Missouri waitress. Maraniss speculates that William Blythe may have been briefly married to this unnamed woman.

The next verified marriage for William was on May 3, 1941, when he wed eighteen-year-old Wahnetta Alexander in Kansas City. That marriage occurred a mere five months after William had supposedly married Minne. Eight days after their wedding, Wahnetta gave birth to a daughter named Sharon Pettijohn. In August of 1993, reporters from the *Arizona Republic* tracked down Sharon Pettijohn. Since then, she has steadfastly refused to be interviewed about her father.

Enter Virginia Kelley. Bill Clinton's mother was working as a student nurse at Tri-State Hospital in Shreveport, Louisiana, when she first met William Blythe. Not surprisingly, William was with another woman. The woman William was accompanying was stricken with appendicitis. In her autobiography, *Leading with My Heart*, Virginia recalls their fateful first meeting: "There is such a thing as love at first sight. When I stepped into that room and saw him standing there, I was stunned. . . . He smiled and the only way that I can describe it is that he had a glow about him. I was weak-kneed and also embarrassed because I was afraid that everybody in the room could see what I felt."

By all accounts, William Blythe was a handsome, charming, and fun-loving man. Described as tall with sparkling blue eyes, broad shoulders, and sandy brown hair, William made an indelible first impression on the obviously smitten Virginia. For Virginia the next step was to find out if this enchanting stranger was married. She called William by the last name of the ailing woman he was with. When he told her that they were not married, Virginia was relieved and elated. Before he left the hospital, William asked Virginia to join him for a coke after she got off work. She eagerly accepted. William and Virginia were soon seeing each other every day.

According to Virginia, William was passing through Shreveport en route to his hometown of Sherman, Texas, to enlist in the army. This is another inconsistency in the life of William Blythe. Maraniss points out that when they met, William was already in the army. He had been drafted in April and he joined in May. Why he told Virginia he was a heavy equipment salesman is an unexplained mystery. There are more inconsistencies. Virginia recalls that shortly after they met, William got an apartment in Shreveport and postponed his enlistment plans, taking a job as a salesman at a local Oldsmobile and Cadillac dealership instead. How William could simultaneously be a soldier and a car salesman and how he could keep Virginia from learning that he was already in the army are two more unexplained mysteries.

Less than two months after they had met, William and Virginia were married by a justice of the peace in the border town of Texarkana. The date was September 3, 1943. A few weeks later, William was on a troopship bound for the Mediterranean.

Most of the records documenting the military career of William Blythe were destroyed in a warehouse fire. It is known that he spent a little over two years in north Africa and Italy rebuilding trucks, jeeps, and heavy equipment while serving as a technician third grade with the 3030th Company, 125th Ordnance Base Auto Maintenance Battalion. The men in that outfit routinely worked ten-hour days with Sunday afternoons off. Their hard work earned the battalion a meritorious unit commendation for supporting the Rome-Arno campaign of 1944–45.

William adapted to the army life well enough to earn himself a Good Conduct Medal for "exemplary behavior, efficiency and fidelity." On December 7, 1945, William received his honorable discharge at Camp Shelby, Mississippi, after two years seven months, and fourteen days' service in the United States Army. He had attained the rank of technical sergeant third class and was given $203.29 as his mustering-out pay.

As Maraniss mentions, William Blythe's discharge date raises another puzzling question. President Bill Clinton was born on August 19, 1946. Nine months prior to Clinton's birth, William Blythe was in Italy. Virginia has maintained that her son William Jefferson Blythe Clinton was born one month early.

After his discharge from the army, William found employment in Chicago as a traveling salesman of heavy equipment. William had purchased a home in Chicago, and he was planning to raise his family there. He was traveling from Chicago to Hope, Arkansas, to take his pregnant wife to their new home when his life suddenly and tragically ended.

William Blythe died late in the evening of Friday, May 17, 1946, while traveling on Highway 60 near Sikeston, Missouri. Accounts of the fatal automobile accident vary, but it is generally believed that a blown front tire caused him to lose control of his car. William's Buick rolled over twice before landing upside down near a service ditch. About two hours after the accident, the lifeless body of William Blythe was found face down in a watery ditch. Apparently William was either thrown from his car or climbed out the driver's side window before falling down in the water and drowning. The only apparent injuries were a scratch on his forehead and a bump on the back of his neck.

A front page story in the May 18, 1946, edition of the *Hope (Ark.) Star* reported: "William Jefferson Blythe, 28, husband of the former Miss Virginia Cassidy of this city, was killed in an auto crash near Skitson (sic), Miss., Friday night. Details of the accident are not known." The story erroneously reported that William would be buried in Sherman, Texas. He was buried in Rose Hill Cemetery in Hope following a Sunday afternoon funeral service at the First Baptist Church of Hope.

After Bill Clinton became president, Virginia Kelley was jolted by the revelations of William Blythe's previous marriages. In her autobiography, she expressed no resentment, explaining, "As for why he never told me about his previous marriage or marriages, when did he have time? Even though we were married for two years and eight months, we were actually physically together for only seven months. . . . I'm convinced that had Bill lived, he would have found the moment to tell me about his past."

Clinton biographers have analyzed the effect on the life and psyche of President Bill Clinton of the early death of a father he never knew. In his book, *Bill Clinton: The Inside Story*, Robert E. Levin records that when Bill Clinton was in his early twenties, he visited the site of his father's fatal accident. In an interview with Bill Moyers, Clinton recalled: "I was just near the town in Missouri and the space of highway where I knew he died, and I had never been there. So I decided to go check it out. . . . He was thrown out of a car face down in the ditch. I was looking at the way the road was and wondering what it might have been like and wishing that he'd landed the other way." In an article in the *Washington Post National Weekly Edition*, David S. Broder writes: "Clinton has always said that he's haunted by the early demise of the father he never knew."

The most insightful analysis comes from Clinton himself. On different occasions he has said: "Most kids never think about when they're going to have to run out of time, when they might die. I thought about it all the time because my father died at twenty-nine, before I was born," and "I never got over . . . never meeting my father. It was always sort of a hole in my life. And I lived with that wistful memory."

Bibliography

Broder, David S. and others. "The Bus Stops Here." *Washington Post National Weekly Edition.* January 25–31, 1993, pp. 6–12.
"Clinton Recalls War Fought by Father He Never Knew." *Chicago Tribune,* May 30, 1994.
Hewitt, Bill. "Blythe Spirit." *People Weekly,* September 13, 1993, pp. 51 & 54.
"Husband of Hope Girl Is Auto Victim." *Hope (Ark.) Star,* May 18, 1946, p. 1.
Kelley, Virginia with James Morgan. *Leading with My Heart.* New York: Simon & Schuster, 1994.
Levin, Robert E. *Bill Clinton: The Inside Story.* SPI Books, 1992.
Maraniss, David. *First in His Class: A Biography of Bill Clinton.* New York: Simon & Schuster, 1995.
Oakley, Meredith L. *On the Make: The Rise of Bill Clinton.* Washington, D.C.: Regnery Publishing, 1994.
Portis, Jonathan and Charles E. Allen. *The Comeback Kid: The Life and Career of Bill Clinton.* New York: Birch Lane Press, 1992.

Roger Clinton
(1909–1967)

Car salesman, automobile dealer,
auto parts manager, and stepfather of
President Bill Clinton

Roger Clinton was not a particularly good father or husband. He was an alcoholic prone to violent rages and abusive behavior as well as a compulsive gambler and philanderer. Yet, in spite of his stepfather's many sins and shortcomings, Bill Clinton has still forgiven him.

The stepfather of America's forty-second president was born on July 25, 1909. Most of the scant information available about Roger Clinton's early years appears in David Maraniss's biography of Bill Clinton, *First in His Class*. Maraniss reports that Roger's parents moved to Hot Springs, Arkansas, from Dardanelle, Arkansas, in 1919, and that Roger was one of their five children (four boys and one girl).

Clinton biographers do not report if Roger graduated from high school. In her book, *Leading with My Heart,* Bill Clinton's mother, Virginia Kelley, reveals that Roger was married for the first time on December 23, 1933. His first wife was named Ina Mae Murphy, and she had been previously married. She had two sons from her prior marriage. According to Kelley, Roger was a good stepfather to the boys, but that did not keep Ina Mae from divorcing him in 1948. When Ina Mae filed for divorce in August of 1948, she charged Roger with physical abuse. According to court papers, he once beat her with one of her shoes. The alleged assault left Ina Mae with a black eye and bleeding from the head.

Kelley reports that she first met Roger when she was attending nursing school, but that there was nothing memorable about their first encounter. In the spring of 1947 they met again and she recalls, "he was attractive, and a lot more dashing, in a dangerous sort of way, than most of the men in Hope. . . . He dressed fit to kill, with sharp-creased trousers and fine-tailored sport coats and two-toned shoes. . . . His hair was dark and curly and his eyes twinkled when he talked. . . . He was the life of the party and he partied a lot."

When Virginia was first smitten with the stylishly dressed carouser, Roger was still married to Ina Mae. Virginia did not know that and she may not have wanted to know. She merely recalls, "I didn't know much about his background, and of course, I didn't pry." She also writes that she assumed that Roger was divorced. Once they started dating, Virginia found that along with his penchant for drinking, gambling, and fighting, Roger Clinton was also a womanizer. She recalls that after receiving an anonymous tip, she paid a visit to Roger's apartment. After finding lingerie strewn throughout his apartment, she gathered up all the garments and hung them on his clothesline. Roger was certainly embarrassed, but there is no evidence that he changed his ways.

When Virginia told her mother of her intentions to marry Roger, the news was not well received. She reports that her mother attempted to get legal custody of Bill. On June 19, 1950, Virginia Kelley married Roger Clinton. She was twenty-seven and he was forty. Her parents and her son, Bill, did not attend the wedding.

Maraniss reports that although Bill called Roger "Daddy," his stepfather never legally adopted him and never spent much time with him. Roger was more interested in drinking and hanging out with his pals than he was in paying attention to his stepson.

In September of 1952 Roger sold his Buick dealership and moved his family to Hot Springs. For a few months, the Clintons lived on a farm on the outskirts of town. Virginia did not like rural living and she did not like leaving Bill with Roger while she was working. The following summer, they moved to a two-story house in Hot Springs. Virginia thought that Roger bought the house in Hot Springs with the money he had received for selling the auto dealership. Actually, the house belonged to Roger's older brother, Raymond. Roger had gambled away the money from the sale of his Buick agency.

Except for the brief moment of tranquility afforded by the birth of their son, Roger Cassidy Clinton, in 1956, the marriage of Roger and Virginia was stormy and tumultuous. Roger's beatings, verbal abuse, and drunken, jealous rages were common and chronic. Once he was hauled off to jail after shooting a gun off in the house. That outburst was caused by Virginia's insistence on taking Bill to Hope hospital to visit her dying maternal grandmother.

Virginia claims that as early as 1959 she had filed for divorce but then relented. According to her, two events occurring in 1960 caused her to finally divorce Roger. The first event was the widely reported instance of fourteen-year-old Bill Clinton intervening during one of Roger's rages and demanding that his stepfather never strike his mother again. The second event was Virginia finally learning that they did not own the house they were living in. She reports that from 1954 to 1960, she had been faithfully turning her paycheck over to Roger. She felt used and betrayed when she learned that the house was not theirs.

Virginia's divorce testimony and Bill's affidavit contain a litany of complaints documenting Roger Clinton's beatings, extreme jealousy, excessive drinking, and verbal threats and abuse. A divorce was granted on May 15, 1962. However, Virginia and Roger were back together about three months later. After the divorce, Roger lost a lot of weight, began going to church, and started sleeping on Virginia's front-porch. As he had done several times before, Roger promised to change. Despite her family's strong misgivings, Virginia took Roger back. On August 6, 1962, they remarried.

About a month after the divorce, fifteen-year-old Bill Clinton changed his name from William Jefferson Blythe to William Jefferson Clinton. It has never been made clear why he would choose to take the surname of an alcoholic, wife-beating stepfather who never adopted him. Bill Clinton has explained that he did it for family solidarity and so he would have the same last name as his younger brother. At other times he has simply said, "The name doesn't matter; it's the man."

In 1965 Roger Clinton was diagnosed with a cancerous growth in a gland behind his ear. Rather than undergo a disfiguring operation, Roger opted for a series of radiation treatments at Duke Medical Center in North Carolina. During his hospitalization, Roger began reconciling with his estranged stepson. Several weekends during his junior year at Georgetown University, Bill Clinton drove from Washington, D.C., to Duke Medical Center to visit his dying stepfather. He also corresponded and once wrote to Roger: "You ought to look everywhere for help Daddy, . . . You ought to write me more — people — even some of my political enemies — confide in me."

In the fall of 1967 Bill Clinton was summoned from his classes at Georgetown to fly down to Hot Springs. He returned to a home that had been transformed into a virtual hospital wing. Virginia's nursing colleagues had volunteered their time to give Roger round the clock attention and care. Because of his uncontrollable drooling, Roger had refused to leave the house. He spent the last months of his life as a recluse. Bill Clinton sat up with his stepfather every night until death claimed Roger Clinton, at age fifty-eight, on November 8, 1967. For the second time in his life, Bill Clinton was without a father.

The weekends when Bill Clinton visited Roger at Duke may have been the only pleasant days of their stormy father-son relationship. Twenty-five years after Roger's death, Bill Clinton wistfully recalled those times by telling an interviewer: "There was nothing else to fight over, nothing else to run from. It was a wonderful time in my life, and I think in his."

The day after his death, the *Hot Springs Sentinel-Record* ran a photo of Roger above a small one-column, five-paragraph obituary. The obituary merely reported that he was fifty-eight, had been assistant manager of the Clinton Buick-Opel Company, and had lived in Hot Springs for forty-eight years.

Bibliography

Allen, Charles F. and Jonathan Portis. *The Comeback Kid: The Life and Career of Bill Clinton.* New York: Carol, 1992.

Carpozi, George, Jr. *Clinton Confidential: The Climb to Power.* Del Mar, Ca.: Dalton, 1995.

Kelley, Virginia with James Morgan. *Leading with My Heart.* New York: Simon & Schuster, 1994.

Kelly, Michael. "The President's Past." *New York Times Magazine,* July 31, 1994.

Maraniss, David. *First in His Class: A Biography of Bill Clinton.* New York: Simon & Schuster, 1995.

Oakley, Meredith L. *On the Make: The Rise of Bill Clinton.* Washington, D.C.: Regenery, 1994.

"Roger Clinton Dies at Home; 48-year Resident." *Hot Springs* (Ark.) *Sentinel Record,* November 9, 1967.

Index

Abell, Chester 98
Abrahamsen, David 203
Adams, Abigail Smith 26, 29, 30
Adams, Charles 28–29
Adams, Elihu 8
Adams, Eliza 29
Adams, Hannah Bass 7
Adams, Henry 7
Adams, John 7–10, 25–32, 41, 65, 146
Adams, John, Sr. (father of President John Adams) 7–10
Adams, John Quincy 25–32, 107
Adams, Joseph 7
Adams, Louisa Catherine Johnson 30
Adams, Peter Boylston 8
Adams, Samuel Hopkins 147
Adams, Susan Boylston 8–10
Addison, Joseph 13
Aitken, Jonathan 198, 202–203
Alexander, Wahnetta 231
Allen, Charles E. 234, 237
Allison, Nancy 114, 116
Allred, James V. 195
Ambrose, Stephen E. 177–178, 197–198, 200–201
Ammon, Harry 23–24
Anderson, Judith I. 127, 130, 132
Andrews, Elizabeth 65
Andrews, Isaac 65
Angle, Paul M. 78
Armistead, Mary 46–47
Arthur, Chester A. 97–101, 124, 132
Arthur, Regina 98, 100, 101
Arthur, William 97–101
Aspinwall, William Henry 163

Baines, Rebekah 193, 195
Bakeless, Catherine 44
Bakeless, John 44
Baldwin, Margaret 218

Baldwin, Orson G. 218
Ballou, Eliza 94–96
Ballou, Mehitabel 94–95
Barnard, Harry 91–93
Barre, W. L. 62
Bassett, Elizabeth 40
Bassett, John Spencer 35
Bauer, K. Jack 54, 57
Belknap, William W. 131
Bell, John 66
Bellamy, Francis Rufus 6
Bemis, Samuel Flagg 32
Bent, Silas 57
Benton, William 227
Berry, Richard 74
Beschloss, Michael R. 178
Beveridge, Albert J. 75–76, 78
Bewley, Thomas 202
Birchard, Sardis 91–92
Birchard, Sophia 89–90, 92
Blair, Francis P. 35
Blum, John Morton 140
Blythe, Lou Birchie 230
Blythe, William Jefferson 230
Blythe, William Jefferson, III (biological father of President Bill Clinton) 230–234
Bober, Natalie S. 14
Bowen, Catherine Drinker 7, 9, 10
Boyarsky, Bill 222
Boynton, Thomas 94
Braddock, Edward 34
Bragdon, Henry Wilkinson 140
Brant, Irving 19–20
Braun, Saul 53
Brendon, Piers 178
Brewster, Kingman 228
Broder, David S. 233–234
Brodie, Fawn M. 14, 197, 202, 204
Brooks, Preston 110–111
Brown, Caroline Athelia 151

239

Brown, Fern G. 67, 96
Brown, Harry J. 94, 96
Brown, Stuart Gerry 23–24
Brownlow, William 81
Bryan, William Jennings 170
Buchanan, James 68–72
Buchanan, James, Sr. 68–72
Buchanan, John 68
Buchanan, Mary 69
Buell, Augustus C. 35
Bullitt, William C. 134–135, 141
Bulloch, Annie 120
Bulloch, Martha 118–121, 164
Bunton, Jane 192
Bunton, Lucius 191
Burke, Robert F. 178
Burner, David 159
Burr, Aaron 38
Burton, David H. 132
Bush, Barbara 228
Bush, George 129, 222–229
Bush, Flora Sheldon 223
Bush, John 226
Bush, Nancy 226
Bush, Prescott 226
Bush, Prescott Sheldon 223–229
Bush, Samuel Prescott 223
Bush, Sara 74
Bush, William "Buck" 226
Butler, Andrew Perkins 110
Butterfield, L. H. 32
Byrd, William 12

Calhoun, John C. 130
Callum 80
Cannon, James 205–206, 211
Cannon, Lou 220–222
Caro, Robert A. 190, 192–193, 195
Carpozi, George, Jr. 238
Carter, Ann 40
Carter, Billy 216
Carter, James Earl, Sr. 212–216
Carter, Jimmy 212–217
Carter, Lillian Gordy 213–214, 216
Carter, Nina Pratt 212, 214
Carter, Robert 40
Carter, William Archibald 212
Cary, Archibald 23
Casso, Peter 79–80
Catherine the Great 28
Cervantes 17

Chamberlain, Neville 187
Charles I 22, 45
Chase, Chris 211
Chessman, G. Wallace 126
Chidsey, Donald Barr 35
Childs, Marquis 178
Chitwood, Oliver Perry 45, 48
Churchill, Allen 118, 126, 166
Churchill, Winston 187
Clark, Edward 195
Clarke, Fred G. 28, 32
Clary, Joseph 61
Claxton, Jimmie Loum Sparkman 53
Clay, Henry 56
Cleaves, Freeman 40, 44
Clements, Kendrick A. 138, 140
Cleveland, Grover 102–106, 165, 179
Cleveland, Margaret Falley 102
Cleveland, Mary 105
Cleveland, Richard Falley 102–105
Cleveland, William 102
Clinch, Nancy Gager 181, 189
Clinton, Bill 33, 228, 230–238
Clinton, George 38
Clinton, Raymond 236
Clinton, Roger (stepfather of President Bill Clinton) 235–238
Clinton, Roger Cassidy 236
Cole, Donald B. 38–39
Collier, Peter 126, 166, 189
Collins, David R. 72, 105, 117
Conkling, Frank J. 37
Conkling, Roscoe 124
Conway, Francis 16
Coolidge, Abigail 149
Coolidge, Calvin 149–154
Coolidge, Calvin, Jr. 152
Coolidge, Galoosh 149–150
Coolidge, Grace 152, 154
Coolidge, John Calvin 149–154
Coolidge, Louis A. 88
Coolidge, Sarah 149
Corimer, Frank 195
Cram, Dr. 152
Cramp, H. A. 198
Cranch, Richard 25
Crawford, Jane 35
Cresson, W. P. 23–24
Crisp, Colonel 170
Cromwell, Oliver 22
Crossier, Barney 154
Cunliffe, Marcus 6

Index

Cunningham, Noble E. 14
Current, Richard N. 74, 78
Curtis, George Ticknor 70, 72
Curtis, James C. 35
Curtis, Jane Will 154

Dallek, Robert 190, 192–193, 195–196
Dana, Francis 28
David, Irene 178
David, Lester 178
Davidson, Dr. 70
Davis, Burke 34–35
Davis, Jefferson 86
Davis, John H. 182, 185
Davis, Kenneth S. 166, 179
DeGregorio, William 83, 88, 96, 147
Delano, Sara 164–166
Delano, Warren 164
deMause, Lloyd 215
Demosthenes 31
Dent, Julia 85–86, 88
DeToledano, Ralph 204
Diamond, Edwin 213–217
Dickens, Charles 116, 135
Dickerson, Deb 143
Dickerson, Elizabeth Ann 143
Dickerson, Malvina 143
Dickerson, Phoebe 142–144, 146
Dillingham, William P. 151
Dix, Dorthea 61
Dodson, E. Griffith 48
Donavan, Frank 6
Downes, Randolph C. 144, 147
Duffy, Herbert S. 132
Dunmore, Lord John Murray 41, 47
Dye, Isaac P. 169
Dyer, Brainerd 57

East, Robert A. 32
Eaton, George 113
Ebel, Henry 215
Eckendore, H. J. 92–93
Edmunds, George L. 147
Edwards, Ann 218
Eisenhower, Abraham 176
Eisenhower, Arthur 175–176
Eisenhower, David 179
Eisenhower, David Jacob 173–178, 200
Eisenhower, Dwight D. 173, 176–179, 200, 203, 227

Eisenhower, Earl 176
Eisenhower, Edgar 175, 177–178
Eisenhower, Jacob 173, 175–176
Eisenhower, Paul 176
Eisenhower, Rebecca 173
Eisenhower, Roy 176
Elder, Betty Doak 53
Ellis, Joseph J. 31
Ellis, Rafaela 39
Ellison, Andrew 86
Emery, Ann 159
Eskridge, George 5
Everett, Marshall 117
Everts, William M. 100

Faber, Doris 1, 6, 57, 83, 88, 93, 96
Falkoff, Lucille 48, 88
Ferling, John 6–7, 10
Ferrell, Robert H. 172, 179
Ferris, Robert G. 44
Fillmore, Calvin 58
Fillmore, Millard 58–62, 111
Fillmore, Nathaniel 58–62
Fiske, John 44
Fitz-Gerald, Christine Maloney 44
Fitzgerald, John Francis 183
Fitzpatrick, John C. 39
Fleming, Thomas 14
Flexner, John Thomas 4, 6
Flynn, John 186
Ford, Betty 205, 211
Ford, George 208
Ford, Gerald 205–211
Ford, Gerald R., Sr. 206, 208–211
Ford, James F. 208
Ford, John 63
Ford, Richard A. 208
Ford, Thomas G. 208
Foster, Charles 131
Franklin, Benjamin 28
Frazier, Mary 30
Freeman, Douglas Southall 4, 6
Friedel, Frank 166
Freud, Sigmund 134–135, 141
Fridlaender, Marc 32
Fry, Joshua 12
Fuess, Claude M. 151, 154

Gale, George 4
Gardner, Dorothy Ayer 205–209

Garfield, Abram 94–96
Garfield, Edward 94
Garfield, James A. 87, 94–96, 132
Garfield, James Ballou 95
Garfield, Solomon 94
Garfield, Thomas 94
Gargan, Agnes Fitzgerald 185
Garibaldi, Giuseppe 161
Garland, Hamlin 82, 85, 88
Garrett, Romeo B. 101
Gash, Minne Fave 231
Gash, Virginia Adele 230–231
George, III 45
Gibbon, Edward 116
Gibson, John 56
Gilbert, Chinard 10
Gilman, Daniel C. 24
Gilman, John T. 65
Goebel, Dorothy Burne 43–44
Gold, Victor 228
Good, Milton 175
Goodrich, Charles A. 44
Goodwin, Doris Kearns 165–166, 180, 185–186, 189
Grant, Jesse Root 82–88, 146
Grant, Matthew 82
Grant, Noah 82
Grant, Peter 82
Grant, Rachel Kelly 82
Grant, Ulysses S. 82–83, 85–88, 131, 156
Greeley, Horace 116
Green, Fitzhugh 229
Green, James A. 44
Greenblatt, Miriam 32, 53
Green, J. R. 154
Grenville, George 23
Grigsby, Charles 76
Grover, Stephen 103
Grundy, James 52
Gunn, Lewis 146

Hall, William Thomas 140
Hamilton, Alexander 38
Hamilton, Holman 54–57
Hamilton, Maxine 231
Hamilton, Nigel 189
Hammond, John C. 151
Hanks, Dennis 75–76
Hanks, Nancy 74–75
Haptonstall, Abraham 55

Harding, Abigail 146
Harding, Charles Alexander 142
Harding, George Tyron, II 142–147
Harding, Mary Anne 142
Harding, Richard 142
Harding, Warren G. 142–148, 151–152
Harney, Gilbert L. 113
Harriman, Averell 225, 228
Harriman, E. Roland 225
Harrison, Benjamin 107–113
Harrison, Benjamin, IV 40
Harrison, Benjamin, V (father of President William Henry Harrison) 4–44, 47
Harrison, Devlin 112
Harrison, Irwin 109
Harrison, John Scott 107–113
Harrison, William Henry 40–41, 43–44, 107, 109
Hatch, Alden 179
Hayes, Lucy 91
Hayes, Rutherford "Ruddy," Jr. (father of President Rutherford B. Hayes) 89–93
Hayes, Rutherford, Sr. (grandfather of President Rutherford B. Hayes) 89
Hayes, Rutherford B. 33, 89–93, 124, 131
Hayes, Rutherford Birchard (brother of President Rutherford B. Hayes) 90
Haywood, John 81
Hearst, William Randolph 187
Heaton, James 115
Hecht, Marie B. 32
Heckscher, August 134–135, 138, 140–141
Henderson, Tom 80
Henry, Patrick 19, 41, 45, 47, 55
Herrick, Myron 117
Hess, Stephen 10, 32, 44, 126, 132–133, 166
Hesseltine, William B. 88
Hewitt, Bill 234
Hill, J. C. 156
Hillman, William 167
Hitler, Adolf 187
Hoehling, Adolph August 152
Hogenboom, Ari 93
Hoover, Eli 155
Hoover, Herbert 155–159
Hoover, Jesse 155
Hoover, Jesse Clark (father of President Herbert Hoover) 155–159

Index

Hoover, Lou Henry 155, 159
Hoover, Mary 156
Hoover, Theodore 156, 158
Hope, Bob 221
Hopkins, James 70
Horowitz, David 126, 166, 189
Howard, Oliver Otis 57
Howe, George 98, 101
Howland, Rebecca Brien 162–164
Hoyt, Edwin P. 39, 48, 57, 72, 117
Hume, David 116
Hyams, Joe 226, 229

Ingham, Albert C. 161
Irving, Washington 6
Irwin, Elizabeth Ramsey 107

Jackson, Andrew 33–35, 66
Jackson, Andrew, Sr. 33–35
Jackson, Elizabeth Hutchinson 33–35
Jackson, Hugh (brother of President Andrew Jackson) 33–34
Jackson, Hugh (brother of Andrew Jackson, Sr.) 33–34
Jackson, Robert 33–34
Jacobs, David 26, 32
James, Marquis 35
Jay, John 28, 38
Jefferson, Jane Randolph 11–12
Jefferson, Mary Field 11
Jefferson, Peter 11–14
Jefferson, Thomas 11–15, 20, 30, 38, 45, 47, 65
Jefferson, Thomas, II (grandfather of President Thomas Jefferson) 11
Jennings, Elizabeth 100
Johnson, Allen 44
Johnson, Andrew 79–81
Johnson, Eliza Bunton 190
Johnson, Jacob 79–81
Johnson, Lyndon B. 190, 192–196
Johnson, Lucretia Knapp 107
Johnson, Sam, Sr. 190–191
Johnson, Sam Ealy, Jr. (father of President Lyndon B. Johnson) 190–195
Johnson, Sam Houston 194–196
Johnson, Valentine 55
Johnson, William 79
Johnston, John D. 76, 78
Johnston, Sarah Bush 75–76

Jones, James Sawyer 81
Jones, Joseph 23

Kane, Joseph 181
Kane, Joseph Nathan 79, 81, 88
Kearns, Doris 196; see also Goodwin, Doris Kearns
Kelley, Virginia 231–238
Kendrick, Anna 65
Kennedy, John F. 32, 180, 183, 185, 188–189
Kennedy, Joseph P., Jr. (brother of President John F. Kennedy) 183, 188
Kennedy, Joseph P., Sr. (father of President John F. Kennedy) 180–189
Kennedy, Kathleen 186
Kennedy, Mary Augusta 180
Kennedy, Patrick Joseph 180, 182
Kennedy, Robert 188–189
Kennedy, Rose Fitzgerald 183, 185–186, 189
Kennedy, Rosemary 185
Kennedy, Ted 189
Ketcham, Ralph 19–20
King, Charles 205–207
King, John 69–70
King, Leslie Lynch, Sr. (biological father of President Gerald Ford) 205–207, 210–211
King, Margaret Atwood 206–207
King, Marietta 205
King, Nicholas 229
King, Patricia 207
Klein, Philip Shriver 68, 72
Kline, Mary Jo 32
Knollenberg, Bernhard 3, 6
Knox, Jane 50–51
Koch, Adrienne 14
Koskoff, David E. 183–184, 189
Krock, Arthur 187–188
Kurnhardt, Philip B. 75

Lamb, Charles 136
Larsen, Rebecca 166
Lash, Joseph P. 166
Lasky, Victor 217
Law, Kevin J. 62
Lee, Henry 54
Lee, Richard Henry 23

Leech, Margaret 94, 96, 117
Levin, Robert E. 233–234
Lieberman, Frank 154
Lincoln, Abraham 73–78, 131, 143–144
Lincoln, Abraham (grandfather of President Abraham Lincoln) 73
Lincoln, Bathsheba Herring 73
Lincoln, Mordecai 73
Lincoln, Sarah 74
Lincoln, Thomas 73–78
Lindsay, John 228
Link, Arthur S. 141
Lisitzky, Gene 14
Lloyd, James, Jr. 30
Longmore, Paul K. 3, 6
Lossing, B. J. 44
Love, Eunice 61
Luthin, Reinhard H. 78
Luvisi, Eudora Kelly 146
Lynch, Dennis Tilden 39, 105
Lyon, Peter 179
Lyons, Eugene 159

McCarthy, Joseph 227–228
McCormac, Eugene Irving 53
McCoy, Donald R. 150, 154
McCoy, Drew R. 21
McCullough, David 119, 126, 167, 169, 171–172
McDonough, Mary 79
McElroy, Robert 104–105
McFarland, Joseph 144
McFeely, William S. 82–83, 86, 88
McGee, Dorothy Horton 159
McKinley, Abbie Celia 116
McKinley, Abner 116
McKinley, James 114
McKinley, Silas Bent 57
McKinley, William 114, 116–117, 126
McKinley, William, Sr. 114–117
McLaughlin, "Chick" 182
McMurdo, William 47–48
McPherson, Aimee Semple 201
MacDowell, Ephraim 51–52
Mackenzie, William L. 39
Maddison, John 16
Madison, Ambrose 16
Madison, Francis Taylor 16
Madison, James 16–17, 19–21, 38, 56
Madison, James, Sr. 16–21
Madison, John, II 16
Madison, Nelly Conway 16
Malone, Dumas 12, 14, 44, 67, 130, 133
Maraniss, David 230–232, 234–236, 238
Marsh, Joseph 9, 25
Martin, Thomas 17
Mazlish, Bruce 204, 213–217
Mee, Charles L., Jr. 142, 148
Milhous, Franklin 200
Milhous, Hannah 198, 200–203
Milhous, Jane 198
Millard, Phoebe 58–59
Miller, Merle 170, 172, 175, 177, 179
Miller, Nathan 126
Miller, Richard Lawrence 169–170, 172
Minthorn, Hulda Randall 156–158
Mitchell, Pames P. 203
Monroe, Andrew 22
Monroe, Elizabeth Jones 22
Monroe, James 22–24, 31, 56
Monroe, Spence 22–24
Montesquieu, Charles de Secondat 17
Montgomery-Massingbred, Hugh 6
Moor, Victoria Josephine 149
Moore, Virginia 16, 21
Morgan, George 24
Morgan, H. Wayne 117
Morgan, James 234, 238
Morgan, Ted 165–166
Morrell, Martha McBride 53
Morrill, David L. 66
Morris, Edmund 122–123, 125–126
Morris, Roger 202, 204
Morse, John T. 32
Moyers, Bill 233
Murphy, Ina Mae 235–236
Musser, Chris 175–176
Myers, Elisabeth P. 93, 113, 133

Nagel, Paul C. 32
Nash, George H. 155, 159
Neal, Ann 102–103
Neal, Steve 179
Neal, William 102
Nevins, Allan 32, 102, 104
Nevins, John 37
Nevins, William 102
Nichols, Roy Frank 65–67
Niven, John 39
Nixon, Arthur 201
Nixon, Don 201

Nixon, Edward Calvert 201, 203
Nixon, Ernest 198
Nixon, Frank Anthony 197–204
Nixon, Harold Samuel 200–202
Nixon, Julie 203
Nixon, Pat 203
Nixon, Richard M. 197, 200–204
Nixon, Samuel Brady 197–198
Nixon, Sarah Ann Wadsworth 197
Nixon, Tricia 203
Nott, Charley 161
Nott, Dr. 161
Noyes, John 89–91

Oakley, Meredith L. 234, 238
O'Connell, Cardinal William 183
Olcott, Charles S. 117
Osborn, George C. 134–136, 138–141
Ovid 17

Parker, George F. 105–106
Parks, Rosa 100
Parmet, Herbert S. 204
Parsons, Theophilius 29
Passmore, John 71
Patterson, James T. 133
Peabody, James Bishop 10
Peden, William 14
Pemberton, William E. 171–172
Perry, Aaron 131
Pershing, John J. 233
Peskin, Allan 94, 96
Pessen, Edward 93
Peterson, Merrill D. 15, 21
Pettijohn, Sharon 231
Phelps, Charles 130
Phelps, Fanny 129–130
Phillips, Cabell 171–172
Pierce, Benjamin (father of President Franklin Pierce) 63–67
Pierce, Benjamin, Sr. 63
Pierce, Elizabeth 65
Pierce, Elizabeth Merrill 63
Pierce, Franklin 65–67
Pierce, Robert 63
Plutarch 170
Poe, Edgar Allan 134
Polikoff, Barbara G. 21
Polk, Ezekiel 50–51
Polk, James K. 50–53, 130

Polk, Samuel 50–53
Polk, Thomas 50–51
Polk, William 51
Pope, Alexander 13
Portis, Jonathan 234, 237
Powers, Abigail 61
Pringle, Henry F. 133
Putnam, James 25

Quarles, Benjamin 136, 141
Quixote, Don 110

Raimo, John W. 41, 44, 49, 67
Rakove, Jack N. 21
Randall, Henry S. 13, 15
Randall, Willard Sterne 12, 15
Randolph, Sallie G. 211
Randolph, Thomas Jefferson 14
Randolph, William 11–12
Rapin, Paul de 13
Rayback, Robert J. 62
Reagan, Bill 218
Reagan, Jennie Cusack 218
Reagan, John 219
Reagan, John Edward (father of President Ronald Reagan) 218–222
Reagan, John Michael 218
Reagan, Neil 221
Reagan, Ronald 218–222
Reep, Jacob 115
Reeves, Thomas 98, 101, 184, 187–189
Remini, Robert 35
Ribicoff, Abraham 227
Richman, Daniel 217
Rice, Allen Thorndike 78
Rice, Asa 61
Richardson, William 35
Ritzenthaler, Henry Lee 231
Robbins, Charles 170, 172
Robertson, Donald 17
Rockefeller, Nelson 227–229
Rockne, Knute 221
Roosevelt, Anna 121, 126, 164
Roosevelt, Corinne 120, 125–126
Roosevelt, Cornelius Van Schaak 118–119
Roosevelt, Elliott 124–125
Roosevelt, Franklin D. 160, 165–166, 184, 186–187, 214, 221
Roosevelt, Isaac 160–161, 163

Roosevelt, James (father of President
    Franklin D. Roosevelt) 160–166
Roosevelt, James Roosevelt 162, 166
Roosevelt, Margaret Barnhill 118
Roosevelt, Rebecca Aspinwall 160
Roosevelt, Robert 119
Roosevelt, Theodore 118–120, 122–126,
    164–165
Roosevelt, Theodore, Sr. 118–126
Ross, Ishbel 127, 130, 133, 154
Russell, Francis 144, 146, 148
Russell, Jane 68
Russell, Joshua 68
Russell, Samuel 68
Rutland, Robert Allen 21

Sandburg, Carl 73–74, 78
Sarnoff, David 184
Schachner, Nathan 12, 15
Schlesinger, Arthur M., Jr. 180, 189
Scott, Carol Lavina 110
Seager, Robert II 48
Sellers, Charles 50, 52–53
Seuling, Barbara 101
Severance, Frank H. 62
Severn, Bill 79–81
Severns, Alice 147
Shakespeare, William 13, 116
Shaw, Peter 8, 10
Shearer, Lloyd 207, 211
Shepard, Edward M. 39
Shepherd, Jack 10
Shriver, Eunice Kennedy 185
Shuler, The Rev. "Fighting Bob" 201
Sievers, Harry J. 107, 109, 113
Silliman, Benjamin D. 162
Simpson, Hannah 83, 86
Smathers, George 185
Smith, Al 221
Smith, Chloe 89
Smith, Gene 159
Smith, Kate 221
Smith, Lon 195
Smith, Mary 25
Smith, Mary Mackall 56
Smith, Page 9–10
Smith, Richard Norton 157, 159
Snyder, Charles M. 62
Sobel, Robert 49, 67
Spann, Gloria Carter 215
Speer, Elizabeth 68–69

Speer, James 68
Spielman, William Carl 116
Stapleton, Ruth Carter 212–217
Stefoff, Rebecca 10, 229
Steinberg, Alfred 21
Stevens, Rita 113
Stickney, William W. 150
Stimson, Henry 226
Stoddard, Samson 64
Stone, Malvina 98, 101
Stover, Ida Elizabeth 174–177
Strother, Sarah Dabney 55
Stryker, Lloyd Paul 81
Styron, Arthur 24
Sullivan, George 222, 228–229
Sullivan, John L. 127
Sullivan, Wilson 88
Sumner, Charles 110–111
Sumner, William Graham 35
Sunday, Billy 201
Swanson, Gloria 185–189
Swift, Jonathan 13

Taft, Alphonso 127–133
Taft, Charles Phelps 130
Taft, Helen 130
Taft, Horace 128
Taft, Peter Rawson 127–130
Taft, Robert 129
Taft, Robert A. 133
Taft, Sylvia 129
Taft, William Howard 127, 131–133
Talmadge, Gene 215
Taylor, Elizabeth Lee 54
Taylor, Hancock (uncle of President
    Zachary Taylor) 55
Taylor, Hancock (son of President Zachary
    Taylor) 55
Taylor, James 54
Taylor, John M. 95–96
Taylor, Richard 54–56
Taylor, William 55
Taylor, Zachary 16, 54–57
Taylor, Zachary (grandfather of President
    Zachary Taylor) 54
terHorst, Jerald R. 211
Thomas, Benjamin 73–74, 78
Thomas, Lately 79
Tod, George 82
Todd, Helen 88
Tom, John 69

Index

Torrey, Louise Maria 130–132
Torrey, Samuel 130
Trefousse, Hans L. 79–81
Truman, Anderson Shippe 167–168
Truman, Bess W. 171–172
Truman, Harry S 167, 169–172
Truman, John Anderson 167–172
Truman, Margaret 171–172
Truman, Mary Jane 167
Turner, Nancy Byrd 4, 6
Tyler, Henry 45
Tyler, John 45–49
Tyler, John, Sr. 45–49

Underhill, Robert 172

Van Aelstyne, Dirckie 36
Van Alen, Marie Hoes 37
Van Buren, Abraham (father of President Martin Van Buren) 36–39, 65
Van Buren, Abraham (brother of President Martin Van Buren) 37
Van Buren, Dirckie 37
Van Buren, Jannetje 37
Van Buren, Lawrence 37
Van Buren, Martin 36–39, 52
Vanderbilt, Cornelius 160
Vaughn, Stephen 222
Vestal, Bud 211
Villa, Pancho 224
Virgil 17

Walker, Dorothy 225–226
Walker, James 52
Walker, Dr. Thomas 13
Wallace, Lew 113
Walworth, Arthur 131
Ward, Geoffrey C. 163–164
Warner, Mildred 4
Washburn, R. M. 154
Washington, Augustine 1, 3–6, 13
Washington, George 1, 3–6, 23, 29–30, 43, 56, 63

Washington, Jane Butler 4–5
Washington, John (cousin of Augustine Washington) 4
Washington, John (grandfather of Augustine Washington) 3–4
Washington, Lawrence (brother of Augustine Washington) 4
Washington, Lawrence (father of Augustine Washington) 4
Washington, Lawrence (granduncle of Augustine Washington) 3
Washington, Mary Ball 4–6
Washington, Mildred 4
Webster, Daniel 130, 136
Weicker, Lowell 228
Welch, Richard E. 106
West, Jessamyn 201–202
Wetzel, Charles 24
Whalen, Richard J. 182–183, 185, 187, 189
White, John 154
White, William Allen 154
Williams, Charles Richard 93
Wills, Gary 220–222
Wilson, Anne Adams 134
Wilson, James 134
Wilson, James Grant 44
Wilson, Joan Hoff 159
Wilson, Joseph Ruggles 134–140
Wilson, Nelle Clyde 219, 221
Wilson, Woodrow 134–141
Winston, Robert W. 81
Wood, Walter 59, 61
Woodrow, James 135
Woodrow, Jessie 135
Woodward, W. E. 4, 6, 88
Wright, Nathaniel 129
Wyman, Jane 221
Wyman, Lutheria 198

Young, Jeff C. 1
Young, Martha Ellen 167–170
Young, Solomon 169, 171
Young, Stanley 43–44

www.ingramcontent.com/pod-product-compliance
Lightning Source LLC
Chambersburg PA
CBHW051218300426
44116CB00006B/618